HOW TO BE A GIFTED PARENT

Also by David Lewis
THE SECRET LANGUAGE OF YOUR CHILD

with Dr Robert Sharpe
THE SUCCESS FACTOR
THRIVE ON STRESS
THE ANXIETY ANTIDOTE

HOW TO BE A GIFTED PARENT

Realise Your Child's Full Potential

by

DAVID LEWIS

SOUVENIR PRESS

First published 1979 by Souvenir Press Ltd,
43 Great Russell Street, London WC1B 3PA
and simultaneously in Canada

Reprinted 1985

ISBN 0 285 62414 8

Printed in Great Britain by
Photobooks (Bristol) Ltd

Contents

Acknowledgements

The continuing research from which the material for this book has been drawn is only possible due to the help and co-operation of parents and teachers in both Britain and the United States. I am pleased to take this opportunity to thank them and their children for the time and trouble they have been prepared to invest in this project. I would like to record special thanks to Mr and Mrs Burke and their son Graham for the very extensive help which they have given to me and for permission to use photographs of Graham in this book.

Mr Henry Collins at the National Association for Gifted Children was especially helpful in allowing me to make contact with the parents of exceptional children through the facilities of his Association. If you feel you have a gifted child who could benefit from the knowledge and opportunities available from the NAGC you might like to contact them at 1, South Audley Street, London W1Y 5DQ. My grateful thanks are also due to the Montessori Society for permission to carry out observations at their nursery schools and particularly to Mrs Hood. If any parents are interested in finding out more about the Montessori approach to nursery education then they should contact them at 26, Lyndhurst Gardens, London NW3 5NW.

My thanks to Professor Richard Lynn of the New University of Ulster for providing me access to his paper on intelligence, and to Professor Alexander Thomas of New York University Medical Centre, for his help in obtaining access to his most recent research findings. I am also grateful to Dr William Mitchell and to James Brannin MA for their helpful advice during the preparation of this manuscript.

I would especially like to thank Mr Stephen Roberts of the Reference Library at the United States Embassy in London for his assistance. I am most grateful, too, for the detailed help and co-operation of James Robinson of the Head Start Bureau in the Office of Human Development Services, Washington DC; and to Dr Dorothy Sisk, Director, The Office of Gifted and Talented at the Department of Health, Education, and Welfare, Office of Education in Washington DC.

I would also like to extend my grateful thanks to several publishers and their authors who have been kind enough to allow the quotation from their books: To Dr Burton L. White and his publishers W. H. Allen and Co. Ltd for permission to use extracts from their book *The First Three Years of Life*. To Dr Glenn Doman and his publishers Jonathan Cape Ltd, for permission to use extracts from their books *Teach Your Baby to Read* and *What To Do About Your Brain-Injured Child*. My grateful thanks to Professor D. H. Stott and his publishers Hodder and Stoughton Educational for permission to quote from their book *The Parent as Teacher*; to Dr Richard Q. Bell and Dr Lawrence V. Harper and their publishers Lawrence Erlbaum Associates, Hillsdale, New Jersey for permission to quote from their book *Child Effects on Adults*; to Dr Susanna Millar and her publishers, Penguin Books Ltd, for permission to quote from their book *The Psychology of Play*. Finally my thanks to Dr J. W. Getzels and Dr P. W. Jackson and to the editor and publishers of Phi Delta Kappa for permission to quote from "The Meaning of 'Giftedness' — An Examination of an Expanding Concept." (c. 1958, Phi Delta Kappa Inc.)

My thanks to Mr Tony Timmington for providing some of the photographs and to Mrs Jane Massey for her usual excellent work in deciphering the usually difficult manuscript. Finally, but by no means least, my thanks to the numerous television and radio producers and interviewers who were kind enough to allow me to broadcast my request for parents of gifted children to contact my research team. I am especially grateful to Wendy Jones of ATV, Birmingham and John Doyle of Westward television for their help.

Introduction

How This Book Will Help You

This is a book about gifted children and the gifted parents who help them to realise their potential. It explains how children can attain inborn promise of brilliance which is the birthright of virtually every baby, and it describes how their parents can help them. It is a book about special children and special adults. It is a book about you and your own child.

There are hundreds of books dealing with all aspects of bringing up a family. Many offer advice and practical information about ways of making the environment more stimulating. Much of what they say is helpful. But it is only a part of the growing-up story.

Why is it, even in environments which seem to equal one another in providing an enriched background for mental growth, that one child develops so much better than another? What creates a high level of intellectual and creative attainment in some cases but seems to diminish and restrict development in others? Why does one youngster grow up with a very positive idea about his or her abilities while another rapidly evolves a highly negative, failure-inducing self-image?

It is with such basic questions about mental growth that my research and this book are concerned. In the following chapters I will be concerned with how you can help your child to a mind-expanding, rather than a potential-inhibiting, view of himself or herself and the world. I will be offering practical advice about ways in which young children can be encouraged to develop a constructive, success-promoting approach to their own abilities and skills. I will be considering the influence of self-image and anxiety on performance, and relating these crucial factors to the adult's perception of the child. And I will look at the vital, but seldom-considered, effects of the behaviour of the child on grown-ups — especially on the mother. This is a subject rarely discussed in books on child care, and one which parents often fail to understand, tending to see the role of the adult as one of giving, and that of the child as one of receiving.

But growing up is not a solitary process, taking place in isolation from the rest of the human race. It involves a multiplicity of complicated interactions: how parents feel towards their children has a profound influence on the way in which each child feels about himself. You cannot adequately examine the developmental processes during infancy without considering this constant, dynamic exchange. The emotions of the mother are no less important than those of her child. The way in which a father regards his son or daughter affects the growth of self-esteem and individuality. Both parents are influenced by the appearance and behaviour of the child and their assessment of the child's ability.

Reading some child-care books, you get the impression that parents are expected to behave like saints. They must never get angry or impatient, tired or depressed. They must always remain loving and tender. The message has been sold so hard and so long that many feel guilty over any lapses from such parental perfection.

Parents are human. They get tired and anxious, unhappy and cross. They endure periods of depression and boredom, and sometimes they feel more hatred than love for their children. To pretend otherwise is to suffer a dangerous illusion. To try and behave as though you lack human weaknesses, desires or emotions will not, ultimately, enhance the child's future, but may easily harm it.

In this book, I will be dealing with the real world of babies, and the day-to-day realities of growing up; not the sunfilled fantasies of happy families created by television soap opera and romance magazines. These are part of a fictional never-never land that is regarded as a factual ideal by many mothers.

The phrase 'gifted child' has come to mean highly intelligent child. But there are many other kinds of abilities and talents which need not necessarily be associated with high levels of intelligence. Those of the creative child, for example, or the socially skilled are no less important to successful development and attainment in the adult world, yet they are often overlooked.

An imbalance of abilities all too easily leads to emotional difficulties later in life. The highly intelligent but socially unskilled child may alienate others by his intolerance for those less able, or by his inability to express opinions in a diplomatic manner.

Both of these qualities are likely to work against successful development. On the other hand, the creative child who lacks the intellectual capacity to keep up with other children may never be given the right opportunities to make his true abilities known. It could well be argued that these are failings of society, symptoms of a lack of understanding for the needs and talents of the exceptional child. This is a point to which I will return in the last chapter. But it must be said that while the fault often lies outside the child, this will make no difference to the damage which may be caused.

Your baby is born with a balanced brilliance, a rounded talent for intellectual development of every kind, and a potential for high intelligence, great creativity, and impressive social skills. Each must be allowed the same opportunity for development to its maximum level.

I hope that you share my belief in the enormous promise of the very young, and that you will want to play your part in ensuring that the promise is fully realised. In helping the child towards a bright future, gifted parents enrich not only the child's world but their own as well.

Chapter One

Are You A Gifted Parent?

Is your child gifted? Even if you are not certain of the answer I am sure you must have given some thought to the question. There can be few caring parents who have not hoped that their children possess some special talent or ability which will help them to do well in life. There is such an interest in the early detection of superior abilities that testing children has become a major part of psychology. Each year millions of youngsters are given some form of intelligence, creativity or personality test the outcome of which can drastically shape the future course of their lives.

I am not saying that such testing is necessarily wrong. Nor am I criticising parents for showing a perfectly natural interest in the abilities of their children. But the emphasis is too one-sided. In our concern for the child we overlook the vital importance of the adult's role. We test the children but not their parents. We question the talents of the sons and daughters but not the child-rearing skills of the fathers and mothers. I wonder how many of those parents who are so eager to discover whether their children are gifted would be equally keen to find out if their children had gifted parents?

The fact is that gifted children begin with gifted parents. By that I do not mean adults who are exceptionally intelligent or highly educated, especially creative or materially successful. They may be any or all of these. But none is an essential component of those very special, and equally rare, skills which combine to produce gifted parents. Exactly what those skills are and how you can make them work to the benefit of your child is what this book is all about.

Parents do not create giftedness in their children. That is neither possible nor necessary. Just as a seed contains all that is needed for successful growth, and requires only a rich soil and the right conditions in order to flourish, so does each infant arrive with a promise of genius just waiting to grow.

No baby is born stupid. With the exception of a relatively few severely brain-damaged infants — and even some of these can be helped to astonishing levels of attainment, as I will describe in the next chapter — all babies have a birthright of brilliance. Tragically, this truly remarkable potential is all too seldom realised. The almost limitless horizons of the new born contrast starkly with the all too limited achievements of the school-age child. Bright babies are the general rule. Brilliant children are very much the exception.

Why should this happen? What limits mental abilities so drastically? The answer to questions like this is as simple as it is sad. Children learn to be unintelligent. They learn a caution which inhibits true creativity. They learn to become socially ineffective. They learn because we, the adults, teach them. It is out intervention which effectively diminishes and so often destroys early promise. It is we who teach them to undervalue their brains and underestimate their abilities. At birth the baby has none of these damaging conceptions. It is we who teach the child that some problems are too difficult to solve. The baby knows nothing about difficulties or about giving up. It is we who teach the child that stupidity can be more rewarding than intelligence; that getting by can be a safer strategy than getting on.

These are the lessons we teach very well, very consistently and very early. By the end of the first five years of life, most children have mastered them to a very great extent. The groundwork for attitudes and beliefs which will restrict intellectual growth, retard creativity and interfere with social success has usually been completed by a child's fifth birthday. Beyond this age, the inappropriate early responses are more likely to become firmly established than they are to be changed. All the available research evidence suggests that damage caused in these earliest months can seldom be repaired.

How Parents Harm Their Children

In Chapter three I will be examining the crucial first five years during which these lessons are learned. But I want to start by considering come of the more basic ways in which parents, often with the best possible motives in the world, can harm their children. It is by avoiding these extremes that the gifted parent provides the framework within which beneficial, ability-expanding interactions can take place.

Some parents are so ignorant, indifferent or incapable of meeting even the most basic needs of their children that permanent damage is almost inevitable. I can say with confidence that none of them will be reading this book! But these gross forms of neglect and inadequacy are not the only reasons why a child fails to develop as nature intended. Parents who are deeply loving and very capable of carrying out their chosen methods of child-rearing may also restrict intellectual, creative and social progress. The difficulties arise not because of the competence with which the child is raised but because the procedures themselves are damaging. Their stringent application merely makes matters worse.

Let me start by looking at a set of parental attitudes which I still frequently encounter. These arise because the adults are firmly convinced that tradition provides the answer to any problem.

Good Old Days — Best Old Ways

The lessons we learn in childhood make the most lasting impressions. If we reach adulthood with a mind receptive to fresh ideas and flexible enough to incorporate new methods, then a child-orientated approach to parenthood — which sees every infant as an individual with particular needs — will seem the most natural one to follow. Such parents will be keen to find new solutions to age-old problems of child-rearing. They will have sufficient confidence in themselves not to have to fall back on responses learned from their own parents. They will carefully consider all the information available and then select those methods — whether ancient or modern — which seem best suited to the needs of the child.

But not all parents are capable of adopting a flexible approach. Some tend to be suspicious of new ideas and to treat child psychology with contempt. In the short term, at least, they may find it far easier to bring up their children, because to every problem there is usually a solution which is simple and direct. The fact that it may also be disastrously wrong seldom occurs to them. Their confidence in the 'good old days — best old ways' approach is such that self-doubt is unlikely to creep in. They *know* their methods are right. If the child fails to respond as anticipated, becomes rebellious, sullen, anxious or under-achieving, then the fault always lies elsewhere — in the child himself or with the school, with television or the kind of friends he makes. At no stage do they experience real anxiety or begin to question their own role in the situation. Their usual line of argument goes like this: 'I was raised in exactly the same way and it didn't do me any harm. I've no patience with modern ideas.'

In such families, each generation's child-raising methods become a carbon copy of the one before. If physical punishment was used by his father, then the man will consider it likely to be effective with his own children. If certain subjects were taboo when the parents were young, then the same topics may never be discussed in the present home. If strict, unquestioning obedience was demanded of them then the parents may require the same from their own children. At the other extreme, adults who were raised in an atmosphere of total freedom, where there were no rules or prohibitions, may follow the same pattern with their own youngsters. One can also get a reversal of the 'good old days — best old ways' pattern, where the new parents reject everything their parents thought of as right and proper and do the exact opposite.

I am not saying that discipline is necessarily wrong or that a laissez-faire approach is right. What I am saying is that blindly following tradition, or rejecting it and doing the opposite, produces a lack of flexibility in child-rearing. No method, except extreme harshness or total indifference, should be considered bad or good in itself. Judgement can only be made as a result of its effects on the child. What helps one infant may hinder another. In order to meet the needs of the child as an individual it is essential to match the methods to his or her requirements. Gifted parents not only have a wide choice of responses from which to choose, they have an acute feeling for the reactions of the child. They are prepared to monitor their own actions closely and, based on the feedback from the infant, to modify, abandon or increase certain aspects of their child-rearing practice.

The Frankenstein Syndrome

Many parents are made anxious by precocity. They see something 'unnatural' in early development, and fear they will create a monster instead of a 'normal, healthy, happy child'.

As recently as 1949, a psychologist stated confidently that: 'A home which nurses a genius may very likely also harbour a future criminal or a downright lunatic.' We know that this fear is quite unjustified. Numerous studies have shown that children with fully developed mental abilities are not less stable than others but probably more emotionally balanced. They tend to be happier, more sociable, more restrained in their conduct and more aware in their judgements. Yet the fear remains, and is fanned by the treatment of giftedness in the popular press:

TORMENT OF A CHILD TOO CLEVER FOR WORDS . . . HAVE THESE
PARENTS MADE A MONSTER? . . . THE NIGHTMARE WORLD OF
BRILLIANT BOY. . . .

These are just a few newspaper headlines I have seen recently.
No wonder many parents are firmly convinced of the old
warning, 'early ripe — early rot', like the mother who told me
firmly: 'I don't want my daughter to be gifted, I want her to be
normal.'

Gifted parents have no such anxieties. They realise that for
their child to reveal talents and skills which the world may
regard as exceptional is nothing abnormal. It is a perfectly
natural event and one which indicates how successfully that
child is developing.

The Desire For Dependency

Many parents do not want their children to be clever. They
want them to be 'cute'. In these households, the child's role is
that of some kind of pet; amusing to the parents. The cute child
best meets the adult's dependency needs. Being cute involves
doing amusing, childish things which can be commented on
amidst general, adult laughter. Cute children ape adult
behaviour and make people smile by doing so. Children who
strive to be independent, to think and act for themselves as
competently and intelligently as they know how, are not being
cute. They are not playing the kind of role these adults demand
of them. They are 'unnatural', they are 'growing up too
quickly'.

When this happens, those adults who need dependency as a
prerequisite for their love may start to reject the child. They
may not do it obviously, they may not even be fully aware that
they are doing it. But the child, being far more perceptive than
they realise, quickly identified their displeasure. Under these
circumstances, it is an unusually bold and self-possessed infant
who continues with the independent behaviour and risks the

loss of parental affection. If there are other children in the family who are prepared to continue playing the 'cute' role, then the position of the persistently individualistic child is likely to be an exceptionally unhappy one. The saddest thing about this type of child-rearing is that the parents are firmly convinced that they are being helpful and especially loving. They usually refute angrily any suggestion that the child's mental development or social progress may be being harmed.

The gifted parent manages to balance the giving of love and attention with a recognition that the child has rights as an individual. They tend to see the child as capable of making important decisions concerning his or her needs at a very early age. Early attempts, however amusing they may appear, are not greeted with patronising interference: 'Here, let Mummy tie those laces for you, you're much too little to do that,' says the mother who wants dependency. What does the child learn from this 'help'? Only that he is little, weak and helpless; not how to tie shoe laces, nor — perhaps more important — how to behave independently. But that, of course, is the last thing his parents want.

The Looking Glass Kids

Michael's father believes children should be able to stand up for themselves and fight back. Michael's father enjoys boxing and so will five-year-old Michael. Clara's mother is an enthusiast for classical music and despises 'pop'. The only music Clara is ever allowed to listen to, or has been allowed to listen to during her four years of life, are the classics. Billy's father is convinced of the superiority of the white race and the inferiority of all others. At the age of five Billy already shares his father's prejudices. Mary's mother thinks that the children in their neighbourhood are too common for her daughter to play with. Four-year-old Mary thinks they are common as well.

These are the 'looking glass kids'. They are being brought up to reflect only their parents' view of the world. If, as they grow older and experience other attitudes and opinions, they shatter the mirror and start to think for themselves the parents will probably be upset and angry.

'How could Mike refuse to go on boxing? Is he a sissy?'

'How could Clara want to listen to that rubbish? Has she no taste?'

'How could Billy date a girl from another culture? Has he no pride?'

If the parental pressures are strong enough, these rejections of the hand-me-down attitudes may never occur, or be short-lived if they do. In any event, it is most unlikely that the children will have sufficient knowledge of the world to reject them, or even seriously question them, before the age of five. During these vital years of development their perceptions of the world will accurately mirror those of their parents. Since the parents are the child's major source of knowledge and information about the world, such a sharing of viewpoints is inevitable. But that does not mean it must consist only of those values which the adults perceive as important. For the child to progress successfully it must enjoy, as early as possible and as often as possible, the widest possible access to different viewpoints. Children should certainly be exposed to the special interests and deeply-felt beliefs of their parents, but not to the exclusion of all else and never in such a way that alternatives are held up as being unworthy of their attention or interest.

It is always very hard to become aware of one's own prejudices, or to consider deeply-felt attitudes as being just one of a number of possible viewpoints. Usually they seem so 'right' and 'natural' that it becomes impossible even to consider that viable alternatives may exist. Part of the skill of the gifted parent lies in an ability to expose the child to as wide as possible a variety of ideas, opinions, attitudes and possibilities. In this way they come to reflect experience brilliantly and in all directions, like a many-faceted diamond rather than the single image of the looking glass.

Some parents may feel that it is wrong to allow a child below the age of five to make up his, or her, mind about anything of importance. They might argue that nobody so lacking in knowledge and experience of the world has any right to make a decision on anything significant. Far better for the parents to do the thinking for the child and to hand over a neatly-packaged answer. An additional criticism which some parents have voiced to me is that children become very anxious when there is any degree of uncertainty. By offering a variety of experiences and possibilities you merely confuse and bewilder the child. It is far safer to provide ready-made verities on which they can build their perceptions of life. Certainly, some children need more reassurance than others. They tend to become anxious when faced with the unusual and take longer to adapt to new situations. But this does not mean they cannot be provided with a range of experiences, so long as it is done sensitively and in constant sympathy with the child's particular needs. How the task is to be accomplished must be a matter for individual parents. Only they have the expert knowledge of their own children necessary for judging the best approach. But playing safe is certainly not the answer if the child's mind is to be allowed to develop.

It should be made clear that I am not saying children must be discouraged from sharing their parents' interests, nor should adults be concerned about expressing their own honest views about life. Maybe the children will find them equally convincing and adopt those interests and attitudes as their own. But the choice has to be theirs, and it can only properly be made once the child has been allowed to experience as many viewpoints as possible.

If the child is persistently moulded to reflect the opinions and attitudes of the adult then a close replica will almost certainly result. But that independence of thought and self-confident awareness so necessary for successful mental growth will be restricted. Under these conditions it is much less likely that the child's inborn potential can ever be achieved.

The Prodigal Son Syndrome

In many families there is a marked difference in ability between one or more of the children and the rest. There is evidence to show that the first born is likely to be advantaged over later arrivals, unless there is a gap of at least four years between the children. But birth order alone is not always sufficient to explain the marked discrepancies which are found. It is by no means always the oldest child who is seen, by the parents, as being the most gifted. I call the recipients of such favourable opinions the 'Prodigal Sons' — although they can equally be daughters!

What happens is that, for any number of reasons, the parents have a more positive attitude towards the abilities of one of the children. This may be because that child is better looking, or of a sex which the adults especially wanted, or because they seemed to show some special talents early on in life. When this occurs, there tends to be an unequal distribution of resources with the favoured child, or children, receiving more than their fair share of opportunities and encouragements. The parents will tell you that this arrangement is only fair because: 'He is so much better able to take advantage of them than his brother.' Sometimes they will add a further justification by saying that the less-advantaged child prefers things that way: 'He gets so anxious when pressured. He's happier not being pushed into situations beyond him.'

Their behaviour often seems to be justified because the children really do exhibit the kind of responses they describe. The favoured child is confident and capable, the other diffident and anxious. But while the judgement seems confirmed, we have a chicken and egg problem here: how can we tell which came first? Was it the behaviour of the children or the initial belief that these differences were present in their behaviour? Was it this belief, translated into the very different responses of the parents towards their children, which produced the results originally predicted? We now know that the role of the self-fulfilling prophecy in child development is a potent one and something which plays an important part in the emergence of ability. It is a subject to which I shall be returning later in the book.

The gifted parent is well aware of these dangers and takes care never to prejudge a child or to advantage one child over the other. All must be given opportunities to experiment as widely as possible with the world, and to determine the extent to which they want to respond in any particular direction. Only in this way can the inborn promise of each be allowed the best possible chance of realisation.

Rich Man — Poor Mind

There is a great deal of talk these days about enriched environments, by which most people mean surroundings which provide plenty of material resources such as books, toys, games and puzzles. To an extent this is justified. Pleasant surroundings will improve performance. Children of all ages develop most effectively in environments which offer an adequate supply of all types of resources, particularly those qualities most precious and difficult to obtain, understanding and patience. But an extravagant expenditure on playthings will not, of itself, provide the key to unlocking mental abilities. You cannot buy your way to giftedness and gifted parents realise this. They realise too that an overflowing toy cupboard may be matched by an almost empty mind. Yet it is a point easily overlooked, especially by parents who are determined to lavish every possible material advantage on their children. To give them: 'All the things I never enjoyed as a kid.' To the casual observer, the homes of such children may appear an almost limitless source of mental stimulation. Yet it is clear that the youngsters have failed to be stimulated. All they have learned, and possibly at great financial cost to their parents, is how to think as little as possible.

This is not as surprising as it may seem. Let me offer a simple analogy which should help to make matters clear. Suppose you handed an infant a tin opener and then locked him in a larder that was well stocked with all kinds of tinned food. Would you be surprised if he grew thinner and weaker with every day that passed? Would you express amazement if he finally starved to death? Of course not. We all know that a can opener is useless unless you have been taught how to use it. We all realise that tinned food provides nourishment only after it has been opened. Put in those terms, the infant's need for the proper training in order to receive nourishment is so obvious that it is almost impossible to imagine anybody thinking otherwise. Yet this is exactly the mistake which is made, time after time, when it comes to feeding the mind. An enriched environment certainly provides a multitude of stimulating possibilities. But without the knowledge of how to exploit them properly they remain just that — possibilities and not realities.

Children can only learn with the help and encouragement of others. The parents are the gatekeepers of the child's world. They stand sentinel over a constant flow of experiences, determining what shall be allowed in, deciding what shall be kept out. The more limited and unexciting the imports, the more numerous the prohibitions, the more poverty-stricken the intellectual diet the child will enjoy. The opportunity for experiences of all kinds is of paramount importance. But it must be first-hand experience because the most effective learning takes place by doing, not simply by looking and listening. This basic fact is often overlooked today when children are bombarded with fresh information from television and radio and books and teachers, which puts them in a passive role. They are expected to learn by absorption, which is difficult, wearying and inefficient, rather than by direct, practical involvement which is not only the most effective and lasting way of learning but also — a damning attribute in the eyes of some teachers — enjoyable! Three hundred years ago the great educationalist and creator of the world's first picture book for children, Bishop Comenius, stressed the need for first-hand experience and active exploration when he wrote: 'Men are taught to become wise not by books but by the heavens, the earth, oaks and beeches; that is they must learn to know and examine things themselves, and not the testimony and observations of others about things.'

Jerome Bruner, Professor of Experimental Psychology at Oxford University, echoes those sentiments today when he says: 'We must talk about enriched *people* not enriched *environments*. Our interventions must enable children to become richer in their intentions, not in their environmental possessions . . . the objective is not passive consumers of enriched environments, but active producers of their own thing.'

How Do You Rate As A Gifted Parent?

In the course of my research into gifted children I have received help 'from many thousands of parents. Amongst the information they provided were descriptions of their approach to child-rearing. From these a clear pattern of responding emerges which seems to typify the most successful approach to encouraging favourable mental development. You can rate yourself on the same scale by ticking those statements below which reflect your own approach to bringing up your children. If you are really interested in learning how you compare to the parents in my survey then it will be essential to respond honestly. Only tick those statements which refer to responses you normally make, not those you sometimes employ. If your child is less than three years old a number of the statements will not be appropriate. In this case tick them if you truly *intend* to carry out those particular responses when the child is older.

1. I answer all questions from my child as patiently and honestly as possible.
2. I take serious questions or statements from my child seriously.
3. I provide a display board where my child can show off his/her work.
4. I am prepared to tolerate an untidy work area if my child has not yet completed some creative task (i.e. painting, model making etc.).
5. I provide my child with a room, or part of a room, exclusively for his/her own use.
6. I show my child he/she is loved for own sake, not for achievements.
7. I give my child responsibilities suitable to age.
8. I help him/her make *own* plans and decisions.
9. I take my child on trips to places of interest.
10. I teach my child how to improve on the tasks he/she does.
11. I encourage my child to get along with children from different backgrounds.
12. I set a reasonable standard of behaviour and see my child follows it.
13. I never compare my child unfavourably to other children.
14. I never denigrate my child as a form of punishment.
15. I provide hobby materials and books.
16. I encourage the child to think things out for himself/herself.
17. I read regularly to my child.
18. I teach my child early reading habits.
19. I encourage my child to invent stories and fantasies.
20. I give careful consideration to the individual needs of each child.
21. I provide a time each day when the child can be alone with me.
22. I allow my child to have a say in planning family programmes or trips.
23. I never mock my child for making a mistake.

24. I encourage my child to remember stories, poems and songs.
25. I encourage my child to be sociable with adults of all ages.
26. I devise practical experiments to help my child find out about things.
27. I allow my child to play with all kinds of junk objects.
28. I encourage my child to look for problems and then solve them.
29. I look for specific things to praise in my child's activities.
30. I avoid general praise which I do not really mean.
31. I am honest about my emotions with my child.
32. I do not have any subjects which I would totally refuse to discuss with my child.
33. I provide opportunities for real decision-making by my child.
34. I encourage my child to be an individual.
35. I help my child find worthwhile programmes on TV.
36. I encourage my child to think positively about his/her abilities.
37. I never dismiss failures by my child with the comment: 'I can't do it either!'
38. I encourage my child to be as independent of adults as possible.
39. I have faith in my child's good sense and trust him/her.
40. I would sooner my child failed by himself/herself than succeeded because I did most of the work.

What the Score Tells You

Work out your score by adding up the ticks. If you find that you frequently, but not invariably, carry out some response then award yourself half a mark.

The parents of gifted children in my study obtained an average score of 30 ticked statements. If you had between 25 and 35 ticked then you are certainly carrying out most of the responses found in families where the children are exceptional in their abilities. You may find it worthwhile to look at any of the statements which you felt unable to tick and see if these responses might not be incorporated into your own family.

If you were only able to score less than 25 statements, then I suggest that you read through the list of responses again to see if more of these helpful activities could become a part of your daily routine. If you would like to increase the number of responses but are uncertain about how to do so, or concerned that your child may respond unfavourably to changes, then I suggest you read Chapter eight at this point.

Chapter Two

Is Genius All In The Genes?

When one considers the enormous potential for brilliance which babies possess and compares it to the subsequent levels of attainment in the majority of children, the outcome seems little short of a tragedy. Not only are individual lives being diminished and opportunities for achievement lost, but mankind as a whole is squandering one of the scarcest and most urgently needed natural resources — intelligent human beings.

That is how it seems to me and to many psychologists. But there are others who strongly refute that suggestion, not because they favour a squandering of inborn abilities, but because they deny that any such wastage occurs on the scale which I have suggested. They do not view intellectual growth as dependent on what we do but on what we are. It is not where we go in life that matters but where we start from. According to their beliefs, intelligence depends, to a very great extent, on a person's inherited genetic make-up. They regard children as programmed from birth to attain a certain level of intellectual achievement. Failure to achieve more, far from being surprising, is inevitable. Genius is written into the genes.

These are widely held views which have profound social and political consequences. After all, if certain races, or some sections of our society, are inherently less intelligent than others then there is little point in trying to change matters by improving the surroundings. An enhanced environment will merely be a waste of time and resources for individuals who are genetically crippled, and whose inheritance condemns them to be intellectual second-class citizens.

If these views are correct then those who argue, as this book does, that the environment is all important must be wrong. Even if one believes that intelligence is largely, although not entirely, determined by the genes — a middle ground position now widely favoured by those supporting a mainly genetic argument — the significance of changes in the surroundings becomes greatly diminished. It might indeed be argued that attempting to change the predestined, genetically determined, intellectual fate of children is a cruel deception, rather like training a cart horse for the racetrack.

The assumption basic to this book is that genetic limitations to intellectual growth do not exist, at least not in any meaningful way. If you are not particularly interested in what has become known as the Nature versus Nurture controversy, I suggest that you skip to Chapter three. It is not important to understand the finer points of the debate in order to make full, practical use of the information given in the book. However, it is essential that I set out the reasons why I reject the naturist arguments, if only in an attempt to defuse attacks which are likely to be made by naturists on the approach I am advocating.

The Great Debate

If you hold the view that intelligence levels are predetermined (mainly) by genes, and that environment (usually) plays a minimal role, then you are a naturist. If you believe that environment is all important and that genetic inheritance (except in a relatively few instances of inherited brain damage) counts for little, then you have joined the nurturists' side of the great debate. It is a debate not quite as old as psychology itself but one which has now been around for more than fifty years. The argument has been fierce and frequently bitter, often more of a no-holds-barred fight than an academic debate. Eminent upholders of the naturist approach have been prevented from speaking at universities and colleges by rioting students. Heated words have been exchanged in the letter pages of newspapers and learned journals. Political extremists have seized on the arguments of one side or the other as 'evidence' that their particular prejudices have been exonerated and 'scientifically' proven. Although the evidence on which each side bases its particular conclusions is rather complex, with disagreements centring on experimental approach and statistical interpretation, the opposing arguments can be fairly simply and briefly summarised.

The naturists hold that intelligence, and the capacity for intellectual growth which the child possesses at birth, is largely decided by inheritance. It depends to a very great extent, they claim, on an individual's genes. Everybody with a normal number of genes has 46 in each cell, half donated by the father via his sperm, and half by the mother in her egg. Four of these genes determine the sex of the child, the remainder are responsible for all other physical characteristics, although not all are 'switched on' in a particular cell. Those which do influence the cell's performance are said to be dominant. If a woman has blue eyes and a father brown eyes, then the genes for blue eye colouring will be dominant if the child's eyes are blue.

Genes do not actually exist. They are simply convenient names for large groups of specific units within the control centre, the nucleus, of the cell. These units make up the chemical blueprint which determines how the cell will grow, what kind of jobs it will do, and the sort of chemicals which it will manufacture. How the genetic blueprint is expressed decides, for example, whether a cell will form part of the liver or the kidney.

Genes determine the colour of the eyes and the pigmentation of the skin, whether a child will have his father's chin or his mother's nose. Some people have ear lobes attached to the side of the face, others have detached lobes. Seven out of ten people can roll their tongues. These characteristics, and many, many others, are genetically dictated.

The naturist would say that the same applied in large measure to intelligence and creative abilities. A child with 'good' genes is destined for a bright future. A baby with a poor blueprint has a gloomy future, which the best and most stimulating environment in the world will do little to improve. In this sense, 'good' genes are those which combine to produce effective brain cells capable of high performance and, therefore, of expressing themselves in better than average levels of intelligence. Certain races are held by some naturists to be a better repository of good genes than others. It is at this point, especially, that racial prejudice and the politics of inborn supremacy enter the scene.

A nurturist holds the view that all children are born equal, and their fate is decided later by the family and social conditions into which they are born. If you improve the environment you will enhance the intelligence. If the child is forced to develop in bad, neglectful and insufficiently stimulating surroundings, natural abilities will be diminished.

Thirty years ago, it was possible to find extremist views on both sides of the argument. There were those who believed that the environment had no effect at all on genetic endowment, and that 'good breeding' would always make itself known. Others held that birthright had no part to play at all. Any child, provided he or she was raised under the right conditions, could be turned into a genius. Since then, as a result of greater experience and knowledge, the two sides have moved closer together. There is now general agreement that both genetic factors and the environment exert an important influence on development. At the same time, there has been growing interest in the effects of other genetically determined characteristics; the temperament of the child, the sensitivity of the individual's nervous system to stimulation, the level of activity or passivity of the baby. All these will be considered later in the book. The remaining dispute between the two sides now revolves around the relative contribution of nature and nurture.

A leading advocate of the naturist position is Arthur Jensen, professor of educational psychology at the University of California at Berkeley. It was an article which he wrote for the *Harvard Educational Review* in 1968, entitled 'How Much Can We Boost IQ and Scholastic Achievement?' which sparked off the most recent bout of controversy. The answer which he supplied to his own question was — not very much. On the basis of his findings, the genetic composition of intelligence amounts to 80 per cent of an individual's ability. Other researchers have disputed his statistics and recalculated them to bring down the genetic component to as low as 25 per cent.

One of Professor Jensen's most vocal opponents, Professor Leon Kamin of Princeton University, considers that there is no inherited factor in an ability to score highly on intelligence tests. My claim that babies are born brilliant may, at first sight, appear to be adopting an extreme naturist approach. But this would only be true if one qualified it by saying that some babies are born brilliant while others are born stupid. By stating that all of them, with the exception of a very few chronically brain-damaged infants, are born with a potential for brilliance, I am, in fact, contradicting a basic tenet of the naturist faith. Naturists consider that genes mean inequality and differences. In theory, there can be no doubt that they are right. It seems to me impossible seriously to dispute the statement that a person's ultimate intellectual capacity must be genetically determined. In practical terms, I would argue, this approach is not so much wrong as irrelevant.

There can be no doubt that the upper limits of mankind's mental capacity are imposed by the way the brain is put together. This incredible piece of biochemical engineering is directed by the genes. It is also reasonable to assume that the upper limits will vary from one individual to the next, depending on the ways in which their genes work. Some are likely to be more effective than others and to construct more efficient brains with higher upper limits of ability. Even the best genes, producing the most efficient brain, will be restricted by the physical characteristics of the chemicals from which that brain is made. There will always be an upper limit to the amount of things we can store in our memories. Some computer experts have estimated that this total, using the language of computer programming, amounts to one billion million bits of information. There must also be an upper limit to the speed at which the brain can function. Just as it takes a certain amount of time for the pain message to reach my skull after I have stubbed my big toe, so too will it require a tiny but measurable amount of time for messages to transfer from one part of the brain to the next.

My contention is that these upper limits that genetically determine boundaries of human intellectual ability, lack practical significance. There are many excellent reasons for supposing that we never come anywhere near to approaching the limits of mental capacity. There are no reasons for believing that we do. It has been estimated that even the world's finest thinkers, scientists, academics, and philosophers, use less than half of their total brain power, while the average person uses only a fraction of his or her available intellectual abilities.

Imagine a computer capable of the most sophisticated and complex reasoning being used merely to balance the household budget, play noughts-and-crosses, or — as seems to be the fate of many computers — print out Snoopy drawings! It would be quite correct to say, under those circumstances, that the limits of the computers's powers were determined by the design of its circuits and the skill with which they had been assembled. But it would be ludicrous to extend that argument and say that noughts-and-crosses or Snoopy print-outs were the peak of its logical attainments. Yet that is what happens, time and time again, during discussions about the potential of the human brain. We focus on its presumed limitations and pay insufficient attention to its potential for expansion.

The Expanding Mind Of Man

The harder you make your brain work, the greater will be its capacity for work. The more use you make of your memory, the better will be your powers of memory. The more confidence you have in your mental abilities, the more that confidence will be justified. The human mind is the only container in the world that grows larger the more things you put inside. That applies to the adult mind, but even more strongly to the still-growing, highly flexible and versatile brain of the very young. The evidence for this is massive and indisputable. Why then do so many people find it so hard to accept?

I have met parents who have deliberately prevented their children from learning new things because they were afraid it might 'wear out' their intelligence. I have been assured by well-educated and articulate mothers that learning poetry was bad for their off-spring because it 'used up' valuable memory space. Professor Parkinson invented the famous law which states that work expands to fill the time available for its completion. Perhaps we should announce a similar law which says that the mind expands to meet the demands we make on it! Were that not so, mankind would still be living in caves, travelling around in hollowed-out logs, and rubbing sticks together to make fire.

Let us look at just a little of the evidence which clearly demonstrates how remarkably responsive the brain is to any demands made upon it. Anybody unfortunate enough to lose their sight at an early age, or to be born blind, finds a great increase in the sensitivity of their touch and hearing. Blind people can frequently hear sounds so faint that a sighted person would fail to notice them. They can discriminate between surface textures far more efficiently than somebody whose eyes are the primary source of information about the world. But this is not because they have better ears or finger tips. It is an expansion of brain power. The disability has forced the brain to seek new ways of doing things; different kinds of connections have been made.

Special skills, the result of an expanding mind, can also be determined by the way we are brought up. A city-born child usually has a sharper eye for the traffic than his country-bred companion. The country child may notice the movement of birds and animals which remain invisible to the town dweller.

In some cultures, special ways of looking at the world are essential to survival. For example, anthropologists have reported that the Murray islanders, who inhabit remote islands in the Coral Sea off the coast of New Guinea, can see many things which are hidden to European eyes. They can spot cunningly camouflaged fish resting motionless against virtually identical coral backgrounds. At sea, they are able to describe objects on the distant horizon while a European in the boat beside them may notice only water and sky. These skills are a result of the way their brains have developed in response to particular needs.

There is experimental evidence, too, for the ability of the brain to grow in a special way on demand. Animals raised in cages which provide no stimulation are found to have smaller brains than animals raised in richly stimulating surroundings. In a rather grim experiment carried out in Russia, puppies and kittens were placed in two groups. One group was raised normally, the other was reared on a slowly moving turntable so that they got a constantly changing view of the world. From ten days onwards, the animals were killed and their brains examined. Those which had been exposed to a moving world were found to have brain cells in the areas concerned with balance which were one third larger and more mature than in other animals.

By stating that the brain grows in accordance with the demands made upon it, one is doing no more than confirming the truth of the well-established biological principle that structure and function are always related. What every living thing looks like has been determined by the activities necessary for its survival. To see this principle in action, you need do no more than glance in a mirror!

Humans, like their near-animal relatives the apes and monkeys, have flattish faces and eyes set side-by-side at the front. We share this common feature because of a once-shared survival strategy. At the dawn of human history, near-man swung from tree to tree in order to escape predators. To do this, you need the ability to judge distances very accurately, since a missed branch or too vigorous a leap could have disastrous consequences. Frontal facing eyes provide stereoscopic vision and allow a very precise perception of distances. The flattish face was preferable to a snout when swinging through the forests for the simple reason that it got less knocked about!

There are other ways, as well, in which the structure of the human form can be related to what early man did to survive. In order to make primitive tools, the hands had to be freed from their original purpose of helping to support the body. This meant walking upright, a change which placed far greater strain on the pelvis. Under a sudden impact, it now had a tendency to crack. Nature's answer was to favour individuals born with stronger, more reliable hip bones. In the female, greater strength was obtained by narrowing the birth canal, a change which led to a clash of survival priorities. Near-man was getting more intelligent. Brain power was starting to replace speed and brawn. A larger brain meant a larger skull, a bigger head at birth. But the narrowing birth canal offered a smaller exit to the world. The solution was to produce babies with fairly small heads and brains at birth, but to give the brain an ability to grow very rapidly during the first few years of life. In this period of dependency on adults, the infant was able to learn the skills necessary for survival.

The increase in brain size probably came about as a result of using primitive tools. Those who managed to fashion weapons from sticks and stones had a better chance of survival. They produced more children, managed to raise them to adulthood, and so were favoured by natural selection.

As tools become more complicated, a greater intelligence was needed to use them. But it was a two-way traffic. Superior intelligence led to the production of more sophisticated tools. These demanded higher levels of intellect to use them. It is a pattern which continues to this day. Every major advance in modern technology makes new demands on man's intellectual powers. Yet that challenge is always met, as it has been throughout the millions of years of evolution. There has never been a time when the expanding mind of man has proved unequal to the tasks it has been required to perform. Yet, in a very real sense, the true potential of the brain has never been tested at all. We have mostly been content to use our computing powers for trivial and undemanding purposes.

We can never be sure what the human mind is capable of achieving until and if ever that goal has been reached. But something of the awe-inspiring possibilities for growth can be seen, by a curious paradox, in the case histories of those who seem to have the least brilliant brains of all: the mentally handicapped.

A few years ago, a young man of twenty-five died suddenly, and an autopsy was performed. The doctor found that the youth's skull was practically an empty vault. Major brain damage, at an early age, had destroyed most of his cerebral cortex. These are two pinkish-grey hemispheres, each about the size of a clenched fist, which should fit snugly inside the head like walnuts in a shell. It is in this area of the brain that all the higher intellectual activities, such as reasoning, language, memory and logic, are considered to take place.

Feeling he should try to comfort the parents over the young man's death, the doctor called to see them: 'A tragic loss' he murmured sympathetically. 'But surely a blessing in many ways. . . .'

'What do you mean?' demanded the father indignantly.

'Well, with that amount of brain injury,' the doctor explained, 'he must have been a vegetable.'

Even more indignantly, the father explained that, far from being mentally retarded, his son had been highly intelligent. He had done well in school, passed his exams with good marks, and been holding down a responsible job in a bank at the time of his death.

Astonished and deeply chastened, the doctor departed. But his mistake had been a reasonable one. With so little brain tissue left, the boy ought to have been reduced to a virtual cabbage. The fact that he had been able to function more effectively than many of his friends, who possessed absolutely complete and healthy brains, demonstrates the brain's remarkable capacity to conquer almost overwhelming odds by finding new pathways, fresh connections, and different ways of carrying out the tasks demanded of it.

This is far from being an isolated case, as the work of Dr John Lorber of the Children's Hospital in Sheffield has demonstrated. For several years, Dr Lorber has been studying the consequences of hydrocephalus, or 'water on the brain', for intellectual growth. In this condition, brain fluid builds up in the skull, forcing out the soft bones of the baby's head and compressing the cerebral hemispheres. The pressure can be released by implanting a special tube inside the skull, to drain the fluid into the blood stream. But by the time the operation is performed, the brain has often been seriously and permanently injured. In some instances, the hemispheres have been so greatly reduced, that it is possible to shine a powerful light through the infant's skull. Here again, one might imagine that these severely brain-damaged children would be incapable of anything but the most elementary mental activities. But this is not the case. Dr Lorber has shown that injuries of this kind are not inevitably associated with retardation. Indeed, the opposite can be true. Many of those he examined had high levels of intelligence. In one instance, the patient had an IQ of 136, and took an honours degree in economics.

Dr Glenn Doman, an American expert on brain injuries, is the Director of the Institutes for the Achievement of Human

Potential, an organisation which helps to transform the lives of thousands of brain-injured children each year. The specialists at these centres, in Britain and America, achieve their results by forcing the brains of injured children to work — and to work hard. They have found that with the right therapies, a large proportion of their young patients can be helped back to a normal life. Dr Doman's files overflow with evidence of the brain's astonishing ability to make-good lost or damaged tissue. Many of the children have emerged from treatment with well above average IQs, and at least one was a genius.

'The world has regarded brain growth and development as if it were predetermined and unalterable,' he explains in his book, *What To Do About Your Brain Injured Child.* 'Instead, brain growth and development is a dynamic and ever-changing process. It is a process which can be stopped (as it is by severe brain damage). This is a process that can be slowed (as it is by moderate brain injury), but, most significantly, it is a process that can be speeded. . . .'

There can be no doubt that the brain grows on demand, whether in response to loss, to injury, or because of special needs imposed by the environment. Is there any evidence that the minds of children can be expanded by deliberately creating surroundings which provide massive amounts of the right sort of stimulation? The answer is that such proof does exist. It is provided by reports from parents who have specifically set out with the intention of turning their children into 'geniuses'. Before describing one such case, I would like to make clear my own attitude to this type of 'hot house' approach.

The cases that are written up, either in academic journals or as popular books, are the success stories. We cannot know what happened where the attempts failed, nor do we know what price — to parents and child — that failure was brought. I am certainly not criticising the desire of parents to encourage the full development of their child's potential. Indeed, that is my purpose in writing this book. Nor am I against many of the methods and procedures which are adopted. They can prove helpful with many children. My main criticism is that such an approach is unnecessary and cannot possibly work with every child. In many cases, the results might be exactly the opposite to what was intended. My main reason for briefly describing the one such case below is to illustrate just how willingly the human mind will expand to meet the demands made upon it.

The Edith Project

In August 1952, Aaron Stern, a survivor of the Nazi concentration camps, called a press conference in a New York hospital to announce the start of the *Edith Project*. Edith was his newborn daughter. The project was to turn her into a genius.

From five months onwards, he took over control of his daughter's life. The family radio played classical music twenty-four hours a day, for years on end. Baby talk was banned. Aaron Stern talked and talked to his daughter, showed her cards with words and numbers printed on them, so that she would quickly begin to understand written symbols. After eleven months, Edith was asked to give her age. She searched through the pile of number cards until she found the one marked with a ten. She held this out to her father, and then held up one tiny finger.

At a year old, Edith could speak fluently. At two, she could read. By four-and-a-half, she had read almost every word in every volume of the Encyclopaedia Britannica. When she entered school, aged six, she was reading two books a day and the *New York Times*. As a child, she consistently scored at well above genius ratings whenever her IQ was tested. By the age of 15, Edith was teaching higher mathematics at Michigan State University, and working for a PhD. Stern's hospital prediction had been proved correct. He had managed to 'create' a genius.

In his thought provoking book *Teach Your Baby To Read*,

Dr Glenn Doman asks this highly relevant question:

'How long could we look at Johnny, who had half his brain removed, and see him perform as well as Billy, who had an intact brain, without asking the question what is wrong with Billy? Why did not Billy, who had twice as much brain as Johnny, perform twice as well, or at least better?'

Why not indeed?

Surely it is time we stopped asking ourselves what makes brilliant children so 'extraordinary' and begin to face up to the rather less easily answered question of what causes the majority of children to so drastically underachieve? Or, to rephrase this crucial problem — what makes gifted children different?

Chapter Three

What Makes Gifted Children Different?

The most obvious way in which gifted children differ from others is in their special skill or ability, whether this is early reading or writing, a flair for mathematics or a particular musical talent; whether it involve high levels of intelligence, great creativity or both. In each case the gifted child is clearly behaving in a special way.

There are other differences as well and I will be examining four of the most important later in this chapter. These are much less obvious and often harder to detect, but no less significant. Indeed, I believe them to be the foundations on which the special skills of the gifted child are constructed. They include the amount of confidence with which a child approaches some unfamiliar task and the span of attention involved in solving problems. The child's image of himself and the way that child is regarded by adults are also important considerations. All of these will be discussed at length in a moment.

At first sight, it might seem as if these attitudes and responses were the result of having some special ability, and not a contributory cause as I have suggested. The gifted child, it might be argued, is bound to have a strong self-image, to be confident and well regarded by adults. None of these is necessarily true. But even when this does all happen, we can only say that there is an interaction — often a very beneficial one — between all these aspects of performance. And the starting point, I maintain, lies in the initial self-confidence and sense of competence which every baby possesses. It is only as a result of inappropriate learning that these basic, inborn characteristics come to be diminished. Where they grow strong and prosper, enabling skills and abilities to develop alongside them, it is as a result of successful interaction with the environment during the early years; interaction which is largely controlled by the parents.

For many years I have been studying this process of interaction and looking at the sorts of learning which occur, both helpful and damaging. I have now come to the firm conclusion that we regard giftedness in children entirely incorrectly, and in a way which not only hinders our understanding but limits our ability to help every child reach his true potential for brilliance — that birthright of which I spoke in the first chapter.

Let me explain what I mean, by comparing different levels of mental achievement with the results of a race. Inevitably there will be winners and losers, some who stride ahead and some who lag behind. We can examine the results and ask two different questions about them. The first is to look at those children who came in the first three places and ask ourselves how they achieved this success. I term this a front-runner approach to ability because it concentrates on those who succeed. This is the attitude we normally adopt when considering giftedness in children. Watching a group of infants drawing, for example, we may notice that one or two are much better than the rest, most are average in what they create and a few are worse than the rest. This is the kind of outcome you are likely to find when any task is performed. When we ask what the results tell us about the children the normal, front-runner, approach is to say: 'John and Mary did much better than the others. They are clearly clever children. What is it that makes them so talented?' At this point we might enter the great debate in the last chapter and discuss the relative importance of nature and nurture in the development of their particular skills.

But there is another way of looking at abilities and, in my

view, it is a far more valuable and constructive starting point than the conventional front-runner approach. Instead of making comparisons based on average performance and saying that some have done better and others worse than average, we could take the best results as our norm. Then we have to ask ourselves what made the other children fall behind. We might conclude, for instance, that the work of John and Mary is what one should expect from children of that age. If that is right what has caused the others to underachieve? What factors could have restricted their performance so badly?

By framing our questions in this way it is no longer the few, gifted children like the imaginary John and Mary of our example who are seen as exceptional, but the rest of the children who are looked on as special for having fallen behind in the realising of their inborn talents.

Suppose one visited a country where a few privileged children enjoyed normal levels of nutrition while the majority were half-starved. Those favoured youngsters would clearly be superior in mental and physical abilities to their unfortunate companions. They would be healthier, stronger, and better able to succeed in a whole range of activities. But nobody would comment: 'The majority are normal. That is what we would expect in children of that age. That is the level of performance they should be able to achieve. What is so different about the minority that makes them so superior?' Anybody who looked at the situation like that would be ridiculed, and with good reason. Yet this is the position adopted by those who advocate a front-runner approach to child development. It is just as absurd and equally unhelpful to both the children themselves and to our proper understanding of how to encourage maximum achievement.

I said in Chapter one that parents do not create gifted children but they do largely create the environments most likely to enable natural abilities to flourish. This applies to all kinds of abilities. You do not need to try and make your baby intelligent, he is born highly intelligent. It is a matter of making certain that the inborn potential is achieved. You do not need to teach your baby to be highly creative. All children are creative if given the opportunities to develop successfully. Children will need to be taught the customs and manners of their particular culture and society so that they can interact effectively in social situations. But you do not need to try and teach infants to be sociable. They have a strong desire for the companionship of other human beings and are socially precocious.

It is now widely accepted that our ultimate, adult, levels of intelligence, creative talent and social effectiveness are determined long before the start of formal schooling, during the first sixty months of life. Successful development during this critical period of growth will be reflected in the achievements of later childhood, adolescence and adulthood. But so too will any failure to realise that inborn potential. And failure, the research shows, is a far more likely outcome than success. One eminent American psychologist, Dr Burton White of Harvard, estimates that only *one child in ten* is raised in such a way as to maximise inborn abilities. For the majority, the advantages of birth are quickly diminished. And it all happens in the first five years of life.

Five Vital Years

During this period your child learns more than he, or she, will ever need to learn — or be capable of learning — during any similar period of time. Infants have an ability and a desire to master new knowledge that would be considered the mark of a genius in an older child. Not one adult in twenty thousand could grasp as much fresh information, or grow as rapidly in an understanding of the world, as every child achieves in just sixty months. Between birth and the fifth birthday, intellectual capacity expands as much as it is going to over the next thirteen years. The brain is capable of prodigious accomplishments and can meet virtually any demands made upon it. Indeed, all the evidence points to the fact that the greater those demands, the more varied and superior the accomplishments will prove. The reason for this is that the brain is still very flexible, with an enormous capacity for expansion. Pathways are laid down for the processing of information. These connect with one another to produce an almost infinitely complex network of passages and junctions along which ideas can flow. The more numerous these pathways and interconnections, the faster and more flexible the information processing will be.

Your baby's brain is eager to be made to work. Every infant has almost boundless curiosity and an inborn need to explore in order to discover everything possible about his, or her, surroundings. In gaining this essential knowledge the infant is greatly helped by an absence of the inhibitions and anxieties which restrict older children. While the toddler may hesitate, the crawling infant experiments without the slightest trace of fear. He, or she, will act impulsively, unconcerned by the thought of doing something silly, or looking foolish or getting into trouble, fears which greatly concern many older children. This freedom does not last long, however. All too quickly the infant learns to avoid certain activities and to behave in ways which conform to adult desires and expectations.

The uninhibited curiosity of the early months can quickly and easily give way to an anxious wariness as the child begins to experience failure. Such anxiety restricts the child's mental development in a number of crucial ways, all of which can interact with each other to increase adverse effects. The child who fails frequently develops a self-image which incorporates that failure. He or she suffers a sharp decline in self-confidence and self-esteem. Instead of seeing themselves as capable of solving problems effectively, such children come to perceive themselves as individuals who are unable to solve problems. This causes their approach to fresh challenges to be different from that of children with a self-image which includes confidence in tackling fresh problems. It also makes it less likely that the child will seek out problems. After all, they are a stimulus for distressing anxiety responses and most of us prefer to avoid things which make us feel worried. When confronted by a problem which he has to tackle, the child with an anxious, negative self-image usually perceives it as more difficult than it actually is and approaches the challenge of finding an answer in an inappropriate and ineffective manner. Finally, the high anxiety levels mean that the child is unable to receive constructive feedback from the problem-solving attempt. If he gets the answer right, such a child may not be able to tell you how or why that correct solution was arrived at. If he fails to find an answer, the child may be unable to explain the nature of the reasoning which led to that conclusion, nor why that particular approach was adopted in the first place.

All these anxiety-based responses damage the child's mental ability, retard progress and restrict the growth of intellectual skills. They are a major cause of failure to realise inborn brilliance. Their presence or absence from the child's pattern of behaviour is a result of different types of learning. These differences lead to the marked contrast of ability between the gifted child and one who is underachieving.

Differences That Make All The Difference

In this section of the book I want to examine four major areas of difference to see how exceptional children, through the intervention of their gifted parents, develop special skills. I shall be describing the kind of things which can go wrong and suggesting ways of overcoming some of the most frequently encountered difficulties. I will begin by looking at the ways in which children come to look at their own abilities.

The Importance Of Self-Image

Gifted children, generally, have a realistic confidence in their own abilities and a positive self-image. This leads to their approaching problems in a way which is must likely to lead to success. Children who lack a positive self-image, who have come to regard themselves as failures, approach problems in a way most likely to lead to an ability to find the right answer. This difference in self-image is, in my view, one of the most important differences between the gifted and the average child. But it does not always apply. There are some highly intelligent children who lack confidence and have a very low self-image. There are also children of limited ability who have an entirely misplaced confidence in their own competence.

This kind of discrepancy between self-image and reality is usually the result of an inappropriate feedback from performance. The child simply does not realise how badly or how well they are doing and so cannot form a reasonable judgement about their own capabilities. This is a topic to which I will return in a moment.

So far as the gifted child with a poor self-image is concerned, there may be other influences at work besides incorrect feedback. One difficulty gifted children always face is their ability to see far more problems in any situation than other children. Because they view a particular challenge so much more realistically they may be far more hesitant about tackling it. Where a child of limited mental abilities may say: 'Of course I can do that. . . .' and then proceed to get it hopelessly wrong, the able thinker may murmur uncertainly: 'It looks difficult. I don't know if I can do that. . . .' and then go on and get a very good result. I will be dealing with this ability to understand the true nature of problems in a moment. Here, I want to make the point that achieving children may be regarded as lacking in confidence simply because they adopt a much more serious and perceptive approach to challenges.

A second difficulty, which can lead some adults to underestimate the self-esteem in which the child holds himself or herself, is that there is a common tendency not to consider as difficult things which we can do easily, and not to regard an ability to do those things which come without much effort as being especially noteworthy. If you are very talented at painting or playing the piano, you will probably look on such skills as being fairly unremarkable. You appreciate that most people cannot do them to your level of expertise, but that is more their problem than an indication of your precocity. Children under the age of five are even more likely to see their special skills in this way. I remember talking to a five-year-old girl who was highly advanced in mathematics. She enjoyed working out number problems, and frequently did the maths homework for her ten-year-old brother, Michael.

'I wish I were clever like Mike,' she told me. 'He writes lots of stories and poetry and things like that. I wish I could.' 'But you are clever in other ways', I suggested. "Look at the way you can do maths. You are much better at that than he is.' 'Oh that,' she said dismissively. 'That's easy. That's just numbers. Anybody can do those.'

An adult who had talked to this girl only about her reading or writing, which were less advanced than her skill with figures, might well have got the impression that here was a very diffident child with a poor self-image and low estimation of her own talents. When it comes to the things they have learned to do well, gifted children almost always have a positive but realistic assessment of their own abilities. The less able child may have either a strong, but unrealistic, impression of their own abilities, or else be generally underconfident about everything they attempt.

Practical Ways Of Enhancing Self-Image

1. Never make a snap judgement about the self-esteem in which a child who has shown well-developed abilities in some direction holds himself or herself. Children who can do something exceptionally well are often so confident of themselves in this activity that they never even consider it something unusual.

2. Help the child who is mistakenly self-confident towards a better understanding of their real abilities. How this can be

done will be described below under the heading **Feedback**.

3.   Because a child hesitates before tackling a challenge, do not assume it indicates a lack of self-confidence. It may just be that they have a realistic understanding of the difficulties involved.

4.   You will not help a child build up a realistic self-image by constantly providing answers and solving problems on his behalf. As Professor Martin Seligman remarks in his book *Helplessness*: 'A sense of worth, mastery, or self-esteem cannot be bestowed. It can only be earned. If it is given away, it ceases to be worth having, and it ceases to contribute to individual dignity.'

The Importance Of Seeing Problems Properly

One of the main differences between gifted children and those of average ability lies in their ability to see problems. The nature of problems and the ways in which children learn to tackle them will be dealt with in the next two chapters. Here I want to consider the ways in which children become skilled at discovering and learning through their ability to notice things accurately — and then to ask questions about them.

In order to realise that something unusual and interesting is happening, the mind must be alert to the unexpected. Anomalies and discrepancies have to be recognised as signs that something novel and perhaps significant is happening; that it may prove useful to find out why things are as they are, and that exciting discoveries could be made with the application of some mental effort and ingenuity. If the environment has proved sufficiently varied and stimulating, these abilities can be identified within the first eight months, as experiments carried out by Jerome Kagan of Harvard University have demonstrated. He showed a series of distorted masks of the human face to children aged from four months to just over two years. Some of the faces had eyes missing, or in the wrong place, and in one all the features had been smoothed away. Up to eight months, there was little difference in the response of the infants. But beyond this age, those who had been able to develop their problem-solving capacity most fully broke into fearful crying when shown the distorted faces, while the remainder were unmoved. What produced these different responses?

The researchers attributed the crying to anxiety. The infants who were receptive to unusual events in their surroundings, perceptions from which problems are generated, were immediately aware that the faces were strange and wrong. They saw them as a problem, and one which it was impossible for them to solve. All they could do was to search through their memories for images of other faces — real, undistorted human features. Nothing they had seen before prepared them for the bizarre masks. These were problems to which they had no answer, and this made them fearful. Those infants whose perceptions were much more limited, on the other hand, simply did not recognise the faces as presenting any kind of problem. There was no conflict, no tension and no tears. The perceptive infants eventually overcame their difficulties with such anomalies however. When shown the masks at the age of 27 months, none of them cried.

Practical Ways To Improve Problem Perception

1.   Seeing problems is a skill which must be learned as early as possible. It is one of the most basic intellectual abilities the child has to master. You can help the infant by providing plenty of the right kind of stimulation during the first few months of life. How this may be done will be described in Chapter eight.
2.   Children who have learned to see problems will want to ask far more questions about their surroundings. I will talk about the ways in which such children can be helped in Chapter eight, and discuss the vital importance of encouraging children to ask problem-solving questions in the next chapter.

3. Give the child plenty of opportunities to work with problems which provide an immediate confirmation of success when answered correctly, such as jigsaw puzzles and construction blocks.

4. Point out problems in daily life. Encourage the child to have an inquiring mind and to ask questions about the things around him. Then help the child to find the answers for himself by means of practical experiment whenever possible.

The Importance of Perceiving Problems Realistically

Gifted children usually confront problems with a confidence based on a realistic appreciation of the exact difficulty of the problem. Children with a less well-developed appreciation of the nature of the task often become anxious before they even start.

During my researches I have been looking at the ways in which a particular problem may be presented and perceived, rather than at the nature of the problem itself, and how this can influence a child's ability to find the right answer. It was quickly apparent that, with most children, seeing the problem as being more difficult than it really was led to a sharp decline in ability to find solutions. In a typical research situation a four-year-old boy was given the task of putting together a collection of coloured blocks to match the design printed on a card. Electronic equipment enabled us to monitor the child's level of bodily arousal, and to give an indication of the amount of anxiety present. On the first run the boy succeeded well and was clearly very pleased with himself. Then he was given another design to match, one which he could have been expected to do equally easily under different circumstances. But this time he was warned that it was very difficult. Staring at the design and then at the blocks he hesitated and frowned unhappily. The monitoring equipment showed a sharp increase in anxiety level. He began to move uncomfortably in his seat. Almost haphazardly he started to push the blocks around. After a few half-hearted attempts involving little thought or concentration he pushed the blocks away and insisted he could not solve the problem.

It was clear in this, and many similar experimental situations, that the child saw the problem as being more difficult because of the warning to anticipate a harder task. This anxiety got in the way of the correct response. Once such an association between some task and anxiety has been formed, the most likely outcome is further anxiety and failure. The child rewards himself, or herself, by refusing to think about the problems. This rejection of the challenge leads to an immediate reduction of anxiety, which makes it more certain that a refusal to respond will follow at the next attempt.

The gifted child, by contrast, does not usually accept a description of the problem as being difficult at face value. He will assess the complexity for himself. On many occasions I have seen set problems being tackled just as rapidly and competently, after being described to the child as difficult, as they were when no such comment was made. In such instances the child looks even more delighted at having found the right answer and remarks: 'You said it would be hard . . . but it was really easy!'

The Importance Of Feedback

A gifted child solves a problem, looks carefully at the answer and shakes her head. It does not check out. A mistake has been made, so she starts all over again. A less-able child tackles the same problem. He comes up with an answer, glances briefly at it and then hands problem and solution over to an adult for checking. He is wrong but unaware of the fact.

In the first case there was constructive feedback from the task. The girl checked her answer against the steps needed to produce it and detected an error. When the right solution was finally found she had not simply solved the problem but learned important lessons about the way problems in general can be successfully solved. The other child was so relieved at finding an answer at all, that the problem was immediately discarded. No feedback occurred to enable the result to be checked.

Children whose minds are growing efficiently are not only aware of their successes, they are very conscious of their failures; but in a constructive way. They use feedback to correct mistakes, and to learn from them. They do not merely check the final answer, but constantly monitor their progress through the problem. They appreciate, correctly, that complex problems are never solved in one mental leap, but in a series of small steps. If the right answer is seen as the opposite bank of a wide river, then these stages on the way to success can be regarded as stepping stones. The child who thinks inefficiently ignores them completely, and flounders desperately as a result, while the capable problem-solver will work out the exact position of each stepping stone and make sure it is firmly positioned before proceeding further.

The result of a failure of feedback was well illustrated by an experiment carried out by Dr Alice Heim of the Psychological Laboratory, Cambridge. She gave a group of 14-year-old boys of average to low academic ability a difficult intelligence test designed for children whose IQ places them in the top ten to fifteen per cent of the population. The aim was to discover just how unsuitable such a test was for this type of student. Most of the boys reached the end of the test, worked faster than brighter children of the same age, and gained very low scores, some of them little better than could have been obtained by sheer chance. Because their feedback was so poor, they did not appreciate either the difficulty of the question or the inadequacy of their replies. 'Part of being a good student is learning to be aware of the state of one's own mind and the degree of one's own understanding,' comments the American teacher, John Holt, in his perceptive book on failure in childhood. 'The good student may be one who often says that he does not understand, simply because he keeps a constant check on his understanding. The poor student, who does not, so to speak, watch himself trying to understand, does not know most of the time whether he understands or not. Thus the problem is not to get students to ask us what they don't know; the problem is to make them aware of the difference between what they know and what they don't.'

Some psychologists believe that people approach problem-solving in one of two quite distinct ways. There are those who are able to extract the task from its surroundings, and concentrate on finding an answer without concerning themselves with anything else. This has been termed the 'field independence' approach, because the problem has been isolated from inessential events and emotions. As a result, it is more likely to be tackled efficiently and the right answer found. The majority of gifted children I have studied were capable of adopting this kind of independent attitude towards problems.

The field independent approach is in marked contrast to that of the 'field dependent' individual, who remains aware of events which have nothing to do with the task in hand. Let me illustrate this by describing how these different approaches might influence an adult in tackling a problem. A company executive has the job of working out a programme for the introduction of some new process. It is a tricky assignment, which needs to be completed quickly and very accurately. The field independent person focuses all his attention on the problem itself. The overall goal is broken down into a series of logical sub-goals, and these are tackled efficiently. The job done, each stage is carefully re-checked before the final report is presented.

The field dependent person sees not merely the problem, but much else besides. He or she is unable to extract that particular task from other events in their lives, from personal feelings and relationships within the office. While tackling the job, they are plagued by fears about how the report will be received by their superiors. If they do badly, how much will this influence their chances of promotion? How will their reputations be affected? Is that subordinate making suggestions out of a desire to help, or as a tactic for gaining points? Does that slight headache mean a dose of 'flu? Are they going through a 'lucky' phase? The field dependent individual is bombarded by these sorts of conflicting thoughts, doubts and anxieties. Inevitably, there is a reduction in efficiency. The feedback he or she receive is less helpful, because it includes so many factors which have nothing to do with the actual problems they are attempting to solve.

The under-fives can also be field dependent or field independent when it comes to carrying out intellectual tasks. As with the adult, the field independent children concentrate on the job at hand, while the field dependent children see many more difficulties. They might, for example, regard the presence of a grown-up as either threatening or helpful, depending on whether they read disapproval or encouragement into the adult's expression. They may worry about whether they are in the right mood to tackle such a problem. Whether they will be praised or punished for their efforts. Whether they will finish in time. Such children will be strongly influenced by immediate past performance on similar tasks. If they have done well on a previous occasion they will see the problem as less difficult and estimate their chances of success as high. If they have just done badly on some task they will be much less eager to try anything new. They quickly become confused and, when this happens, are likely to fall back on old problem-solving strategies even if these have failed them in the past.

Which approach the child adopts depends on his or her experience. But we must always remember that the underlying desire is to reduce anxiety as quickly and effectively as possible. The gifted child does this, very largely, by finding the right answers to problems. The child who has failed to develop successfully may achieve it simply by offering the first answer that comes to mind.

This brief description of the major differences between

gifted and average children will, I hope, have provided some useful insights and a little practical advice. It should serve as an introduction to the important topics of problem-solving which follow in Chapters four and five.

The best starting point for our examination of the ways in which children learn to use their brains is with an objective appraisal of your own child. This can be achieved by using the analysis check-list below.

What To Look For In The Gifted Child

In the last chapter I provided a check-list of responses which, my survey has indicated, are found in gifted parents. The same study has also produced interesting information about the behaviour of children who are developing their mental abilities to the full. By using the forty-statement analysis below you will be able to gain a general impression of your own child's intellectual, creative and social growth. I should emphasise that the results must be used as a guide only. It would be wrong, and potentially damaging, to categorise any child absolutely on the basis of this analysis. However, the answers should provide you with a useful and informative check of his progress. The responses described are normally seen only in children older than two years; many of them clearly do not apply to the much younger child, although you may find it interesting to carry out the analysis on a child of less than two years, answering those statements which can reasonably be applied to his or her behaviour. This will offer certain insights and provide a means of monitoring progress during the years to come. Complete the analysis by ticking, or noting, those statements which can be applied to your child's behaviour and then refer to the analysis chart at the end of the list.

MY CHILD. . . .

1. Is observant, alert and quick to pick up new things.
2. Is able to carry out mental tasks with enjoyment.

3. Is able to learn rapidly and well.
4. Uses a large number of words correctly.
5. Asks a great many questions.
6. Has original ideas.
7. Pays close attention when being shown something new.
8. Has a good memory.
9. Enjoys reading.
10. Takes the lead when playing with children of about the same age.
11. Provides ideas for games when playing with others.
12. Is given duties by teachers at nursery school or play group.
13. Spends much time painting and modelling.
14. Has a good sense of perspective and detail when drawing.
15. Produces original drawings which do not look like other children's attempts.
16. Likes looking at pictures and commenting on them.
17. Has a good sense of rhythm and enjoys moving to music.
18. Uses expressive body movements to reflect emotional mood.
19. Has good co-ordination.
20. Enjoys beating time when music is played.
21. Expresses ideas clearly when speaking.
22. Is not easily discouraged when things go wrong.
23. Is/was an early reader.
24. Enjoys working with numbers.
25. Is eager to find out why things happen.
26. Has a steady hand and can manipulate small objects successfully.
27. Becomes very absorbed in subjects that interest.
28. Is constantly experimenting with things.
29. Prefers to work out solutions to problems for himself/herself.
30. Is ingenious at finding new answers to problems and new ways of doing things.
31. Has a vivid imagination and creates a fantasy world.
32. Is excited when solving a problem or making a discovery.

33. Is a source of ideas for new projects, does not rely on others all the time.
34. Has a great enthusiasm for life.
35. Is self-confident about his or her ability when facing a new challenge.
36. Has a great many friends.
37. Is always eager to explore new surroundings.
38. Is looked on as a leader by other children.
39. Makes up imaginative stories and enjoys telling them.
40. Has a very independent attitude towards life.

Statement Analysis

The answers you made to those 40 statements provides information about mental development in general and the growth of abilities in five specific areas which are listed below.

Let me start by listing the statements you will have ticked if your child is starting to realise some of his or her inborn potential. The key responses such children should be making are found in statements: 1;2;3;4;5;6;7;8;9;22;23;25;27;28;29;30; 32;35;37;40. The average score for children aged from two to five years, who are considered gifted by adults other than their parents (i.e. teachers, psychologists and so on) is 14 ticked responses. If you scored ten or more as being appropriate to the behaviour shown by your child, then a high level of successful mental development would seem to be taking place. The more statements you were able to tick, the more satisfactory this growth of abilities would seem to be. The statements also provide insight into some of the particular ways in which a child may be developing.

Intellectual/Scientific Abilities

These are particularly suggested by statements: 1;2;3;4;5;6;7;8; 9;21;22;23;24;25;26;27;28;29;30;33;34;35;40. The higher the number of statements you were able to tick, the greater ability in these important areas is likely to prove. If you ticked a large number of the statements from 21 through to 30 there may be a greater interest in science subjects and tasks demanding a logical approach to problems. The average score amongst gifted children with these abilities is 16 statements ticked.

Leadership Abilities

These are indicated by agreement with statements 10;11;12;22; 34;35;36;37;38;40. Children who show above average leadership abilities normally respond according to at least five of these statements.

Artistic/Creative Abilities

These are indicated by agreement with statements 13;14;15;16; 18;25;28;31;33;39. Children who show better than average creative and artistic abilities usually score on at least five of these ten statements.

Musical Abilities

These are indicated by agreement with statements 17;18;19;20; 31;39. Children who have a higher than average ability will score positively on the statements 17;18;19;20 and usually on the other two as well.

These, then, are some of the major ways in which children who are growing brighter through their experiences of life are likely to respond. If you study the statements you will see that many of those relating to behaviour, and certainly all those concerned with intellectual growth, deal with some aspect of problem-solving. The child who is observant and alert will spot many things which interest and puzzle him. He or she will see problems waiting to find a solution where the less able child finds nothing of interest. The child who is able to carry out mental tasks with enjoyment, who learns rapidly, asks a lot of questions and pays close attention when being shown how to do something, is developing valuable problem-solving strategies.

It is in an ability to see and solve problems that the gifted child differs most profoundly from the youngster who is underachieving, who is learning all the wrong lessons from life. Because this is such a fundamental and important aspect of giftedness, I will be devoting the next two chapters to considering problems and problem-solving. Only by understanding how, when and why we identify problems and discover answers to them can the nature of intelligence and creativity be properly appreciated.

Chapter Four

How Problems Help Your Child

The reader of a detective story who is trying to solve the mystery before the last chapter and a five-year-old doing a jigsaw puzzle have something in common. Each is trying to find the answer to a problem and doing so for no other reward than the satisfaction and entertainment involved.

Most adults see problems as things to avoid. Yet they have an importance in our lives which is seldom appreciated. It is only by solving problems that we progress; that we gain new knowledge and fresh insights; that we come to a greater understanding of those things which matter to us. Our success or failure in almost every activity we undertake, from promotion at work to social effectiveness, depends on our ability to solve the problems with which those situations confront us.

For the under-fives, problem-solving can be seen as rungs in the ladder of mental attainment. It is only by solving problems at one level that the child can climb to the next. Every answer which is arrived at enables a whole range of other problems to be tackled efficiently. Before those preliminary problems have been solved, it is often impossible even to understand the nature of tasks further up the problem-solving ladder. The more rapidly problems can be solved, the greater number of problems which can be resolved in a certain amount of time. The more problems which are solved the greater the mental development. For example, before we can count we have to learn a numbering system. Before we can manipulate numbers we have to appreciate the ways in which they can be moved around. As children, we progress in mathematical knowledge from the most basic problems towards those of increasing complexity, each forward step built on knowledge gained from the last. Without a logical progression there could be no real understanding of later steps. Indeed, when we are faced with something we do not understand it is often because some essential, preliminary problem-solving steps have been insufficiently completed.

To understand how gifted parents can help their children's mental growth we must appreciate the nature of problems and problem-solving. In this chapter, I shall be looking at this important topic in some detail, explaining what problems are, how we set about solving them and why we often find the challenge presented by problems so entertaining and stimulating. Detective stories, crossword puzzles, games of chess and cards, puzzles and brain teasers may seem very remote from the world of the under-fives. But while adult problems and those facing the very young differ markedly in content and complexity, each share important attributes. Furthermore, the essential skills needed to solve those various types of problems remain the same. The five-year-old doing sums and the fifty-year-old trying to work out what sort of a hand his opponent holds in a card game are both engaged in the same kind of mental activity, and using much the same thinking process. Most people enjoy being puzzled. They like the stimulation provided by the unusual, the unexpected and the unfamiliar. Such variety is seen by many as essential to job satisfaction, a way of avoiding mind-cloying routine. People with jobs they define as 'interesting' may tell you there is always something new to think about, or say that they have to be on their toes, constantly alert and ready for new challenges. What they are actually describing is a continual flow of fresh problems to be solved.

Away from work, there is a tendency to seek out artificial problems as an aid to relaxation, hence the popularity of

Scrabble, chess, wooden and metal puzzles of all shapes and sizes, crosswords, detective stories, and mystery dramas on television. Especially popular are those crime novels where the author plays fair, provides all the necessary clues, and challenges the reader to unravel the web of problems he or she has woven. The very popular American crime writer, Ellery Queen, actually emphasises the problem-solving nature of the story by stating, at some point, that the reader now has all the clues necessary to find out 'whodunit'. Nor is it any coincidence that Agatha Christie, whose books have sold more than 300 million copies all over the world, specialised in just this problem-presenting approach. Her plots, which are really no more than a series of ingeniously constructed problems, provide an unfailing way of appealing to one of the most basic psychological drives.

But why should such a drive exist? Why do we so enjoy being puzzled? What makes variety at work so much more popular than far less demanding routine? Where does our appetite for problem-solving spring from?

The Drive To Discover — The Need To Know

The problems of the jungle are all concerned with survival of the individual and of the species. The need to find food, water and a secure lair, to escape from predators, to mate and to raise young. Each species has evolved different strategies for solving these life or death challenges. Some employ a single problem-solving tactic, such as camouflage, speed, protective armour or warning pigmentation. Others have evolved a wide range of skills. The fox, it has been said, knows many things — the hedgehog only one big thing.

Man's survival strategy is to be more intelligent than any other animal in nature. So far, at least, it has proved enormously successful. So successful that the day-to-day survival problems which confront wild animals no longer affect us. We have sufficient security and leisure to set our problem-solving machines to work on tasks which have nothing to do with staying alive.

We have an inborn drive to discover and a need to know. We arrive in the world pretuned by nature, by millions of years of evolution, to seek out and solve problems. We live in a constantly changing environment which has to be made sense of. Anything novel or unexpected presents a possible threat to survival. Only when it has been explored and made familiar by investigation can we be certain that it presents no real hazard.

Stone Age man saw an unusual object, detected a fleeting movement, heard a strange sound. Was it something dangerous he should flee from, or something edible he could have for lunch, or something neither useful nor harmful? The only way to find out was to make a very cautious series of experiments; to look carefully, being prepared to run if it seemed to become more dangerous, then to approach more closely; to touch it, smell it, taste it, chew it. All these are practical, information-providing tactics. You see exactly the same sequence of behaviour with the toddler out for an airing in unusual surroundings, perhaps an unfamiliar area of the park or playground. Some novelty, such as a sight, sound or smell which cannot be identified by reference to anything he has so far stored up in his memory, attracts his attention. He stops and stares, perhaps referring to his mother for guidance, by looking directly at her while continuing to point at the thing which has caught his eye. As I explained in another book (*The Secret Language of Your Child* — Souvenir Press, London, 1978), this kind of reference back to the adult who is most prominent in his life is a valuable survival strategy. By standing motionless he avoids attracting attention to himself if there is danger. Checking with his mother provides a rapid means of obtaining accurate information. Is she worried, or unconcerned? If she is scared, he will be. If not, then he will remain undisturbed and continue to investigate further. He will approach the object more closely; sniff it, touch it, if possible put it into his mouth. Having answered the question

— what is it? — he then moves on to answer the question — what use is it? What can I do with it? If it has possibilities for further exploration, he will play with it. Finally, everything that can be learned having been learned, the child quickly grows bored and probably moves away.

The initial arousing of the system, by the sight of novel objects or situations, is a physical as well as a mental response. Certain hormones flow into the bloodstream to trigger off a number of interconnected bodily events. The heart rate will be stepped up, blood flow to the brain will increase to improve alertness, the limbs will grow tense, ready for flight if danger threatens. These and several other responses are automatic. They form an inbuilt survival response which it is not under the control of the 'thinking' mind to prevent. The same kind of changes occur when we become very anxious by something seen or heard, or by a worrying thought circling in our minds. I shall have more to say about this alerting system later in the book, since it can be incorrectly triggered — as a result of the wrong kind of learning — with often disastrous consequences for the individual, whether adult or child.

Anything which we are unable to understand, but which *seems* significant to our way of life, produces an initial tension, a sense of unease, or a feeling that all is not right with the world. For example, children and adults can watch television without understanding the electronics by which the picture reaches their front rooms. Such knowledge is not necessary to their lives, and, because of this, is not significant. But if you were studying to be a television repair man, and about to take an important qualifying examination in the subject, then your failure to understand some part of the process would be likely to produce tension, because there are problems which you feel unable to solve. Now, imagine a programme you especially want to watch, perhaps the last in a series which has engrossed you for weeks. You are finally going to find out what happened to all the characters whose lives have become so familiar to you. An hour before the show is to be broadcast, your set goes blank; then the picture flickers back on. Here your lack of understanding is significant. What is going wrong? What can you do? Will the picture vanish again? You have suddenly been presented with a significant problem that you cannot solve, and the result is increased tension and anxiety.

It has been shown by a number of experiments that the unfinished, the undecided, the not-fully explained, do lead to increases in arousal. You tend to remember work which has still to be completed and forget jobs which have been finished. If you eat half a bar of chocolate and then absent-mindedly put the other piece down, you often have a niggling memory that something has been left undone. (This phenomenon is termed the Zeigarnik effect, after the psychologist who first studied it.)

The level of tension which an incomplete action can create is illustrated by the story of the lodger whose bedroom was just above his landlady's. On several nights each week, he would return home late, sit on the bed and remove his shoes, which he would then drop with a loud clatter on the floor. His landlady complained that the noise woke her up, and warned he would be given notice unless this behaviour stopped. The following night, he came home, removed only one shoe and let it fall with a crash. Then, remembering her warning, took off the other and placed it silently on the floor. Thirty minutes later, just as he was dropping off to sleep, came an anguished cry from below: 'For God's sake, drop the other shoe!'

We can summarise the situation as follows. There is an inborn attraction towards situations and objects which are both novel and of some importance to our lives. This attraction towards the unfamiliar arises from a primitive survival mechanism and the need to make sense of a changing environment. In situations of genuine danger, the arousal which results from the unknown, the bodily changes which take place, still fulfil their traditional role of aiding physical survival. Because society now presents us with few immediate and genuine threats to life and limb, the attraction for novelty — that is, for fresh problems to solve — has been diverted into all kinds of channels. As adults we find pleasure and stimulation in such artificial problem-solving situations as crosswords, games of skill, and detective mysteries.

Your Baby Adores Problems

In a fascinating series of experiments, a baby of only a few weeks old was given a pillow fitted with a microswitch. By turning his head to the left, a bulb could be made to light. In a while, by chance movement, the baby discovered this fact. At first, he was not certain that the light really had come on as a result of something he had done. When he realised there was a connection between turning his head to the left and the light coming on, his response was surprised delight. He constantly turned to the left, saw the light, and wriggled with delight. Then he grew bored with the discovery. There was no longer any novelty. The mystery had been explained, the problem solved. He mostly avoided turning to the left, but every so often, would give a quick flick over just to check that the light still obeyed his command. For a while it did. Then the experimenter changed things round so that the light came on when the baby turned to the right. In a few moments, this change was discovered. The baby grew extremely agitated, and kept turning to the left. Nothing happened. After a little while longer, perhaps by chance, a right turn of the head was made. The light came on. The baby was once more thrilled. He constantly turned to the right, watched the light come on and wriggled in ecstasy. Then, with the problem once more solved to his satisfaction, he grew bored and contented himself with an occasional right side turn to check his solution. The experimenter once more changed the set-up. Now the baby had to make two right turns and one left turn before the light came on. It took a fair while for him to solve that far more complex problem, but he got there. The same excitement was observed, following by a gradual decline in interest, with just the infrequent repetition of the pattern of movement to satisfy himself that all was well. In time, the experimenter was able to build up an enormously complex problem-solving situation for the baby, with many turns to right and left before the light would come on. This was not a form of conditioning in which the light triggered a particular series of responses. As, for example, the sounding of a bell caused the specially conditioned dogs of Pavlov to salivate. The light only came on *after* the movements had been made. The baby was solving a series of increasingly demanding problems out of an inborn need to do so.

A baby playing for the first time with a rattle is solving problems too, although of a much less demanding nature. The infant is carrying out experiments with the object to answer such basic questions as: What does it feel like, taste like and sound like? If I drop it, what happens? All this information is stored away, so that the next time an object is encountered, it will be more easily identified. The baby given a plastic brick finds out about it by reference to familiar objects already handled. Does it feel the same as a rattle, or taste the same? Does it make the same noise? Does it do the same kind of thing if I drop it?

I am not suggesting that these actual questions go on inside the baby's brain. They obviously do not. But the effect is the same, as though that kind of problem-solving process was being worked through. It is a method of learning about the world through answering problems — the more answers, the greater the learning and the wider the range of problems which then demand a solution.

The Inquiring Mind Of The Infant

As soon as your baby is old enough to crawl, the scope for exploration and discovery is enormously increased. The desire to discover becomes even more apparent, and the kind of problems which can be sought out and solved grow more complex. Your baby wants to find out everything as quickly as possible; to investigate by sight, taste, touch and smell all the objects in his world. There is novelty on every side, things to be understood through direct enquiry and experiment.

In time, often in a depressingly short space of time, this uninhibited eagerness to discover is replaced by anxious uncertainty. The early desire to make sense of everything all too rapidly gives way to an apathetic acceptance that things are as they are, and there is no purpose in trying to find out why. The desire for discovery is lost. The need to know diminishes.

It cannot be too strongly emphasised that *the loss of this sense of excitement at problem-solving, the decline in the urgency with which explorations are made and novelty sought, are major elements in the failure to realise early promise.*

As the child's mind comes meekly to accept instead of constantly to question, that brilliant potential becomes duller and more permanently tarnished. We will look, in a moment, at the reasons for this.

Man is not the only animal with this inborn preference for novelty and stimulation. If rats are given an equal opportunity for entering a familiar section of a Y-shaped maze, or one which provides some kind of fresh stimulus, they will usually choose the latter. Monkeys are prepared to solve problem games for no other reward than the pleasure of finding out how things work. Even baby monkeys, who have had no previous experience of problems, and clearly cannot associate solving puzzles with gaining food or some other reward — as might be the case with more mature laboratory animals — will play endlessly with problem toys.

In the early weeks of life, when the human baby's movements are still clumsy and largely unco-ordinated, there is little chance for the infant physically to experiment with his surroundings. But babies are still choosy about what they want to look at, and what they like best is novelty. In one experiment, a group of infants, ranging in age from six weeks to nearly six months, were shown a series of magazine photographs. One picture was put before them ten times for one minute per session, the other photos were shown once only. It was discovered that, although both pictures were studied by the babies, there was a decreasing interest in the constantly displayed illustrations.

When the infant is old enough to handle objects — rattles, skittles and bricks, for example — he will show an increasingly strong preference for more complicated playthings. A rattle that makes a noise will soon be preferred to one which is silent; a toy which can be made to change shape comes to hold the attention for much longer than a solid, unyielding object.

At one year old, most are bold explorers. How eager they are to investigate fresh surroundings was demonstrated by an experiment in which twelve-month-old infants were put in a large room with their mothers. A second, smaller room, containing a toy, opened off the first, and they were free to go and explore it. All but one of them did so immediately. Crawling at high speed, it took an average of 29 seconds for the infant to cover the 17 feet separating the two rooms, in order to play with the toy. On a second occasion, the same children were given a choice between the same room with the same toy and a second room which held a different toy. Again, all but one of them preferred the novel toy.

These are just a couple of the many dozens of experiments carried out with infants and young animals which confirm the innate need to know. By searching out and becoming familiar with every aspect of their environment, animals increase their chances of survival. Not only do they come to appreciate what is safe, but the unfamiliar can be instantly identified, so providing an early warning possible danger. Exploration also offers learning experience in many skills which can be applied to other problems. The importance of such early training has been clearly demonstrated in a number of experiments using animals and children.

In one study, for example, the differing skills of two groups of chimpanzees were compared. One group had spent the first twenty-four months of life in a cubicle which provided no novelty or stimulation. The second group had been trapped in the wild around the age of two years and brought straight to the laboratory. At two years, the caged chimpanzees were allowed to join others in a large, outdoor enclosure which offered a great deal of stimulation and many opportunities for problem-solving.

Five years later, the two groups were examined with a wide range of artificial problem-solving tasks. On every count, the animals caught in the wild were so superior to the caged-reared chimps that there was simply no comparison between them. Especially noticeable were differences in the span of attention. The chimpanzees who had been reared in isolation for the first two years were unable to remember important parts of the problem for any length of time. Although both groups had experienced the same kind of stimulation in the same surroundings for five years, the differences during the first-four months of life continued to exert a marked influence on performance even after five years.

These differences were due to the different experiences which each group had had with early problems-solving. The wild chimpanzees learned a lot, and they learned quickly so as to survive. The caged chimpanzees were fed regularly, and provided with a secure home. They had no need to solve problems, and no opportunity for doing so. Because of this, they failed to learn not simply particular skills but the right approaches to problems in general.

The same thing can happen with children. Unless they are able to start solving problems within the first few weeks of life, unless they learn the mental strategies demanded by such problem-solving, they may find it impossible to catch up with their more fortunate and more stimulated companions.

Most parents try to provide their infants with simulation and novelty. Even when they know nothing about child psychology, they are well aware that a new plaything may stop the baby crying and give them a few minutes of much-needed peace! Others will take the trouble to think up ways in which the baby can be enjoyably and successfully stimulated. They may buy books which give practical information about the best games and toys for each age group. As I said in Chapter one, such guidance is very helpful, but it frequently results in a cook-book attitude to child-rearing. Although the best 'ingredients' are bought and mixed exactly according to instructions, the results are not always what were anticipated.

I believe that a much sounder approach is to attempt to understand, as far as possible, *why* things work rather than accept on trust that they are bound to do so. Only by appreciating the reasons for things happening as they do can one successfully handle set-backs and make advances confidently and competently.

For this reason, I want to look in some detail at the underlying processes of problem-solving. By gaining such insights into the nature of problems, it becomes easier to provide the child with the right kind of stimulation and novelty — in the right way and at the most appropriate time.

What Problems Are All About

I have mentioned several different kinds of problems in this chapter, all instantly recognisable as such; problems generated by games of skill, mysteries created by detective writers, crosswords and so on. Many of the problems in our lives can be seen as demanding some kind of specific activity on our part. We create a problem for ourselves, and then set about solving it by carrying out a particular course of action. The second main group of problems which confront us are those imposed by other people, or by circumstances.

For example, a woman tells her neighbour that she has a *problem* in getting a new recipe to turn out right. She has a *problem* in making her housekeeping money last the week. She has a *problem* getting along with her mother-in-law. In the first instance, she has introduced the problem into her life quite deliberately and knows that, to solve it, she must do certain things in the right way. The second problem may be a result of her own mismanagement, or have been imposed on her from outside by such things as rising food prices. Finally, her problem of family relationships might have been imposed on her by an unreasonable mother-in-law.

Because problems can mean so many different things to different people, and even different things to the same people from one day to the next, we need to define what a problem really is. Until that is done, 'problems' can only be thought of in a very subjective way. Let us look at a number of problems, pick them to pieces, and see what they are made of.

I am sure there will be general agreement that the following all come into the category of 'problem'.

1   Multiply 5 by 30, subtract 10 and add 15. What is the answer?
2   A squad of fifteen soldiers has to cross a deep, wide river. Their only way across is to commandeer a small rowing boat owned by two boys. The boat is only capable of carrying either the two boys or one soldier. None of them is able to swim across. How does the squad reach the other side?
3   Take six matches and put them together so as to form four equal-sided triangles.
4   What relationship exists between the following words? — Uniform; dungeon; stunning; immunity; tribunal; thereunder; excommunicate; superabundance.

Here we have four very different kinds of problems. The first is easy, the others not so simple, perhaps. (If you are stuck, answers to the last three can be found at the end of this chapter.) My reason for posing them was not to test your powers of logical reasoning, but to demonstrate the similar nature of all problems.

First, all these problems contain certain pieces of information, which are either given to us, or can be deduced from the nature of the problem; or they have to be selected from a wide range of possible information. For convenience, we will call these building blocks of the problems 'givens'. In the above problems, the givens are immediately clear: the numbers; the soldiers, the river and the carrying capacity of the boat: the matches and the shape required; a list of words and a demand to relate them to one another in some way. Without such essential pieces of information, these problems would be insoluble.

Because the problems have been constructed in a special way, all the givens are relevant to the problem. Nothing has been included merely to confuse or to divert our minds from the real issues involved. Unlike a good detective story, there are no red herrings! Many problems used in schools adopt this formal approach. Nothing is mentioned which is not essential to solve the problem, and nothing is excluded which could be considered vital to finding the right answer. In real life, very few of the problems which confront us have such a tidy set of givens. Often the judgement of what is important and what can be discarded is a very subjective one. We are constantly solving problems on the basis of personal opinions about the number of givens we can or should include. Sometimes, as we shall see, we may choose the wrong sort of givens and so come up with an incorrect answer.

This brings us to the second common component of all these problems and, indeed, the majority of problems — that is, a solution. There is a goal towards which we are expected to work. This is stated clearly within each of the examples given. In many academic problems, at all levels of education, a similar approach is adopted. The problem-solver is expected to work toward a particular answer. The psychologist, J.P. Guilford, has called this kind of reasoning 'convergent thinking', because all the ideas circulating in the brain as the problem is tackled are expected to converge at a single point to find the solution which the problem setter had in mind. The four problems above are all examples of convergent thinking tasks. But goals are not always as obvious. Indeed, half the difficulties which people find in handling real life problems is that they lack a specific goal. They cannot decide what they really want. To glance back at our example of the women with a mother-in-law problem, her goal might be to smooth out the ill feelings, to insist that she behaves more reasonably, or to learn to live with the situation. Which goal she selects will obviously have a major influence on how she sets about solving her problem. Open-ended problems like this require what Guilford has called 'divergent' thinking, the opposite of convergent thinking. Often the answers can only be found by breaking away from conventional ways of thinking about things and looking at the givens in a more creative manner.

In order to arrive at a goal, the givens must be moved around in certain ways. They must be manipulated to produce the required answer. In the first of the problems above, the manipulations were clearly stated. The givens (the numbers) had to be manipulated in a specific way, and those manipulations carried out in exactly the order stated; first a multiplication, then a subtraction, finally an addition. If any other manipulations had been used, or any other order followed, the wrong answer must have resulted. In the other problems, the manipulations necessary to arrive at the stated goal were not supplied. Indeed, to discover them is the main challenge of those particular tasks. It is very often the case that finding out which manipulations are the most appropriate to a particular problem goes straight to the heart of the problem. Unless we find and understand how to use the necessary manipulations, and then use them in the correct sequence, the answer will either elude us or prove incorrect.

The well-trained mind of the experienced thinker has a wide range of problem-solving manipulations at its disposal. They include many which are specific to certain types of problems, such as would be needed for changing a flat tyre, finding the fault in a television circuit, or pulling a light aircraft out of a stall. All job training, however simple the task and elementary the skills needed, involves mastering a certain number of specialist manipulations. The more complex the task, the more specialised the necessary strategies required to accomplish it. Consider your own job for a moment, and it will become clear how many problem-solving strategies you have, in fact, had to master. A number of these may have little application or value outside that particular occupation. Others, although quite specialised, will have a wider range of applications. For example, a knowledge of mathematics enables engineers to build bridges and buildings. But the same ways of manipulating the same sort of givens, that is the addition, multiplication, division and subtraction of numbers, can be put to the far simpler and more mundane tasks of adding up a restaurant bill, calculating how much overtime will be earned, or dividing a bar of chocolate equally between several children.

In addition to fairly specialised strategies, there are some types of manipulation which form the basis of reasoning in general — the ability, for example, to deduce an answer from a selected number of givens. You notice that milk has been left uncollected from a neighbour's porch; that bedroom curtains have remained undrawn; that the car is still in the garage. From these givens, you deduce that the neighbour is ill in bed. Of course, you could be wrong, and the same givens and the same manipulation could as easily have produced a different answer. You might conclude, for instance, that they have gone on holiday by train or forgotten to cancel the milk. Or they might have been attacked, bound and gagged. They might even be playing a long hand of poker! Which deduction you make from those givens will depend on other information you have about the habits of your neighbours, about the time of year — is it the holiday season? — and, to an extent, how you view the world. Do you think that robbery is a likely or improbable event?

The ways in which we manipulate the givens and the goals which are reached on open-ended problems such as this are many and varied. There are a large number of logical, and illogical, ways of using information. But I am not primarily concerned with these here.

In order to understand how the under-fives learn to solve problems, there is no need to consider such concepts as inference, casual connection, syllogisms or negation, nor do we have to concern ourselves with such matters as the difference between inductive and deductive logic. What matters is how the very young come to select their givens, how they learn to use manipulations, and the kind of goals they are interested in seeking. In all of these, the exceptional child differs markedly from the child of average intellectual ability.

Before going on, let me just summarise what we have looked at so far, in order to finally arrive at a definition of what constitutes a problem.

This analysis of problems has revealed three main components.

1.   We have the essential information necessary to solve the problem at all. These facts have been termed the givens.
2.   There are the mental strategies by which the givens are moved around, taken apart, made to associate with one another in a logical way, and so on. These are the manipulations. We all know a large number of different manipulations and use them with varying degrees of confidence and success almost all of the time.
3.   There is the goal, which has to be reached, the conclusion which results from manipulating the givens. With many problems, the goal is the same thing as the right answer. But this is not always the case. Sometimes, because of the very subjective nature of the problem, there can be no such thing as a 'right answer'. For example, how could the woman with a disagreeable mother-in-law be certain that any course of action was the best possible one? There are problems where insufficient information is available to reach a conclusive answer, or where the wrong answer is, in fact, produced, but still proves very valuable. Many examples of this can be found in the history of science. We can now define a problem as

follows:

A problem is a task requiring the manipulation of givens in order to achieve a goal.

Consider any problem you wish, whether from everyday life, or some textbook, from your practical experience, or the realm of ideas, and you will find it can be defined.

All of this may seem to have taken us a long way from the nursery, from the world of the under-fives, and from the main purpose of this book. In fact, an understanding of problems and problem-solving, as I said at the start of this chapter, is fundamental to an appreciation of mental growth in the very young.

Infants Solve Problems In Order To Understand The World

Infants are driven to solve problems by an inborn attraction for the novel. That is, they are attracted towards objects and situations which provide stimulation by presenting new problems. Until one set of problems has been solved, it is impossible to proceed to problems of greater complexity. We climb to a knowledge of ourselves and our surroundings on stepping stones built of solved problems. Without the experience of solving problems, there can be no mental development. The more problems, of the right kind, which are offered to a child to solve, the more rapidly mental growth is capable of taking place. The more success the child experiences in solving problems at one level, the more successful he or she will be at solving problems at the next level. When we have mastered a problem, we no longer see it as a problem. In fact, we may never have even the awareness that it existed as a problem in the first place.

At every moment of our lives, we are at the end of a long line of solved problems which stretch back to the moment of birth, and at the start of another line of problems-to-come which will exist until we draw our final breath on this earth.

The more successful we are at solving these problems, the more contented we will feel, the more we shall achieve, and the greater will be our understanding of life. The greater the number of problems we are capable of perceiving, and of attempting to solve in an efficient and constructive manner, the more interested and mentally active we will remain. How capable we are at problem solving, how well able are we at perceiving problems, the level of problem-solving ability we have achieved in adulthood can all be traced back to the way we learned to deal with problems during the first five years of life.

Learning About Problems

Let me return to a statement I made a moment ago: *'When we have mastered a problem, we no longer see it as a problem.'* This is a very important point. As soon as a manipulation, or a series of them, appears to provide a solution to a problem, that strategy will be adopted. Often, we are perfectly justified in doing so, but sometimes, it can have dire consequences. I recently met a girl who had become phobic about parties. The strategy she found to the problem of anxiety over invitations was to avoid them. This worked in the sense that she no longer felt anxious. But it was a bad manipulation, because the solution presented a lot of other problems. Her goal of reducing anxiety should have been tackled quite differently. When it was, as a result of therapy, the anxiety disappeared, and she was able to enjoy a full social life once again.

Learning to read and write once presented you with a whole series of problems. Today, it is so easy that, most of the time, you will hardly think about the problems involved. The manipulations (memory associations) of the givens (letters and words) are so well established, that you no longer have to consider them.

What sort of problems were involved in learning to decode

the ink marks which form the symbols which produce these words? First, each letter had to be learned — including the different ways it might sound — and the various relationships it could have to other letters understood. Then you had to learn what groups of letters meant, what the words they formed stood for, and how to put them together to form meaningful sentences. Quite a task! But before any of this could even start, you had to grasp an even more fundamental idea — the fact that words and the things they stand for are not one and the same.

Young children, and some primitive people, do not understand this. They confuse the name of an object, for example a 'brick', with the object itself. Once you understand the difference, it becomes very difficult to think yourself back into the state of mind where the distinction was not immediately obvious. Perhaps the story of the peasant and the astronomer will help to make matters clear. A Russian farmer was talking to an astronomer about scientific discoveries. He explained that he found it astonishing that scientists could calculate the distances to the stars. 'But even more remarkable', he went on, 'is the fact that you have managed also to discover what all the stars are named'.

Until the child comes to realise that the word 'brick' is just a name given to a particular type of thing which exists in its own right, he cannot appreciate that the object can be represented by five symbols (letters) on a sheet of paper.

When all of these problems have been solved, you were able to read fluently. There may still be occasions, however, when reading can suddenly, once again, present a problem. An unfamiliar word, a phrase in a foreign language, handwriting which distorts the symbols to such an extent that your memory manipulation breaks down, can abruptly confront even the most experienced reader with the fact that problem-solving is involved.

During the first five years of life, every successfully developing infant finds answers to a legion of problems; not all at once, but by mastering the numerous component problems which have to be solved before progress can be made. Just consider all the sub-problems which make up a complex activity such as talking, doing even the simplest calculations, riding a bicycle, swimming, dancing, painting, and so on. When the learning has been completed, we tend to regard it as having provided one answer to one particular problem — talking, mathematics, cycling and so on. In fact, like some extraordinary complex mosaic, each consists of thousands of small problems successfully solved. From a distance, as with a mosaic, we see only the overall picture. To understand how some children fail to think properly or act effectively, it is essential to come in close, to break down each problem into the component problems, and then into their components, until, finally, the underlying difficulty has been discovered.

It can be stated quite firmly that, however difficult they may appear, *there is no such thing as an intrinsically difficult problem*. There is only an impression of difficulty, which arises from not having mastered all the component problems existing between the level of understanding required to make sense of the problem, and the level of understanding which you have reached at that particular moment. No matter how complex a piece of machinery, a building, or an electrical circuit may appear, the starting point was always one line on one sheet of paper.

How does a child learn about problem solving? Our definition makes the three essentials clear:

1.   The child must understand the givens — that is, when provided with certain information necessary for solving the problem, there must be an accurate and adequate understanding of what this means. When the givens have to be found from a wide choice of possibilities, the child must be able to understand what can be discarded and what is significant.
2.   The child must understand the manipulations — what they are, and how to use them. When they are not supplied, the

child must be able to select the right ones from those which have been learned, and use them in the correct sequence.

3. The child must understand what goal is sought. Sometimes, children misunderstand the kind of answer they are expected to give, as in the case of the schoolboy who, asked in an examination where glue comes from, replied: 'Both ends of the tube!' A wrong answer does not, however, mean that the wrong goal has been selected. There may just as easily be an error in the choice of givens or the selection and use of the manipulations. After the goal has been presented, there is a response, at some stage, to the answer. The child learns, one way or another, whether the solution found was right or wrong. When, how and why this feedback is provided can have an important effect on the way problems are tackled in the future. This is something which will be dealt with later in this chapter.

From this analysis of problem-solving, we can draw one vitally important lesson. *There is no such creature as an inherently stupid child.*

Many adults fail to understand this. They tell you that a child fails because he or she is 'dumb' or 'daft', 'unintelligent' or 'slow witted'. They confuse description with explanation. They believe they are offering a reason for intellectual failure, but they are not. It tells us nothing about the inborn capabilities of that child, how thinking occurs, where the mistakes are being made or why the errors arise. It may, however, tell us a great deal about the way adults regard that child and that in itself might be part of the answer we are looking for. . . .

Children fail to answer correctly, or to solve a practical problem effectively, for one of three reasons:

1. Because the givens are incorrectly selected, or, if right for that particular problem, inadequately understood.

2. Because the essential manipulations are incorrectly chosen

for the particular problem, or, if correctly chosen, are wrongly used.

3. Because the assumed goal has been wrongly identified. This may lead to the choice of the wrong givens and/or the wrong kinds of manipulations to produce the particular goal required by that problem.

Although the givens and the manipulations may be used perfectly correctly, and may even produce the right goal for that combination of givens and manipulations, it will still be wrong so far as the problem under consideration is concerned. These errors may all be due to a failure in learning — the child does not understand enough about the givens to choose appropriately and/or to use them properly. The same is true about manipulations. If an incorrect goal is assumed, and this easily happens, the child is likely to go off at a tangent and come up with an answer which is miles off target. It may well appear to be a very 'stupid' response. And yet the actual strategy by which the problem was tackled is entirely correct. It is as if an adult misunderstood an instruction to drive from London to Paris and went from London to Berlin instead. The navigation and driving might be perfect, the trip made efficiently, and in record time. But the end result would, of course, be totally wrong so far as that particular task was concerned.

Incorrect choice of givens, manipulations and goals may also be due to anxiety, a panic state which overwhelms the child, (it can easily happen to adults too) and makes a reasoned choice impossible. The information is all there, but the brain is too confused to make an appropriate selection. The wrong goal is selected, the wrong givens may be chosen, the wrong manipulations applied. The following examples, taken from video-tape recordings made during recent research, will help to make each of these points clear:

Julie, aged 30 months, is working at the nursery modelling

table. She is shaping a lump of clay, trying to copy a crude horse figure made by an older child. But she rolls the legs out too long, makes the neck too thin, and the head and body too heavy. Her model collapses instantly and Julie is desolated. Here, the givens were the clay, the goal was to produce a model similar to her older companion's, and the manipulations were the movements she made to roll out, shape and press together the material. It was her lack of knowledge about physical properties of the givens, the modelling material, which made her fail. She had still to learn that clay can only be made to form or support certain shapes and weights. A perceptive adult, understanding the three basic stages of problem-solving, would know at once where her problem-solving strategy was going wrong. The girl might be encouraged to play with different shapes of clay, forming columns and arches, perhaps building a table and chairs with the material, so that she could practise fitting the clay together and learn how it worked. An adult lacking this essential understanding might well say: 'You shouldn't try to make a horse, dear. That's far too hard for a little girl like you. Why not make a nice snowman?' That is, in fact, what the child was told. What will she learn from such a comment? Nothing about the properties of her given, nothing which will help her understand the basic properties of clay as a modelling material; she will only learn, as a general rule, that some tasks are too difficult for her to tackle. She will learn to avoid anything that looks complex. She has had one small lesson in the art of behaving less intelligently.

Andrew, aged three, wants to make the play-group clockwork train function. It is quite a complicated toy, involving several different manipulations. First, the train must be detached from the carriages and held while the motor is wound up, with the brake lever in the 'off' position to prevent the wheels racing round. Then it must be placed back on the rails and coupled to the carriages. Andrew manages to wind the motor, and, after a few false starts, finds out how the brake works. When he puts the train back on the rails, he couples it up back to front, so that the engine is now pulling the guard's van. It works perfectly well. But a supervisor, who comes over to watch, immediately kneels down and stops the train: 'That's not right, is it, Andrew. You can't have a puffer pulling a guard's van, can you? We must get it right. That's better. . . .' and the engine is replaced at the front of the train.

Here, the givens were the train, the rails and the carriages. The manipulations were to wind the motor, operate the brake, and put the train together in the correct order. The goal was to make it work, as it had been doing when the supervisor was showing the children the way to play with the toy. Andrew made an error in manipulation, but it was a very minor mistake, and the goal, so far as the little boy was concerned, had been achieved. There was no point in correcting the error at that stage, because it taught Andrew nothing and can only have confused him. What had he done wrong? Why was his toy interfered with? What was the difference that was so important? The boy would have understood none of these things, and must have been bewildered by the adult response. The slightly critical tone with which the correction was made, the suggestion that he had done it wrongly — 'We must get it right' — could all have increased his anxiety about the task. It might have made his interest in playing with that toy, or perhaps with any complicated mechanical toys, slightly less than it had been before.

Finally, we have a group question-and-answer session. The children have been asked: 'Where do we get milk from?' Four-year-old Stephen replies: 'From a little van in the road.' The adult, after a moment's hesitation — perhaps wondering whether the boy is being impudent — says slightly crossly: 'Well, that was a very silly thing to say, Stephen. Of course we don't . . . does anybody know the sensible answer?' There are giggles, sly glances in the boy's direction, and several hands go up. The adult gets her 'sensible' answer, and Stephen learns to associate questions and answering in public with humiliation and reprimand. In an older boy, or even a less serious boy of the same age, it might have been a joke. But Stephen means his answer quite seriously. He had understood the givens correctly. He had carried out the correct manipulations, in this case, memory association. He had thought about everything he knew on the subject of milk. And what he knew was that it arrived every morning on his front step in a bottle, delivered by a man who drove a small electric float. From his point of view, the answer was perfectly correct, and he gave it without hesitation. He had misunderstood the goal which the adult had in mind.

Even when you have all the information needed to answer a question, you can still put the wrong interpretation on those givens by an incorrect understanding of the type of goal being sought. This happens time and again on examination papers written by secondary school children, and even adults in higher education. The parent who understands the components of problem-solving is in a very strong position to help the child quickly and effectively. Whenever a failure to provide the right answer occurs, the following possible explanations can be considered:

Does the child understand the givens? Have the right ones been chosen?
Does the child understand the manipulations? Have the correct ones been selected?
Have the necessary manipulations, in fact, ever been learned?
Does the child understand the goal? Are both adult and child talking the same language? Has the problem been presented clearly and unambiguously?
Never assume an understanding on any of these points.

It is rather like tracing a fault in a complex electrical system. If your radio goes wrong, you do not immediately conclude that the set is useless. Nor, if you are wise, do you poke around at random. You continue to have faith in its ability for working once the temporary fault has been repaired, as you set about tracing the trouble in a logical manner. Is the set plugged into the mains? Has a fuse blown in the plug? Does the on/off switch work? Is the aerial attached correctly? The more knowledgeable you are about radios, the more manipulations you have at your disposal, and the further it is possible to take this step-by-step elimination of possible sources of breakdown.

Children are frequently treated much less generously than radio sets. If they fail to answer what we regard as a simple question, they may be regarded by some as stupid, inferior, indifferent, lazy, or deliberately unco-operative. We may try pleading, scolding, bribing, shouting or punishing. All these responses will produce certain effects, although seldom the ones intended. The child becomes anxious, fretful, tense or frustrated. The problem remains unsolved, and the problem-solving capacity is diminished. Our impression of the child, and the image the child has of himself, is influenced. We may begin to predict a continuation of failure. The child may come to accept that he really is unable to answer questions or solve problems. New strategies are adopted in place of reasoning. The child may become aggressive or highly dependent, indifferent or impulsive. Which of these responses will be chosen depends on the nature of the child, the relationship with the adult concerned, and the kind of feedback which has been received from others in response to goal presentation.

How We Know When We Are Right

The child has manipulated the givens and arrived at a goal. How does he know whether the problem has been correctly solved? There are only three ways in which we know whether we have got something right.

1.   The correct goal may be self-confirming. If you fit a piece of a jigsaw puzzle correctly, it is immediately obvious that you have done so. Many problems in the child's world, from

putting on a coat to building with toy bricks, are self-confirming.

2.   We may be told that the answer is right. The child produces some writing, and offers it to an adult for comment. By the adult's reply and the way in which it is delivered, the child will be able to judge how well the goal has been achieved. Later, the problem will become increasingly self-confirming. An adult who has written a letter, for example, usually knows whether it is 'right' and may be posted, or will need to be rewritten.

3.   We can believe, often despite strong evidence to the contrary, that a problem has been solved correctly. This requires considerable confidence in one's ability, and either a very extensive knowledge of the subject — so that you know that all possible givens have been taken into account and all the necessary manipulations carried out — or a very limited knowledge, so that you are unaware of the reality of the problem. Highly subjective problems, where there is no 'correct' answer, almost always come into this category. You usually 'feel' that you have received the right answer over a personal problem, for example.

For the under-fives, confirmation from outside is almost always needed before they accept that a problem has been solved. When and how this confirmation is given, and how errors are treated, play an important role in deciding how the child will approach problems on future occasions.

Behavioural psychologists stress the crucial importance of rewards, or reinforcements, as means of establishing patterns of behaviour. If you want somebody to behave in a particular way, you reinforce all those actions which meet your requirements, and refuse to reinforce those which fail to do so. Very rapidly, the number of desired responses increases, while the number of unwanted ones declines.

To take an everyday example; if you want your child to help with the washing-up, it is best to reward every attempt at doing so by thanking him or her, and by making it clear that you are glad of such assistance. If you ignore the behaviour, or take it for granted, then the child may be much less ready to offer help again.

It has been clearly established, through laboratory experiments and observation, that reinforcers which immediately follow some activity ensure very rapid learning. Delayed reinforcers are less effective in doing so, and the longer the delay between the behaviour and the reinforcer, the weaker the influence of the rewarding situation. If you ignore the child who has just finished washing up, but add a little extra to the pocket money a week later, it will prove very ineffective as a means of increasing help with the dishes. A hug and a few words of thanks at once are far more powerful and efficient reinforcers.

There are two kinds of reinforcer. The first, called a 'positive reinforcer', is a pleasant consequence which follows some activity; words of praise, congratulations, prizes and similar rewards. All of these increase the chances of a repeat performance by making the outcome so agreeable.

The other kind of reinforcer is a 'negative' one. The reward comes as a result of avoiding unpleasant consequences. This is the classic way in which a phobia develops. There is usually an initial association of fear with some object or situation. The next encounter produces anxiety, which is removed (negative reinforcement) by avoidance. Soon avoidance has been firmly established as an appropriate response. The claustrophobic can no longer go into confined spaces, the dog-phobic avoids places where there might be dogs, and so on.

By putting this knowledge of the effects of reinforcement on learning into the context of feedback to goals, we can see how the child comes to learn various responses to problems, and to problem-solving in general.

Katie, aged three, proudly shows a drawing to her mother, who comments: 'That's lovely, dear. It really looks nice. Aren't you a clever girl.' This is a very positive reinforcement, which will ensure that Katie continues to show work to her mother, and is highly motivated to produce drawings and paintings. There can be one or two problems about such an uncritical approach, however, and I will be dealing with these in more detail in later chapters where we will look at intellectual, creative and social learning.

John, aged three, hesitantly offers his far less sympathetic mother a painting: 'What a dreadful mess,' she sighs. 'Can't you paint more neatly?' She thrusts it back. "Go away and do it again. I don't want to see any more splodges!' This is a very harsh and critical response. It may be intended to make John try harder next time. Perhaps his mother advocates a 'no nonsense' approach to child-rearing. But all the little boy has learned from this lecture is that showing work to adults, especially his mother, can be a distressing experience. It becomes associated with a high level of anxiety. He no longer offers work so willingly for comment. He approaches the task with greater anxiety too, and does worse as a result. Without sufficient constructive help from adults, shackled by excessive anxiety, the child begins to fail consistently. This leads to greater avoidance of showing his work to grown-ups and an increasing reluctance to attempt any tasks involving painting at all.

The first approach is certainly less anxiety-inducing than the second. It will be more likely to encourage a positive self-image and the desire to attempt fresh challenges. But both fail in so far as they provide no constructive advice about how the child might improve on the task. This may be rather more tricky when he or she comes to other activities, such as early reading and writing attempts, where there are more objective standards by which to judge — such as fluency and understanding in reading and clarity of words in writing. In all instances, however, the child is seeking two sorts of information when offering work for inspection by adults. The first is — Am I right to be doing this at all? The second — Am I doing it correctly?

The first is a reassurance-seeking ploy. The child wants to know if the adult sees the task as worthwhile and values it being tackled at all. The second asks for constructive advice about the quality of production.

Straightforward praise of the kind: 'That's lovely dear; aren't you clever!' will provide reassurance and, as a result, will satisfy the first part of the information-requesting strategy. But it does nothing to help the child with constructive feedback about the level of achievement. Furthermore, by avoiding any kind of legitimate and reasonable comment or criticism, the child gets no practice in dealing with critical reactions. The youngster who has had nothing but unqualified praise from adoring parents for the first five years is unlikely to have any accurate perception of his or her abilities. In addition, the critical remarks of teachers will be much harder to accept and to learn from, and as a result, anxiety may rapidly rise together with a decline in the child's belief in his or her ability. This can quickly lead to all sorts of learning and self-image difficulties.

Ten Ways Of Enriching The Child

1. *All children have a natural, inborn need to discover and explore.*
Do not inhibit this quality any more than is absolutely necessary. You will find further information on this important subject in Chapter eight.

2. *Children learn about the world by solving problems.*
They need the opportunity to solve as many problems as possible, as early as possible and for themselves. Do not deny them this opportunity. Again, you will find more information in Chapter eight.

3. *No subject is intrinsically complicated, and no child is inherently stupid.*
A failure to understand a problem reflects a lack of knowledge

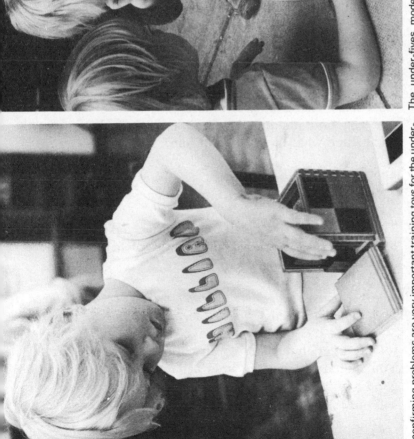

The under-fives model very closely on adult behaviour. Grown-up objects can make valuable playthings for this age group. An old telephone will provide the basis for a whole host of social and problem-solving games, especially if the child is allowed to take it to pieces.

Self-confirming problems are very important training toys for the under-fives. This little boy at a Montessori nursery school in London is discovering how to place coloured blocks in a container in the right sequence. It is immediately obvious to him when the answer is correct.

about one of the three components of problems. A failure to solve a problem can always be attributed to a similar breakdown in understanding.

4. *When the child fails, look at the failure in terms of the three components of problem-solving. Do not regard it as a sign of mental inferiority in the child.*

5. *First check that the givens are fully understood.*
Does the child have all the basic information needed to produce an answer? Has the right set of information been selected?

6. *Now check the manipulations.*
Does the child possess the correct strategies for solving the problem? If so, have the right ones been chosen and used correctly?

7. *Finally, check the goal concept.*
Are you both talking the same language? Does the child understand what is expected of him?

8. *Failure may also be due not to a lack of knowledge about the above three components but to an ability to use them correctly.*
This is usually the result of excessive anxiety. I will be discussing anxiety in describing ways of helping the over-anxious child in Chapter eight.

9. *We can only discover whether or not we have solved a problem correctly from the feedback received.*
Many toys and games which involve some kind of problem-solving offer immediate confirmation of a correct strategy. You should see that the child has the chance to play with a good number of these: jigsaw puzzles, building blocks which will only slot together in a certain way, toy trucks which can

only go if differently shaped figures are inserted into the correct slots, and so on.

But children also depend to a very great extent on the responses of adults. Remember that they are seeking two kinds of feedback from you: confirmation that they are right to carry out a particular task, and information about the skill with which it has been accomplished. It is wise then to avoid sharply critical responses, and never tell the child that he or she is stupid, careless, lacking in ability or less able than a brother or sister. Encourage the desire to tackle problems and to make attempts. If mistakes are trivial, ignore them at first.

10. *While encouraging and reinforcing attempts at problem-solving, remember that you are also a primary source of facts about the world for the under-fives.*

You are a walking reference library, a mobile dispenser of wisdom and knowledge. Nothing must be done to make the child anxious about referring to adults for advice and information — which does not mean that you should solve every difficulty or put the finishing touch to every task for them. But it does mean that you must be willing to offer constructive information about the way a job has been done, or comment on the skill shown in solving a particular problem. The anxious child who has learned to fear the reactions of one or two close adults may find it impossible to respond effectively to any adult. He or she will avoid presenting work for comment, will become highly anxious when forced to do so, and will be likely to transfer the anxiety aroused by the reception of the work to the task of producing that work itself. In this way the child is doubly disadvantaged.

In this chapter, I have looked at the main components of problem-solving and have described ways in which mistakes can occur. I have also briefly described the effects of anxiety on performance. In the next chapter, I want to apply this new way of thinking about problems and problem-solving to intelligence. What exactly do we mean by this term and how does the highly intelligent child differ in his or her approach to problem-solving from the less successful youngster? Can we teach intelligent problem-solving strategies and so help the child to reveal inborn mental abilities? These are some of the important, basic questions to which the gifted parent needs to know the answers.

Solutions To Problems On Page 74

BOAT AND SOLDIERS

The essential manipulation here is to divide the boys so that there is one either side of the river. First, they both row to one side and one boy gets out. The second boy rows back across the river and gives the boat to a soldier who rows it across. On the opposite bank he hands over to the second boy who returns the boat to the other side. This allows the first stage to be repeated. Eventually all the soldiers are on the far bank.

MATCHSTICK PYRAMID

The essential manipulation here is to transform a two-dimensional problem into a three-dimensional one. Without this approach it is impossible to solve the problem. Build upwards from a triangular base using the remaining three matches to form the sides of a pyramid.

WORD PROBLEM

The manipulation needed here is to break down the words into component parts and to observe a rule of construction which applies to each. You will then notice that the two letters u and n move to the right by one letter with every word in the sequence when reading normally from left to right.

Chapter Five

Bright Babies Who Think Themselves Dim

Long before they blow out the candles on their fifth birthday cake, some children have come to consider themselves rather stupid. They have lost confidence in their ability to solve problems and have begun to fear them. The way they now approach the challenge of life makes failure a more probable outcome than success. Bright babies have thought themselves into dim children. How and why should this damaging self-image have been formed?

It is important to remember that while we can never know what a person is thinking we can usually judge the efficiency and appropriateness of those thoughts by the way he or she behaves. There are two processes involved here. The first is the invisible mental functioning and the second the visible response which the other person makes.

When a child, or an adult, produces an answer we know to be wrong, we must decide where the mistake occurred. Was it in the mental functioning or because the right thought was incorrectly translated into behaviour? The explanation most people consider first is that the thought processes have been at fault; the problem-solving has failed. As we saw in the last chapter, this may occur because the givens are not fully understood; the manipulations are inappropriate or incorrectly carried out, or the wrong goals have been selected. These will produce errors and may well be the cause of the mistaken answer.

But the second possibility should also be considered — that

the right mental processes have been translated inadequately into action, the wrong words were spoken even though the right ones had been formed in the brain. The wrong activities were performed even though the individual knew the appropriate responses to make. This cause of failure is a common one in young children. It is not that they lack the mental ability but that they are unable to effectively transform thoughts into behaviour. It may simply be a case of insufficient dexterity. Motor functions (control over movements) are not sophisticated enough to permit the very subtle manipulation of objects which a correct answer demands. The infant trying to complete a jigsaw puzzle may experience enormous frustrations because of this. Another possible cause of failure is anxiety, which will be discussed later. Very anxious children, especially the under-fives who often find it difficult to understand or express their anxieties, are certain to approach problem-solving with far less confidence in their ability than relaxed and self-assured youngsters. Anxiety is a common reason for under-achievement when children take intelligence tests. The challenge presented by a new, unusual and seemingly inexplicable task generates so much anxiety that performance declines sharply.

The child who is easily bored can also fail to translate appropriate thoughts into the right answers. Interest and motivation are quickly lost, turning active minds to more stimulating problems. This is why gifted children may appear rather unintelligent when given problems to solve which are well below their problem-solving capacity. Some children warm very slowly to new tasks. They are so uncertain that they take a long time to adapt to a fresh situation. This is not always the same as the anxiety response although it may appear quite similar, and produce equally damaging responses. Finally there is the very active child who may respond very quickly, become confused and do things in the wrong order.

All these are temperamental characteristics which can have a profound effect on mental performance, not because they directly restrict the brain's ability to solve a problem — although this may happen as confusion or anxiety mount — but because they get in the way of effective thought/action translation. There is no way of knowing how often this happens, but the probability is that failure to achieve a good IQ test result is more often due to temperamental difficulties than intellectual failings. This is certainly the judgement of psychologists who have investigated the effect of emotional states on IQ scores. In one study, kindergarten children were tested on entry to the school, and then six months later, when a considerable improvement in IQ levels was noticed. The researchers concluded that the change had been due to shyness during the original test. Once the children had settled into their classes, and learned how to get on with groups and with adults, they were able to tackle the tests much more confidently. Other research has shown that practice in solving problems similar to those contained in an IQ test can make a big difference to the results. This suggests that it is the strangeness of the problems which suddenly confront them which throws some children off balance. Especially confused by the type of questions included in many tests may be children from educationally deprived backgrounds, who lack not only the experience of handling those particular problems, but have never had the chance to think about the world in the way which these tests require.

In one investigation of this problem, the same test was given to a group of four and five-year-old children on two separate occasions, one week apart. Some of the children came from impoverished homes, the rest from affluent ones. The IQ scores for children living in poverty rose by ten points between the first and second test, while the IQs for the advantaged children increased by only three points. In another study, two similar groups were made to take the test with or without a prior period of playing. It was found that the disadvantaged children, because they had been relaxed by being allowed to play, did better. There was no significant increase in the scores of advantaged children, whether or not they played beforehand.

A New Way To Look At Intelligence

I have already said that coping with changes successfully means being able to solve problems efficiently. Intelligence tests set out to measure this problem-solving ability in a variety of ingenious ways. They seek answers to such questions as: 'How quickly are the essential elements of a problem seen?' 'How effectively are key manipulations carried out?' 'How rapidly can goals be identified?' The better a person is at these intellectual skills, the more readily the right thoughts can be transformed into the proper actions, the more intelligent the tests will show them to be.

But intelligence cannot just be a matter of solving problems which have been neatly presented. If that were the case then a pocket calculator would be as 'intelligent' as a trained mathematician. Certainly the machine can carry out remarkably complicated calculations at high speed and with great accuracy. But nobody would claim great intelligence for such a gadget. It can only do what the programmed instructions allow. The problems solved have first to be presented in a specific manner. The human brain seeks out its own problems and then sets about finding ways of solving them. It is a self-programming computer as well as a self-assembling one. In this capacity to *see* problems, our minds differ in a fundamental way from the most advanced of today's electronic brains.

The history of scientific discovery is really the story of people who saw problems where nobody had previously noticed them. Sir Isacc Newton watched an apple fall, an event which had never before attracted any attention. For him that commonplace posed a problem. Why did the apple fall down and not up? What force compelled it to drop from the branch to earth? Seeing problems which others miss is one of the important ways in which an intelligent individual differs from one whose intellectual potential is not being realised. No wonder the mentally active child asks so many questions — the world presents so many problems!

We can now define intelligence in a way which allows us to consider it in practical terms: *It is the ability to perceive problems and to set about solving them in the most efficient and logical manner.*

The child knows that a problem really is a problem for one of three reasons. The first is that an adult has presented it as such: 'Here are some coloured beads on a string, John. Can you tell me how many red ones and how many blue ones there are?' The second is when a problem arises out of some activity in which the child is involved. How can the parts of a jigsaw be fitted together? How does a clockwork car run? What will make the pile of building blocks stand up?

The third type of problem, which is the rarest, especially in the majority of young children, is the self-presented problem. It arises out of something which has happened, but is not immediately obvious, and involves that problem-seeing ability talked about above. An interesting example of this kind of self-evolved problem cropped up when I was talking to a bright five-year-old and her mother. She had just told me that she hated milk, but her younger brother loved it:

'Does it taste the same for me and Mike?' she inquired thoughtfully. Her mother laughed. 'Of course it does. Don't ask silly questions.'

But, far from being foolish, her comment was extremely perceptive. How do we know that everybody tastes the same food in the same way? The answer, of course, is that we do not and cannot know for sure. We can only assume that it is so. The little girl had seen a problem where her mother saw only a matter of common sense.

Let me give you an example of how all three problems might arise, and how they could be solved.

A bright child is offered a fizzy drink. 'In the kitchen, on the second shelf from the right, you will find a red bottle. You can pour yourself a glass,' his mother says. He has been presented with a problem: how to find the right drink. This can be solved easily enough by reference to his memory of the kitchen, the shelves, and what a red bottle will look like.

The bottle found, and the first problem solved, a second arises. This is presented by the nature of the cap on the drink. It is a type he has not seen previously, and he is unsure how to open the fastener. With some help from his recollections of similar bottle-tops, plus trial and error manipulations, the second problem is solved. As the cap comes flying off, the bright child notices streams of bubbles in the liquid. A less intelligent child might not notice anything unusual about them, but this one wonders why they suddenly appeared. It is a problem which can only be solved by reference to an adult. He will ask a question, and, if he is lucky, receive an interesting and satisfactory response which may provoke further questions.

How children approach problems, the interest they show, and the motivation they have to work for an answer depends on two main variables. The nature of that problem in particular, and the previous experience of the child in solving problems in general.

The chart opposite illustrates what happens after the child has been confronted by a problem. The most successful outcome is shown at the top. The givens and the manipulations, which we considered in the last chapter, have all been correctly understood and properly used. The result is the correct solution. This is seen almost immediately, with the same speed and ease as if you were asked which letter follows in this sequence A. C. E. G. I. ?

You would know that it was K, and, having worked out the very simple relationship between the letters correctly, you would also know that your answer must, logically, be correct. But being certain you have got the right answer is seldom as straightforward as that. Often, there is considerable doubt until a confirmation or a denial has been received. How the child 'knows' that the right solution to a problem has been found will be looked at in a moment. It is important, because

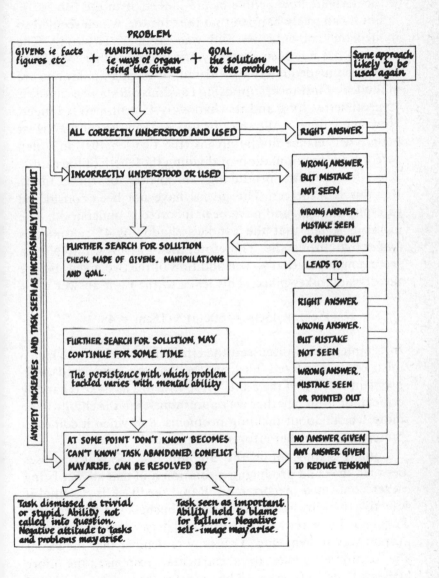

when and how an answer is confirmed as correct will influence the lessons learned from that attempt at problem-solving, and will determine how problems are looked at in the future.

But it can easily happen that the 'answer' which seemed so immediately obvious — and was given — is wrong. The problem has not been correctly understood; either the givens have been inadequately considered, or the manipulations are at fault. For instance, supposing I ask this question: a candle is 15 centimetres long and its shadow is 45 centimetres longer. How many times is the shadow longer than the candle? Most people will glance at the givens (the two lengths) and then perform the manipulation of dividing the length of the candle into the shadow, producing an answer of three times. But this is incorrect. The givens have not been considered carefully enough, and have been incorrectly understood. The problem stated that the candle's shadow is 45 centimetres *longer* than the candle. Therefore, the right answer involves a second manipulation — the addition of the two givens before the division takes place. This leads to the right answer of

$$(15cm + 45cm = 60cm) \div 15cm = 4$$

In Chapter five, I discussed the effect that the way in which a mistake is corrected has on the anxiety associated with problem-solving. If the adult's response to a mistake is harshly critical, or in some other way punishing, then the child will be more fearful about tackling problems, and when it comes to presenting his or her efforts for appraisal.

Equally significant is the amount of time which passes between the child producing a solution and that answer being either confirmed or corrected. Rapid feedback is essential if effective thinking habits are to be established. In Chapter four, I explained how rewards (positive and negative) help to teach a certain way of behaving. You may remember that the closer the reinforcer comes to a particular response, the more powerful its influence. The greater the delay between behaviour and reinforcer, the less effective it will be in establishing that pattern of response.

We have already seen one way in which reinforcers are able to set up particular kinds of attitudes towards problems — through the response of the adult. Now I want to describe how the time interval between an answer being produced and it being confirmed or corrected can also play a highly significant role in the development of a child's problem-solving ability. Reaching an answer which you believe to be correct is rewarding in two ways. First, there is a feeling of pride in achievement, a delight at being clever enough to find a solution. Secondly, there is the relief of having completed the task. Any tension or anxiety associated with the challenge drains swiftly away once an answer has been given.

Suppose the young child is never told that his answers are right, but believes them to be correct. If he has got them right, no harm will be done. But if they are really wrong, then considerable difficulties may result. Inappropriate mental strategies have been used to arrive at a solution, and these faulty tactics have been rewarded. They are, therefore, very likely to become established and to persist; possibly at the expense of better, more effective strategies. When tackling problems in the future, the child will continue to use the same approach. If the mistakes are then pointed out, he or she may often feel bewildered and lost and unable to understand how ways of thinking which they had always believed led to 'success', could suddenly let them down. Faced with this unexpected setback, he or she may lose confidence in their abilities and become much less motivated to attempt problems at all.

Let us look at what happens when mistakes are corrected by an adult after a lengthy time lapse. The errors are pointed out and the reasons for them explained. New ways of tackling that kind of problem are suggested. However carefully and kindly these corrections are made, the fact that the initial strategies — the wrong ones as it happened — were immediately rewarded by a sense of relief in having found an answer, makes it more likely that these strategies will be followed in the future. Here is an example of what I mean.

Tim is a very impulsive child who has learned not to pay much attention to what he is told. When given a problem, he looks at it briefly and comes up with the first answer which occurs to him. Sometimes, almost by chance, he gets it right, but more often than not, he is hopelessly wide of the mark. It is often a couple of hours before his efforts are seen by his teacher, and the mistakes pointed out: 'You must be more careful, you don't give yourself a chance,' she tells him. The teacher cannot understand why six-year-old Tim continues to approach problems in such an ineffective manner, although the answer is really not so hard to find. Tim's behaviour makes excellent psychological sense. His rapid methods produce a quick reduction in the anxiety which problems cause him. They are immediately rewarded. Sometimes they even give him the right answer as well, although he can never understand how or why this has happened. Therefore he persists with them. There are many, many children in primary and secondary education like Tim. Their tactics are hopeless and make them appear stupid; and yet they are not stupid. It is just that the wrong lessons have been learned.

Let us imagine that, faced with a problem, the individual cannot come up with any quick solution. At this point, there are two possibilities, giving up or going on. If the decision is made to continue, it is very likely that the problem will be more carefully examined. The givens may be juggled around and the memory searched for new kinds of manipulations. Fresh facts may be sought, clarification of some part of the problem asked for. This process is known as 'brainstorming', and the more efficient a person is at problem-solving, the longer and more imaginative will be this period of intense mental activity. The more complex a problem, the longer it may take to find a solution. The greater the persistence with which it is tackled, the better the chance that such a solution will be found —

provided the mind continues to work logically. But this seldom happens. Failure to find an answer usually leads to an increase in tension and anxiety. The greater the pressure to solve the problem correctly, the more rapid and powerful this response is likely to prove. Suppose that the candle-and-shadow problem described earlier had been one of the questions in a qualifying examination for a job which you badly wanted. As you write down 'three centimetres', a friendly neighbour leans across and whispers: 'That's wrong!' You believe him, but cannot see why you have got it wrong. As you search desperately for another solution, your anxiety increases sharply. You start to sweat; your mouth goes dry; your heart races, and your brain becomes more and more confused, less and less able to provide you with any logical strategies. In the end, you throw down your pen and think: 'To hell with it. I may be right after all.'

The under-fives approach problems in exactly the same way. If they fail to find the answer expected of them, anxiety results. The greater the pressure to succeed, the more intense their fears and the more rapidly they arise.

There are four factors which influence the amount of anxiety which adult and child will experience in any problem-solving situation:

1. *The personality of the individual.*
Some people have an inborn ability to remain fairly calm and collected, while others rapidly go to pieces. This results from many of the temperamental characteristics we looked at in the last chapter; the speed of adjustment to change, response to novelty, level of activity, and so on.

2. *The experience which the person brings to bear on the problem.*
The more problems of a similar kind which have been successfully answered before, the less the anxiety which is experienced over new, but vaguely familiar problems. This is

why children who have had practice at IQ test questions do so much better, as a rule, than those presented with them for the first time.

3.   *The pressure to find an answer.*
These may be a question of time; the less there is in which to come up with an answer, the greater the urgency to find a solution quickly. This is a problem which faces children every time they take an examination, and is one of the reasons why intelligent, hard-working children sometimes produce such poor results. Or it may be a matter of personal pride. The child wants to do it right because his friend got the correct answer, or because his parents expect him to do well. Very often, the expectations parents have for them exert enormous psychological pressures on children, and generate high levels of anxiety in situations where this response is very counter-productive.

4.   *How difficult the problem is thought to be.*
This is usually a very subjective reaction. Two individuals of equal ability may look at an identical problem and come to completely different conclusions about how hard it will be to solve. Let me give you an example of such a question which often floors young adults. Working from the left, multiply the second whole number by the fifth decimal: 0.5; 6; 4; 0.8; 7; 9; 0.3; 2; 5; 0.1; 7; 6; 0.5; 3; 3; 5; 0.9. Could you do it? Or did you flinch away in horror, your mind refusing even to consider such a seemingly complex mathematical challenge? If you did skip hastily on, you are not alone. Most people give it one glance, imagine that an extremely tough problem has been presented, and refuse to believe they could be capable of finding the right answer. But look again. All that is being asked is this. Multiply the second whole number, which is 4, by the fifth decimal, which is 0.5. When the problem is put in those terms, the answer becomes obvious. It is 2. The difficulties which you saw in the task, if you reacted as the majority of

people will react, were all in the mind. The panic produced by the sight of numbers was an emotional and not an intellectual response.

The amount of anxiety produced by a problem determines the motivation and the persistence which are brought to bear on finding an answer. But anxiety is not the only response children give to an inability to answer problems. An equally common reaction is frustration. This can be expressed in many different ways, ways which have been investigated by a number of psychologists. In one experiment, carried out in the 'forties by three American researchers, children were given incomplete toys to play with. They had, for example, a boat, but no water to sail her on; an iron without an ironing board; a telephone dial without the phone; a chair but no table, and so on. Within minutes, they had invented ways of making good the missing parts. A sheet of paper became the ocean, the telephone dial part of a futuristic machine, the chair was turned into a motor car, and so on. The children played with much pleasure, and showed a great deal of creative ability. The following day, they went into the same playroom, but this time a screen had been removed, and, through a wire mesh, they could see the parts needed to complete their toys. The frustration of being able to look at these missing pieces without being able to get hold of them produced a variety of reactions. Some of the children became aggressive, and broke up the toys, others became listless and apathetic. Instead of playing happily, they sat around, staring through the wire mesh, or looking helplessly at the half toys. Some grew anxious and tense, running aimlessly about.

Aggression, apathy and anxiety are common reactions to frustration both in children and adults. Consider the motorist who, unable to solve the problem of his unresponsive engine, savagely kicks at the car. Or the overburdened housewife, swamped by the problems which confront her, who sits helplessly amongst the muddle of her life. You may remember a similar response on your own part to a seemingly insoluble problem, and you will almost certainly have observed some or all of them in your children from time to time.

Billy cannot make the jigsaw puzzle fit together. With a sudden scream of rage, he hurls it across the room. Sally has tried to read one of her books and got stuck on some tough words. She sits and stares at them hopelessly, unwilling to try any longer. Tom wants to put together a building kit, but the pieces keep coming apart. He freezes up, his arms and body go stiff with tension, and his face becomes expressionless.

There are other ways in which children can respond to frustration, too. They may drift off into a day-dreaming world of their own, replacing unacceptable reality with much more agreeable fantasies. They may revert to much more childish conduct, growing sullen or sulky, kicking and mumbling their discontent.

Probably the most patience-testing response to frustration, so far as the watching adults are concerned, is when children adopt stereotyped patterns of behaviour. They insist on tackling a problem in the same way, time after time, despite the fact that it has failed previously and has no chance of succeeding in the future. 'For goodness sake, think!' begs the infuriated adult as the child mechanically tries and fails yet again. 'You know that didn't work just now. Find a better way of doing it.' Faced with such comments, the child will probably look miserable, hesitate, and then repeat his attempts, using the same method as before. It is as though the child were locked in some astonishing sequence of try-and-fail, try-and-fail. Why should this happen? Research using animals gives us a clue to the answer. In one experiment, rats were trained to jump from a small platform towards one of two specially marked cards. When a rat jumped at one of the cards, identified, let us say, by a black circle, it landed on another platform and found food as a reward. If the rat jumped towards the other card, marked with a black cross, it hit a solid wall and dropped into a net. Not a painful experience, but an unpleasant one. With a little practice, the rat quickly identified the correct symbol and always received a reward. At this point, the experiment became an exercise in frustration for the rat, as the experimenter transferred the cards, so that successful prediction was impossible. Half the time, the rat landed safely on the platform and enjoyed a meal, but the remainder of the jumps finished up in the safety net.

After a short time, the rats would adopt a stereotyped response. Instead of using a variety of left and right sided jumps, they would constantly leap to either one side or the other. Because of the way in which the situation was manipulated, this led to success 50% of the time. Once established, the stereotyped jumping response proved very hard to alter. The experimenter could remove one card completely so that the rat was able to see both the platform and the food. But if this was on the opposite side to the established jumping platform, they would be ignored. The animal would carry on jumping incorrectly, and continue falling into the net.

This may seem an absurd response, but it does make psychological sense. In games theory, there is a strategy called 'minimax' in which a player adopts tactics which will minimise any losses and maximise the chances of rewards. The rat's stereotyped leaps were a minimax approach. If it had continued to leap randomly, first to left, then to right, there could have been many more successes. But there might also have been a larger number of failures. A fixed response exactly halved both the risk, and the rate of achievement. It was certainly not very intelligent of the rat to ignore such obvious clues as the sight of the platform and the food, but then rats, despite the apparent belief of some psychologists, do not always think like human beings!

When a child is denied feedback about whether or not a problem has been solved correctly, the release of tension, perhaps coupled with a belief that the answer is right, may quickly establish faulty problem-solving strategies. Occasional correction or criticism is the equivalent of the rat's fall into the net. It too can lead to the persistence of inappropriate, stereotyped approaches. Some of the time there is a reward; either chance has led to the right answer or, at worst, there is a sense of relief at having disposed of the problem. On other occasions, there might be a punishing response, criticism, or adult disapproval and the need to do the task again. Under these circumstances, the child may lose flexibility of thought, and stick to the inappropriate methods which always produce an answer of some kind, and, very occasionally, the right answer.

It is vitally important to give children rapid feedback in a constructive and non-punishing manner, so that mistakes can be discovered and corrected quickly, before they become a part of the normal problem-solving approach.

You may well have observed some of the frustrated responses described above in your own child. And you may have put them down to bad temper, babyishness, lack of interest, or even stupidity. You may also have punished them, or insisted that the child continue with the problem until the right answer has been found. Perhaps you never managed to find enough time to look at the child's work and point out mistakes. Now that you understand why these reactions occur, and that difficulties can be created by a delayed or inconsistent response, it should be easier to accept them more calmly and handle them more constructively. If failure continues, do not become over-anxious or cross. Both reactions hinder rather than help. Observe carefully, not through the eyes of love which may blind you to your child's failings, but with the objective detachment of a scientist. At what point is the mistake occurring? Can you identify whether the failure lies in the givens, the manipulations, or the goals? Only when the source, or sources, of difficulty have been identified, can you give your child the most constructive and effective assistance.

There will come a point in any unsuccessful attempt at problem-solving when even the most persistent and capable person will give up, having reached the reluctant conclusion that, for some reason, the task is beyond him. If that person has confidence in his mental abilities, such set-backs will not prove damaging to long-term success. A realistic approach to the failure will be adopted, causes looked for and remedied. The person may ask: 'Did I have all the information I needed? Did I have sufficient knowledge about the ways in which these facts could be moved around?'

Individuals who lack confidence in their abilities, and this includes many young children, look at failure very differently, however. To them, it is not just a temporary difficulty, but confirmation that they are 'stupid' or 'incompetent'.

When 'Don't Know' Becomes 'Can't Know'

Having faith in yourself is essential to any kind of success. Gifted children usually have a lot of confidence in their abilities; they have learned to trust their brains. Just because they fail to solve a problem, they do not gloomily accept this as evidence of their lack of intelligence. 'I don't know how to read that word, it's too difficult', said four-year-old Grahame while I was making a video-tape recording of him reading from his favourite encyclopaedia. You notice that he said 'don't know' and not 'can't know'. This is another important difference between children who are being allowed to develop their inborn brilliance and those whose potential intelligence is being diminished. The number of occasions on which 'can't know' is used instead of 'don't know' is significant. Only one word separates the two, but it implies a world of difference in mental attitude.

'Don't know' leaves the door open for finding out. It implies further desire to investigate the possibilities. It is a statement of the current position and not a prediction of future achievements. 'Can't know' is a final admission of defeat. It declares that no further effort will make any difference. The inability is complete, the failure absolute. It is an acceptance by the child that such skill or knowledge will always be out of reach: 'Can't know maths'; 'Can't know swimming'; 'Can't know painting'; 'Can't know. . . .' The fruits of this sort of failure may not appear until primary or even secondary school, but the seeds are sown during the first five years of life. The bright child has thought himself dim.

The effect of saying 'Can't know' and meaning it, is dramatic. When something 'can't be known', either the topic itself or the intelligence of the person who says it, or both, will be devalued; and it may happen without that individual ever being aware of the fact.

In 1959, an American psychologist called Leon Festinger conducted a revealing experiment. He persuaded volunteer students to spend about an hour on a very boring job. Each was then asked to go outside, where the next volunteer was waiting, and 'sell' the task to them. The instructions were to make what was, without doubt, an extremely tedious chore sound as interesting and fulfilling as possible. To persuade them to tell these lies, a cash payment was offered; some students received one dollar, the others twenty dollars. Afterwards, the students were asked what they had really thought of the job. It was found that those who had been paid twenty dollars for describing it glowingly had no doubts about just how dull it had really been. But those who had received only one dollar for their selling efforts had come to believe that it was really quite interesting. Festinger explained this curious change of attitude by what he termed his theory of 'cognitive dissonance'. That is to say, there was a conflict in the minds of those who had received only one dollar for telling lies. The students who had been handsomely rewarded could tell themselves: 'I just did it for the money.' There was no conflict. But those who had been given only one dollar could not persuade themselves that they had told lies in return for payment. They had to find some other explanation for the fact that they had described an immensely boring task in such glowing terms. The only way this could be done, argued Festinger, was by coming to believe that what they had said was true; that the task did have some merits, that it was not entirely dull, that perhaps it had been quite interesting after all. By changing their mental attitudes, they removed the dissonance.

According to this theory, a conflict arises whenever our beliefs conflict with the way we behave. When this happens, something has got to give. Either you behave differently, or you think about life in another way. Usually, it is the beliefs that change. Take the case of a wife who has been brought up to regard the marriage vows as sacred. One day, she falls in love with another man which produces a powerful conflict between what she considers right and what she wants to do. Either she gives up her new love, or she alters her opinions. She could convince herself either that '. . .marriage vows are sacred, but love is more important and we love one another', or that '. . .that's an old-fashioned view. It doesn't apply in modern life.'

Children who fail to achieve what grown-ups have expected of them are in that same position. They have been led to believe they have considerable ability, a belief which conflicts with the reality of their failures. How can these contradictory facts be resolved? Here there are only three possibilities. Firstly, the children could change their behaviour to match the beliefs; in other words they could start succeeding. But this, given the circumstances, is an unlikely, although not impossible, outcome. Far more probable is a change of attitude towards their own capabilities, or towards the merit and importance of the problem itself; or both. Only in this way can the conflict created by changing 'don't know' into 'can't know' be eliminated. When this type of situation is looked at through the eyes of the child, you may find the view surprisingly similar. As adults, we often employ very much the same tactics to get rid of conflicts between anticipated performance and actual results. 'What a waste of effort,' says the exasperated crossword-puzzle solver when the words remain stubbornly elusive. 'I could do it if I really tried, but I've better things to do with my time.' 'I would have got that job if I'd really wanted,' insists the adult turned down for promotion, 'but who really needs that kind of responsibility?'

One child thought himself capable of solving a particular problem, an opinion others seemed to share. But it turned out to be a mistake; the child tried and failed. After a while and in such a way, 'don't know' can finally and fatally become 'can't know'. At this point, the child no longer sees it as a question of trying a different approach, or of persisting in the hunt for a solution. Now he or she must explain to himself why others solve that problem while they can't. One answer is to say 'They are cleverer. I am stupid', which is a common way of resolving the conflict; all is explained in a moment. Clever people can do things, stupid people can't.

The child with a stronger self-image may refuse to accept this conclusion. He prefers to see the fault not in himself but in the task: 'I could do that if I wanted, but it's boring. You'd have to be stupid to want to do it. Who cares? . . .' Sometimes, a child will try a little of each, seeing himself as not very intelligent, and the task as really rather uninteresting. This is an attitude one finds depressingly frequently amongst adolescents.

How It Pays To Be 'Stupid'

Being thought stupid can be very rewarding for some children; they wear their ignorance like a badge of honour. It is a wonderful excuse for not attempting to do things which are difficult or taxing. They no longer have to cope with the painful anxiety of worrying whether they will get a problem right, and life becomes more tranquil once they have opted out of the mental rat race. Let other children try to do things. They do not have to bother any more. They are stupid, and the world is suddenly a whole lot more agreeable. At first, adults may pester them to try harder, make more effort, show greater interest. From time to time, there may be dire warnings from teachers or parents. But adults quickly come to accept the child's own assessment of himself, and soon they stop insisting that the child attempt things which are 'too hard'. They let him idle along; being stupid is no cause for shame. Indeed, it can make the social life of the school-age child a great deal easier, and even in the nursery or playgroup it has considerable advantages for some children. Being especially gifted means being different and this makes many children, perhaps the majority, unhappy. These are attitudes likely to become most noticeable after the age of five, but they have their roots in the earliest years of life.

The small child who decides to adopt the 'I am stupid. . . .' strategy for getting along can find life pleasant and rewarding. Adults tend to give such children a great deal of attention, in an attempt to raise their levels of ability. The obviously talented child, on the other hand, is usually left to his or her own devices, and may be denied the attention and encouragement which less capable infants enjoy. What is worse, the child who usually achieves great things may be more harshly criticised for failure and less praised for success than the normally underachieving infant, because more is expected of him. No wonder so many bright babies decide to switch off their brilliance. It can be easier to think yourself dim.

How The Gifted Parent Helps

There are six important, practical steps which gifted parents can take to prevent the child from thinking himself, or herself, into a state of increasing stupidity.

1. *Beware of tests – they can be dangerous.*
These days, it is not uncommon to give children under five some kind of IQ test. If your child is tested it is wise to treat any outcome with great reservations. The relationship between intelligence test scores at this early age and intelligence later in life is tenuous at best. At worst, a disappointing test result which fails to confirm a parent's belief in the child's mental

ability, can produce a damaging lowering of image. The parent sees the child as less intelligent which easily results in the child acquiring the same, harmful self-image.

2.   *Give the child problem-solving feedback.*
I have described three ways in which the child learns that a problem has been solved correctly. You can help provide the correct feedback by using all of these at the appropriate time. Answer all questions sensibly and seriously. Even if the question seems foolish, ask yourself whether the child might not have seen a problem you missed. Turn it around in your mind, and it may well be transformed into a very serious point indeed. (See Chapter eight for further help here.) Give the child toys which provide self-confirming problems, blocks which only slot together in a certain way, various types of jigsaw, construction kits and so on. Finally, when you have set the child a problem, make sure you check the answer as soon as it is presented. If a mistake has been made, identify the reasons and proceed from there.

3.   *Frustration results when problems cannot be solved.*
It can show itself by a whole lot of unhelpful responses, including aggression, apathy, a step-back into babyishness, day-dreaming, anxiety and stereotyped responses. Recognise these for what they are, and understand what has caused them. Do not punish the child, but provide help in overcoming the obstacles which are causing the failure. Training in persistence through the use of an adult model, as I describe on page 146, is also very helpful.

Constant aggression or anxiety, even when there are no apparent frustrations, are a different sort of difficulty, and I will discuss ways of helping this kind of child in the next chapter.

4.   *Conflict results from a clash between belief in abilities and the results obtained.*

One way out of the conflict is for the child to devalue the task; another way is for the child to devalue himself. Sometimes, there is a bit of both in the reaction. These are very damaging ways of looking at life. They limit ability, and cut down on the number of things the child will ever regard as interesting. Conflict can be avoided if the child starts to succeed. This will generate confidence, and help to produce further success. Again, track down the difficulties to their source. What problems are causing the trouble? How can the child be helped to solve them for himself? Note that this does not mean finding all the answers for the child, which is not helpful. It simply confirms that adults can do something the child is unable to achieve. This can create more conflict, so great care and skill often necessary here. I will discuss ways of helping effectively in Chapter eight.

5.   *Failure in a four letter word.*
There may come a point where 'don't know' in any failure to solve a problem becomes 'can't know'. Never accept a statement like this from a child. Remember there is no such thing as an intrinsically difficult problem; there is only a failure to understand what is involved in solving that problem. Because you had difficulties with a particular subject as a child, do not transfer your failures to your own child. For example, some parents say: 'Can't you do sums? Don't worry. I couldn't do them either!' This is simply providing a licence to fail. 'Can't' is the most potentially damaging word in any child's vocabulary. Failure is that four letter word.

6.   *It sometimes pays to think yourself dim.*
Being dim will only prove rewarding for a child if parents let it. I am certainly not saying that you should punish a child for a failure to understand or to succeed. This is entirely the wrong approach. It does not mean driving children unreasonably, or having an unrealistic expectation about their current capabilities. Nor does it mean that a child should be denied

your help for fear such assistance will reward him for not trying. What it does mean is that successful attempts are always rewarded with recognition and praise, not accepted without comment as the way that child 'should' behave because he or she is bright. It means offering help to the underachieving child in overcoming the difficulties which are creating those failures. How this may best be accomplished will be considered in Chapter eight.

Chapter Six

Making Up Your Mind About A Child

Here is a simple experiment designed to test your skill in assessing the personalities of children. All you have to do is to look at the photographs opposite and then match each to one of the four descriptions below. Study the pictures carefully and try to decide how you would categorise the child shown if you met him or her for the first time. Only when you have completed matching all four pictures and texts should you turn to the next page to see if you were right in your judgements.

CHILD A
Agressive and a disruptive influence in the playgroup. Prefers active games to quieter pursuits and tends to boss others around. Not very bright but good at practical tasks like building models. Self-willed and rather obstinate at times.

CHILD B
Intelligent and thoughtful. Does best at subjects which need to be thought out rather than those where a quick decision is required. Neat and confident in the tasks which are familiar but reluctant to tackle fresh challenges. Finds it hard to make friends and prefers the company of adults.

CHILD C
An anxious child, easily unsettled by any change in routine. Does not like to be separated from mother for long. Tends to be the victim of bullying and makes little attempt to retaliate.

Often hangs around the outer fringe of a group of children in the playground and is reluctant to join in. On occasions can be quite clever but is unwilling to tackle fresh challenges readily. Needs constant reassurance.

CHILD D

A rather dull child, with a drab and unattractive personality. Makes it difficult for adults to relate well to the child. Never seems to try as hard as the others. Tends to lack an imaginative approach, and is unlikely to do well at school.

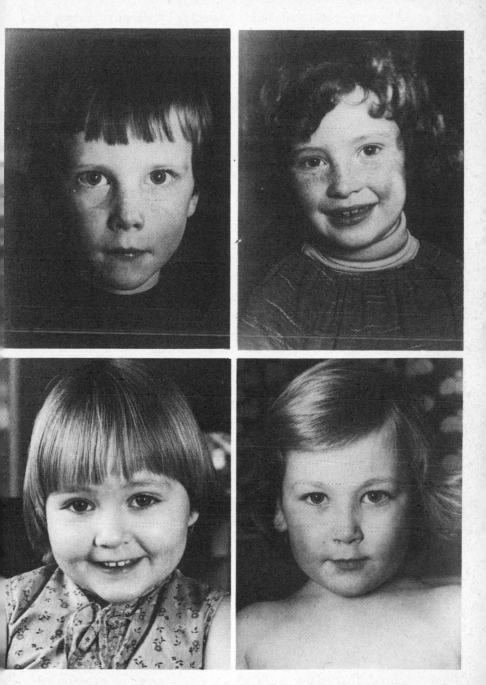

How hard did you find it to decide which picture matched which profile? Do you think that enough information was provided by the photographs for you to reach any firm conclusions?

If you found it fairly easy to assess the likely personality of each child, and did, indeed, glean sufficient clues from the illustrations, then the experiment has achieved what it set out to prove.

The truth is that no connection exists between the profiles, which are completely fictitious, and the children pictured. The intention was to make you believe that there was, in order to demonstrate how few clues, how little information, need be available in order for us to form quite firm conclusions about others. When it comes to deciding our feelings towards somebody, whether adult or child, we typically rely on much less extensive and reliable information than a prudent motorist would be willing to depend upon when buying a second-hand car! Yet these assessments play a crucial role in determining the way that any relationship is likely to develop. How we feel about somebody after the first meeting will influence our wanting, or not wanting, to see them again; whether we trust them or feel that they are basically dishonest; whether we consider them sincere or shallow.

Where judgements about a child's temperament, personality and potential are concerned, the role of such initial impressions can be even more critical and all-pervasive. It has been claimed that the function of prediction is not to prophesy the future but to shape it. When the assessment of a child's character and abilities are the subject of such predictions, this comment is as valid as it is serious in its implications, because children are willing and capable of conforming to a truly astonishing extent with the expectations adults have about them. To test the effects of adult expectation on intellectual performance, two American psychologists fooled a group of teachers at one school into believing that some of their students were brighter than was actually the case. They selected the children, at random, from those who had never shown more than average academic ability, and then told the teachers that each child had been assessed using a newly developed intelligence test which was able to pick out late intellectual developers. The results had been positive for each of the children. The teachers were told: 'You can expect them to make really significant strides during the coming term.' No such tests had been carried out, of course, and the researchers had no reason to suppose that those particular children would do any better than they had previously. But they did. The teachers reported considerable gains in ability. Because they believed the children to be doing better, they responded to them in a different way. The image they had of the children had switched from 'average' to 'potentially gifted', and the prediction, although it had no foundation in truth, came true.

I said in Chapter three that children with unusual talents and exceptional skills behave differently in many ways, some of them obvious and others much harder to detect. Their gifted parents behave differently as well, and they have a different image of their gifted child or children. While the majority of parents consider their children to be 'fairly average', and a minority regard them as 'not really bright', the parents of gifted children almost always see them as especially talented. It must also be said that sometimes parents of children who show no particular abilities also claim that they are exceptionally intelligent or talented. In these cases, where the assessment is largely wishful thinking and based on the wrong kind of evidence, a likely outcome of such predictions is failure and disappointment. This is something I will discuss in more detail in Chapter eight.

How adults regard a child plays a crucial role in determining the child's self-image. The way children see themselves, as I have already noted, has a major influence on how they will respond to intellectual, creative and social challenges.

A self-image is never formed in isolation, and people seldom, if ever, form an impression about somebody which has nothing at all to do with the way that person behaves. There is a constant, dynamic interaction between self-image and outward-image. Each influences and is influenced by the other. Where parents and their children are concerned, this relationship is especially intimate and intense.

What leads parents to decide whether their children are clever and creative or intellectually limited?

What makes them believe that they are outgoing and friendly or self-centred and anti-social?

One would like to think that such important personality assessments would be founded on strong and incontrovertible information, and that no child would be presumed less than brilliant without very strong evidence to the contrary. Everything we know about the way in which parents make up their minds about the abilities of their children, however, suggests that the opposite is frequently the case. Many parents come to firm conclusions about the intelligence of their infants on the basis of a few, trivial, incidents early in life. Sometimes this works to the child's advantage because he or she is seen as being especially bright. As a result of this, the attitude of adults towards them is likely to be different and more positive than if they had been perceived as of average or less than average ability. The subtle nature of these differences was demonstrated by an experiment in which a small boy was tutored by different groups of adults. Some were told, before meeting him, that IQ tests had shown the child to be of higher than average intelligence. They were assured he would prove a quick and adept pupil. The second group was informed that tests had shown the boy to be slower than average and not especially intelligent. The ways in which the different groups of adults responded to the child were then analysed. It was found that those who believed him to be very intelligent were far warmer in their attitude. They gave him greater encouragement, more eye-contact and more frequent rewards for his responses. So being categorised as intelligent does have important consequences for the relationships between infants and adults.

When early impressions are negative, a far less constructive attitude is likely to be adopted. Adults who come to regard their small child as of below average ability are likely to find their impression confirmed as he or she grows older. One of the reasons may be that the child soon accepts the adult's evaluation and develops a very negative self-image. Another factor may be the fact that once we have made up our minds about anything we tend to notice things selectively. Incidents which confirm our viewpoint are more likely to be taken note of than those which contradict it. We have lowered what psychologists term our 'threshold' of perception for certain kinds of events. Once a child has been categorised as 'stupid', adults are predisposed to notice all the 'stupid' things which that youngster does, and to pay less attention to any intelligent responses. Children who are seen as being specially gifted produce a similar but, for them, far more agreeable form of selective perception. Their clever behaviour is taken more notice of than their failures. If they do something we consider 'stupid', it is much more likely to be explained away as a lapse from normal, intelligent conduct.

How much information do we need to make up our minds about children? I have already shown that we will often come to quite positive conclusions on very little real evidence at all. What is more, not all the evidence we have will be given equal weight. We have a tendency to pay special attention to the first items of information which reach us, and to disregard later information which goes against the first impressions. This is called the 'primacy effect' and it has a powerful influence on the ways in which we estimate the abilities of others. An experiment to demonstrate the primacy effect involved people watching students attempting to solve a series of problems. It was arranged that every student solved 15 out of 30 questions. Some students solved the first 15 and then failed on the others. A second group began by failing but scored much better towards the end of the test.

It has been anticipated that those students who did better towards the end of the test would be rated as more intelligent by the observers. After all, their performance had greatly improved during the exercise. But the reverse happened. Those who had done best at the start were seen as being far more intelligent and, furthermore, the observers recalled them as having answered more questions correctly — an average of 20 — than was the case. The students who had scored best at the end of the test were regarded as less intelligent and their score was recalled as being lower than was actually the case. Observers judged them to have got only 12 questions right. The primacy effect caused the observers to make errors of judgement. It also influences the way in which parents form an impression of the abilities of their infants. A child who manages one or two successful problem-solving situations at an early age is likely to be regarded as more intelligent than a child who makes early mistakes in problem-solving. Once the judgement has been arrived at, it tends to be self-confirming and to mould the child towards a particular way of responding. It is not only parents who make up their minds in this way. All adults do — about each other and about other people's children. The danger is that where children are concerned, they have no chance of hitting back at those who define them adversely, while the power to influence their behaviour, and thus possibly the course their lives will take, is obviously all the greater.

While working in nursery schools I have been saddened and shocked by the speed with which some adults are prepared to define newcomers to the group. Personality labels are often pinned onto children who have just arrived within minutes of their joining. 'Jimmy's rather a bully,' I was warned on my first morning at a new playgroup. The supervisor pointed in the direction of a small, fair haired boy of four, playing in a pedal car. 'I knew he was going to be trouble from the moment he arrived. He needs careful watching, and to be kept firmly in his place.'

When Jimmy was watched carefully and objectively, it became apparent that he was much more sinned against than a sinner. Far from being overtly aggressive, he was a rather anxious, unhappy child who frequently got into fights through no fault of his own. After several months of observation and filming, I had dozens of examples, on video-tape, which painted a far more accurate picture of Jimmy's true character. I showed these tapes to the supervisors and explained how and why I felt they were doing Jimmy an injustice. Instead of picking on him, singling him out for punishment whenever there was a general rumpus, and generally treating him like a little savage, he really needed encouragement and help in overcoming his anxieties. He wanted assistance in becoming more socially assertive so that he could learn how to defend his toys against the stronger, bigger children without resorting to physical violence. I could see that the supervisors, despite the evidence of the recordings, were not convinced. So I was not at all surprised when Jimmy continued to carry the 'bully' label around his neck for the rest of his time in that group. Not only that, but his reputation followed the unfortunate child to primary school. About three years after I first met him, I was talking to a supervisor from his nursery school: 'You remember Jimmy, of course,' she said with a laugh. 'Everybody's favourite child! Well, we were right and you were wrong. He really is a dreadful little thing. I heard that he punched a boy and made his nose bleed. He'll end up in serious trouble one day.' There was almost, I felt, a note of triumph in her voice. How satisfying to have a prediction come true!

Every Baby Is Different

In Chapter two, I talked about the Nature versus Nurture controversy and looked at the role which inborn factors — the genetic contribution — were likely to play in determining levels of intelligence. I concluded that, while there is undoubtedly a genetically imposed upper limit on intellectual growth and ability, this ceiling has little practical significance, since nobody ever makes anywhere near full use of their mental potential.

But there is another, and far more critical, way in which built-in characteristics can determine the course of development. This lies in the way the genes decide the temperament of the child, the emotional make-up which gives every baby a unique personality from the very moment of birth. These characteristics are the result of a constant interaction between inborn factors and the ways in which these innate responses to external events are received. We can often liken this effect to the relationship between a river and its banks. The banks decide the course of the water, but the water changes the shape of the banks.

The importance of the inborn contribution — the river banks in our analogy — was largely ignored by psychologists in the years immediately after the war, when the importance of environmental influences were stressed in discussions of the origins of personality. Studies were devoted to examining the effects of such factors as rejection or over-protection by the mother; rivalry between brothers and sisters; authoritarian attitudes on the part of the father; social conditions and cultural traditions. In the early 'seventies, however, the results of a detailed and long term investigation appeared to challenge these widely held assumptions. For more than a decade, two New York psychiatrists, Dr Alexander Thomas and Dr Stella Chess, and a clinical psychologist, Dr Herbert Birch, had followed the development of 141 children from 85 families. They began their study when the children were born, and continued their observations through the pre-school period and into formal education. Parents were regularly interviewed in such a way as to provide objective information about the behaviour of their children in specific situations. The children themselves were examined by a variety of psychological tests so that statistical, as well as descriptive, data could be obtained.

They concluded that children do show distinct and individual temperaments within the first weeks of life, which are independent of either the personalities of their parents or the ways in which they are cared for. Their investigations also showed that these characteristic ways of responding to the world persisted over the years. Although they could be slightly modified by different upbringings — a particular set of circumstances might increase or diminish a particular characteristic, for example — they were incapable of drastic change. A passive, withdrawing baby was almost certain to grow into a rather quiet child with a tendency to avoid unfamiliar situations. An active, responsive baby was most likely to grow into an energetic and inquiring infant. Where original characteristics were, apparently, replaced by other responses, the research showed that these were merely lying dormant rather than gone for good. The researchers commented that: 'The characteristics usually remain present and may assert themselves in new situations, even in the form of an unexpected and mystifying reaction.'

To illustrate this point, they quoted the case of a girl who, at the age of ten, was well adjusted to life in her small school. When she was moved to a much larger one, however, the more formal and less intimate atmosphere badly affected her. She became extremely anxious and worried, a response which puzzled her parents, who had always found her a friendly relaxed child, capable of sound, academic work. When the researchers examined the records of how she had behaved in babyhood, her change in attitude was less mysterious. During infancy, and when starting at kindergarten, she had shown clear withdrawal tendencies. They concluded that her fear over being transferred to a new school stemmed from a fundamental tendency to back away from new situations and to take a long time to adapt to changes.

As a result of their study, Thomas, Chess and Birch were able to describe three general categories of behaviour, personality profiles into which most — although not all — the under-fives in their survey could be fitted. One type they characterised by a positiveness of mood. These children, regarded as 'easy' by their parents, were regular in their habits, adaptable to changes, and showed eagerness when approaching novel and unfamiliar situations. They were cheerful and quick to accept new people and new routines. When they started school, the regularity and adaptability of temperament which had been noted from the first few weeks of life enabled them to learn new rules quickly, join in group activities without anxiety, and adjust readily to the fresh demands made on them. About 40 per cent of the children in the study could be placed in this category.

The second type was in complete contrast to this 'positive' group. They were intense in their reactions, and often irregular in bodily habits such as eating and sleeping. They cried a great deal, and took a long time to adapt to new circumstances. They tended to withdraw from the novel or unfamiliar, were slow to accept strangers, or to learn different ways of doing things. If frustrated, they were likely to fly into tantrums. They were generally negative in outlook, and were frequently described by parents and teachers as 'difficult' children. Some ten per cent of the children included in the survey came into this group.

The third type of behavioural profile included children the researchers described as 'slow to warm up'. Like the 'difficult' group, they were reluctant to adapt to change, had a low level of activity, tended to withdraw from novelty and to avoid the unfamiliar. They made up 15 per cent of the sample.

This means that 65 per cent of the 141 children studied by Thomas, Chess and Birch could be categorised under one of the three headings of 'easy', 'difficult' or 'slow to warm up'. The remainder showed a mixture of characteristics which defied such neat compartmentalisation. Of the children being studied, 42 had behavioural difficulties which required psychiatric help. About 70 per cent of the 'difficult' children required such assistance, while only 18 per cent of the 'easy' children did so. The important point to remember is that these differences in temperament are inborn. They result from the type of genetic blueprint from which such key bodily controls as the nervous and hormone systems are constructed. Whether the baby responds sluggishly to fairly strong stimulation, or vigorously to the mildest external changes, depends on the sensitivity of these physiological mechanisms. Similarly, the amount of activity shown by the baby — the regularity or otherwise of patterns of sleeping and feeding, whether they are fretful or placid, whether, in fact, they possess those qualities of behaviour which will make them an 'easy' or a 'difficult' baby — depends on biological mechanisms over which neither baby nor parent have any control.

To condemn small children for being fussy and fretful, for rejecting unfamiliar types of good or unusual situations, for crying and appearing fretful, for having irregular patterns of sleeping and feeding, for being sluggish instead of alert and active, and so on, is no more logical than to blame them for having brown eyes rather than blue, or blonde hair instead of black.

Yet, while no parent would see such physical characteristics as being a 'fault' on the part of the child, the basic responses of temperament, which are no less innate, are considered voluntary behaviours. They form the foundation on which adults, parents and strangers build their opinion as to the child's personality. As we have seen, these impressions, having been formed, persist through the years and resist evidence which tends to contradict them. They are the main components in predictions which will dramatically influence the child's development. Two cases from my files clearly illustrate the ways in which assessments of personality are derived from the earliest interactions between a baby and its surroundings.

Tom was born prematurely. He was a small, weak child, who spent the first few days of life on a tightrope between life and death. Tom survived to become a 'difficult' baby. When I first saw him, at five weeks, his habits were irregular. Awake, he cried a great deal, and was hard to comfort. He was an unattractive baby and even his mother commented unfavourably on his appearance.

At six months, his irregular habits and intense reactions troubled his parents. He screamed when bathed, woke up at all hours of the night, and often cried for long periods. If picked up, he would struggle violently. He was easily frightened and provoked to tears.

Although they tried hard to express their love for him, his parents had already compared him unfavourably with his older sister, who had been a 'model' baby. By eighteen months, Tom had quietened down, although he still burst into tears at the slightest opportunity. He was slow to crawl and appeared anxious in anything but the most familiar surroundings. He had very strong likes and dislikes. When required to do something against his wishes, he had violent tantrums. By this time, his parents had formed a strong and extremely negative opinion about his personality. They saw him as obstinate, not very bright, awkward in his physical movements, inconsiderate and unfriendly.

Tom was nearly two before he could walk with assurance, and he seldom ran around. He was a messy little boy who played with his food and took a delight in tearing up books, papers and magazines. He was frequently punished by his father, who now felt that the child had been 'spoiled' by his mother. When struck, Tom would cry loudly, but became silent and withdrawn immediately after chastisement.

He was a clinging child who showed great distress when left by his mother. On the first half dozen occasions he was taken to the play group, he made such a fuss that she had to bring him home again. It was not until the age of three that he was finally persuaded to stay. To everybody's surprise, he settled in well after an initial period of tears and tantrums. By the age of four, his social adjustment was greatly improved. He joined in games, although he never took the lead in organising them, and appeared to have lost many of his earlier fears. But he still cried frequently, and usually for no apparent reason.

When he started primary education at the age of five, Tom was a far 'easier' boy than had seemed possible two years earlier. But although increasing maturity and experience of the world had diminished the 'least attractive' aspects of his personality and enhanced his 'good' qualities, both his parents and teachers continued to see him in negative terms. His father punished him physically for the mildest disobedience, explaining that it was necessary to 'keep him in his place'. He believed that Tom was basically a wilful, obstinate child who required strict discipline to control him. Both parents compared Tom unfavourably with his sister. His mother felt that he was too dependent on her, and believed that he would always be one of life's victims. She worried about him a great deal, and constantly fussed over his health. He was kept away from school for every minor ailment, and soon fell behind in his studies. His teachers considered him shy, erratic, unsociable and unreliable. In short, his future was not seen by anybody, including probably Tom himself, as being in any way bright.

Margaret, on the other hand, was regarded — from the start — as an attractive and easy child. She was an adaptable baby, who rarely gave her parents a disturbed night's sleep, soothed easily when crying, took her feed without complaint, and, from the first, was eager for new experiences. At two months, she had regular bowel movements, took about the same amount of food at each meal, and woke around the same time each morning. She smiled a lot, and enjoyed being fussed over.

At six months, she was an active infant, crawling fearlessly and enjoying novelty. She was the apple of her parents' eyes, and a firm favourite with relatives and friends.

By the age of one year, Margaret had grown into a pretty child, with a healthy complexion and dark hair. She would settle easily with strangers and, although clearly attached to her mother, seemed to accept separation from her without too much anxiety. Her parents felt that their original impression of her personality, which had been formed by the third month, was correct. They regarded her as a sweet-natured, intelligent and confident infant, friendly and agreeable to be with. They were extremely proud of her.

Margaret went to a play group at the age of 30 months and, after a slightly unsettled start, soon became very much at home. She was liked by all the other adults, who frequently took her side in a dispute over toys. She rarely cried or lost her temper, and appeared relaxed and happy most of the time. She had walked confidently by 14 months, and started to read when she was four. By five years, Margaret had fulfilled the early predictions of her parents and grown into an affectionate, tolerant and intelligent child whom teachers were glad to welcome into their classes.

The futures for Tom and Margaret are likely to be very different. Only time will tell, of course, but today — some eight years after the first observations were made — Tom's path through life is a hard one. He is not popular at school, and his father regards him as a failure. His school work is slightly below average, and his reports make dismal reading. Margaret, by contrast, achieves academic and social success with seeming ease. She is a confident little girl with many friends and a lot of interests which she pursues with enthusiasm. She is learning the recorder, goes to dancing lessons, and is fond of swimming. Tom has few interests or friends outside the home, and spends much of his free time watching television or playing alone.

You may feel that the early assessments which were made of these very dissimilar personalities were fair and reasonable. Tom is not a very attractive child, while Margaret is liked for very good reasons. Yet if we examine just why these early judgements were made, it becomes clear that factors over which neither child had any control played a key role in the assessments of their personalities. Tom was not an attractive baby. He was small and thin with pinched features, which gave him more the appearance of a little, old man than a healthy, bouncing infant. He had a delicate constitution and a low threshold for stimulation. This meant that he suffered more discomfort and was far more sensitive to stimulation of all kinds than a child born with a less finely tuned nervous system. Changes in his surroundings, which another child might not even have noticed, were intense and frightening. Minor pains, which a more resilient baby might have tolerated without complaint, caused him to protest noisily. Because his nervous system was acutely aware of changes and so slow to adapt to them, he took a long time to accept even minor variations in routine, cried anxiously for long periods, and was hard to distract.

None of these responses was Tom's fault. But he was treated as if they were. He was blamed and sometimes punished for them, and as a result, became even more anxious and helpless. Because he was so intensely aware of the world, it seemed an extremely frightening place. Naturally, he explored it fearfully, sticking close to the one major source of security in his life — his mother. To his parents, Tom's behaviour seemed 'silly' and inexplicable. As he grew older, his father, who had very firm ideas about what constituted 'manly' behaviour, and clear views about how small boys were supposed to behave, found him less and less acceptable as a son. He became the scapegoat for his parents' anxiety and bitterness. The ways in which Tom was biologically programmed to respond, and the way his parents, for a wide variety of reasons, came to treat those responses, were as unfortunate as they were damaging.

Margaret, by contrast, arrived in the world with an inborn system that was perfectly adjusted to the demands of her environment. She was no more responsible for the responses which made her such an 'easy' baby than Tom was for all the behaviours which made him so 'difficult' and unrewarding to deal with. Margaret fitted the world perfectly, and so regarded it as a safe and rewarding place. She was temperamentally suited to her surroundings, and so received far kinder and more understanding treatment than Tom ever enjoyed. The ways she discovered for winning praise, for making friends and meeting the challenges of childhood reflected those more favourable and rewarding interactions.

You might still consider that, however unfair and unfortunate it was for Tom, such an outcome was inevitable. After all, a child born with any kind of a disability must expect to be treated rather differently from a 'normal' baby. Tom's handicap happened to be one which showed itself by psychological rather than physical problems, but the world is not to be blamed for that.

Is this really a reasonable assumption? Must there always be Toms who will grow up condemned because they fail to fit in with the child-rearing methods to which they are subjected? Should we abandon the child to his fate, or question the attitudes that shaped and confirmed that fate? Is the infant wrong for being born with a particular temperament, or does the fault lie in the adults who are unable or unwilling to accept the special handling care needed? Henry Ford used to sell his cars with the slogan: 'You can have any colour you like so long as it's black.' Many parents seem to be telling their new-born babies much the same thing. You can grow up any way you choose, so long as it is our way.

A responsive, flexible approach to child-rearing, which tries to satisfy the inborn needs of the infant, is far harder for parents than a more dogmatic, rule-book approach. It requires one to abandon comforting stereotypes of the ways in which babies should, ideally, behave. It demands that each child be treated as an individual rather than a possession. Instead of 'my baby' to be moulded into the ideal child of the mind's eye, the new-born must be seen as a human being in his own right; a unique individual with a unique way of looking at life. In my experience many parents, especially mothers, find this a difficult attitude to adopt. Perhaps this is because the baby has been a part of their own body for so long that an almost tangible link remains long after the umbilical cord itself has been cut. For satisfactory development, however, the child must be allowed to shape his or her own destiny to the greatest possible extent. One of the major skills of the gifted parent is in knowing how to achieve this very subtle interaction between growing independence and necessary dependency during the first five years. I cannot provide any rules by which such behaviour can be regulated because all those involved, parents and children, are unique individuals. What will work well with one child may prove disastrously ineffective with another. You frequently see this in families where one child has developed successfully while another, who apparently received identical treatment from the parents, has failed. It brings me back to a comment which I made earlier in the book about our definition of good and bad environments. Such judgements can only be made in relation to a particular child. While some surroundings are so obviously damaging that the child has to be removed from them for reasons of health and safety, the majority cannot be assessed in this way. Ask yourself if the child is growing happily and successfully. If this is happening then the environment, whatever your views on it, must be providing the right kind of stimulation for that child's effective development.

Assessing The Temperament Of Your Child

When some parents are asked to described their child's personality the answers are surprisingly vague. This is often because they are too close to their children to form an objective assessment. However, an accurate analysis of some of the child's basic ways of responding to the world is essential if you are to make up your mind about him or her correctly. The 30 analytical statements below have been designed to help with this task. Because of the physical changes which occur, it is not possible to produce a single analysis which would cover behaviour from birth to the age of five. This one has been devised for use with children aged between about 18 months and five years, although with the older child in this range you will have to recollect how he or she responded to some past event with certain of the statements. By slightly rephrasing some of the statements, you will find that most can be applied to infants younger than 18 months.

To carry out the analysis, simply read the statements and note those which most accurately describe your child's response to certain situations. Then refer to the score chart which follows the list. These will provide you with information about the child's behaviour under four important categories of response. You can then use the results in conjunction with the practical guidance given in the remainder of this chapter and in Chapter eight.

1.   *During meals.*
     Child wriggles and fidgets when finished.
     Child sits quietly and waits until everybody else has finished.

2.   *On a long car drive.*
     Child constantly asks for stops in order to run around and play.
     Child sits still and looks out of the window.

3.   *When playing alone.*
     Child can amuse himself/herself with a game, puzzle or book.
     Child wants to explore and play actively most of the time.

4.   *When doing a task which requires concentration, i.e. writing or drawing.*
     Child concentrates hard and works methodically.
     Child rushes through work so as to go and play.

5.   *When first introduced to nursery school, play group, or group of friends.*
     Child soon settled down and began to play happily with

companions.
Child was unhappy, anxious and needed a lot of adult reassurance.

6. *If taken to unfamiliar surroundings (i.e. strange house, zoo, park etc.).*
Child explores without hesitation if allowed to do so.
Child remains close to family group most of the time.

7. *If engaged in some activity which is enjoyable.*
Child is totally absorbed in pursuit.
Child is easily distracted by new interest.

8. *If unable to do something through lack of strength or skill.*
Child continues to try despite setbacks.
Child becomes anxious and gives up.

9. *When meeting strangers.*
Child makes every effort to be sociable.
Child tends to be shy and uncertain.

10. *If offered unusual food.*
Child tries it eagerly.
Child refuses to try anything new.

11. *When given a new toy which is difficult to operate.*
Child carries on trying to make it work by trial and error.
Child quickly loses interest and finds an easier toy.

12. *When given some factual information.*
Child asks a large number of questions.
Child accepts information without further discussion.

13. *When confronted by an unfamiliar task.*
Child attempts is enthusiastically.
Child is anxious and uncertain.

14. *When being read to during the day.*
    Child would sooner be playing a game.
    Child enjoys sitting quietly and listening.

15. *When being shown how to do something.*
    Child watches carefully and makes a good first attempt.
    Child does not seem to pay attention and fails to follow instructions.

16. *When playing with other children.*
    Child tends to take the lead and invent games.
    Child prefers to follow others or watch them playing.

17. *When playing with own toys with friends.*
    Child tends to make spontaneous offerings of toys.
    Child prefers to play with his own toys and not let others near them.

18. *If a mistake is made in some piece of work.*
    Child notices and attempts to correct error unprompted.
    Child does not seem to notice mistake unless it is pointed out.

19. *When dressing in the morning.*
    Child pulls on clothes without much care.
    Child puts on clothes carefully and slowly.

20. *When invited to a friend's party.*
    Child accepts eagerly and at once.
    Child is uncertain and prefers not to go.

SCORE AS FOLLOWS: the top statements each receive a +2 score, the lower statements score –2 in every case. They have been designed to provide information about four basic characteristics.

1. Level of Activity.
2. Response to Novelty.
3. Social Attitudes.
4. Span of Attention.

The statements which provide these totals are as follows:

1. Level of Activity: Total the +2 or –2 scores from statements 1:2:3:14:19
2. Response to Novelty: Total the +2 or –2 scores from statements 6:10:12:13:18
3. Social Attitudes: Total the +2 or –2 scores from statements 5:9:16:17:20
4. Span of Attention: Total the +2 or –2 scores from statements 4:7:8:11:15

These totals give an indication of the child's position along a continuous line from one extreme of behaviour — for example 'very active' — to another, for instance: Very passive; use the scores to place your child on the continuum lines shown below. All you have to do is put a tick opposite the total positive and total negative score on each of the four response lines. For example, if the child scored +8 and –2 on the 'Level of Activity' statements you would tick those numbers on the line. Do this for each of the four categories of behaviour.

1. Level of Activity +10 +8 +6 +4 +2 0 –2 –4 –6 –8 –10
Very active   Very passive

2. Response to Novelty +10 +8 +6 +4 +2 0 –2 –4 –6 –8 –10
Very responsive   Avoids the unfamiliar

3. Social Attitudes +10 +8 +6 +4 +2 0 –2 –4 –6 –8 –10
Very sociable   Very unsociable

4. Span of Attention +10 +8 +6 +4 +2 0 –2 –4 –6 –8 –10
Very persistent   Very easily distracted

Using The Analysis Scores

You may find that you have scored some plus and some minus points on each of the four categories of response. This is perfectly normal. Few children, or adults, will behave in exactly the same way in similar situations. The important scores are the *highest number of points*. In the first category ('Level of Activity') a score greater than either +4 or –4 should be considered significant. In the remaining three categories only negative scores of –6 or greater are important.

These high scores indicate patterns of behaviour which usually play a key role in determining the way adults, including parents, assess children under the age of five. A high positive score on 'Level of Activity' is often found in conjunction with a high negative score on 'Span of Attention'. This is because the very active child is too energetic and easily distracted to play close attention to any task, especially ones demanding passive behaviour such as writing or working out sums. This inability to attend may lead adults to underestimate the child's actual intelligence. Very active children are sometimes considered untestable by teachers and psychologists administering IQ assessments. They never settle down for long enough to give their brains a chance to work efficiently. The overpassive child, on the other hand (a score of –6 or greater on the 'Level of Activity' scale) appears sluggish and slow witted, uninterested in trying new tasks. A high negative score on the 'Social Attitude' scale suggests a child who is failing to learn important basic lessons in social responses. These may result in increasing behaviour problems after the start of primary school. The child who has a negative score greater than –4 on the 'Response to Novelty' scale may fail to progress rapidly enough up the problem-solving hierarchy which I described earlier in the book. This can severely retard mental growth and mean that later learning is a slow, painful distressing affair.

Children with these difficulties can be helped, as such help is easiest to give, and most effective during the first five years. How you can help the child will be described under five headings which correspond to the categories of response listed above. Against each will be an analysis score. If this matches the score obtained for your child on that particular scale, I would suggest that you pay those sections particular attention.

The Over-Active Child ('Level of Activity' score of +6 or more)

At two months, the highly active babies in the survey carried out by Thomas, Chess and Birch wriggled protestingly when their nappies were changed, moved restlessly in their sleep, and were alert and vigorous in their movements during the waking hours. By two years old, they were eager explorers, refusing to settle when put to bed, and constantly climbing around on the furniture.

A high level of activity need not disadvantage the child. Indeed, it can be turned to their benefit by the right approach. But problems are likely to occur when parents try to over-curb this inborn need for movement in action. Forcing such children to spend long periods in passive pursuits can easily breed boredom and resentment. They will soon become frustrated when things do not happen quickly enough for their liking, and may demonstrate their dissatisfaction by aggressive behaviour. The worst response to such conduct is a punishment which further restricts their activity — for example, being made to stand in a corner or sit quietly for some specified period of time.

Start by allowing the child as much opportunity as possible for physical exercise. I realise that this may be very difficult in some circumstances, particularly if you live in a high-rise apartment. But 20 minutes of vigorous activity in an adventure playgroup is much better for this type of temperament than a quiet walk to the shops and a fairly passive game in the park. They must be allowed to burn up their energy. When aggression occurs as a result of frustration with some task, the adult should bring it under control not by punishment but through the introduction of a more constructive approach. Demonstrate the right way to tackle a problem, so that the child does not simply learn how to do it, but how to bring persistence to a task. If the adult simply demonstrates something which the child found especially hard and frustrating, thus making it look very easy, then only half the lesson may have been learned. The child might now understand how it should be done, but might not have grasped the fact that the adult, when learning to do it so skilfully, had to persist in the face of set-backs. Never make a task look too simple if a child has found it hard. Deliberately introduce errors on your part. Put things around the wrong way, fit pieces together incorrectly, and so on, but notice your mistakes almost immediately you have made them and then do it correctly. Say something like: 'Now, does that go there . . . no. Well, how about this, then? That looks better. But this part is still wrong, isn't it?' In this way, you are providing the child not only with a model of how to complete that particular type of task, but also a model of persistence, coupled with good, constructive feedback from what has already been accomplished.

If you feel that punishment of some kind is unavoidable, in order to curb destructive or aggressive behaviour, for example, then try and incorporate active responses on the part of the child. One way of doing this is to use an over-compensation tactic. In this, the child is forced to carry out the misconduct in an exaggerated way, and then make good the damage. For example, a child who deliberately spills water on the floor might be made to spill water all over a suitable floor surface, the bathroom or the kitchen, for instance, and then mop it all up. Repeat the performance a number of times until the child is tired and very fed up with it. A child who has thrown mud against the windows and refuses to stop could be compelled to throw mud against all suitable windows, and then to clean them carefully under adult supervision. In this way, a behaviour which once seemed interesting and desirable ceases to be quite so attractive. But consider carefully why the child is doing any of these things before applying any punishments. Is it a result of boredom, frustration, loneliness, or a lack of adult attention? Try and remedy the situation, even if you still feel obliged to introduce some kind of punishment. In Chapter eight, I shall have more to say on this point, when I discuss the needs of the aggressive child.

The Over-Passive Under-Fives ('Level of Activity' score of –6 or more).

The Thomas, Chess and Birch research has shown that both 'easy' and 'difficult' children were equally likely to have variable levels of activity. By contrast children who were categorised as 'slow to warm up' usually had moderate to low levels of activity.

Parental attitudes towards the very passive could vary greatly, depending not only on the sex and other personality traits of the infant, but on the sex and personalities of the parents. A passive baby makes life much easier for parents, and is generally well thought of. But, as the months pass and the child remains quiet and slow to respond, this can cause concern and irritation.

At two months, the passive baby does not move very much when asleep, and is docile when being changed or dressed. As he grows older, he may prefer solitary pursuits, such as reading, listening to music, or playing games alone. On long car trips, he will sit quietly and look out of the window; he will dress slowly and carefully.

Such passivity in the older child is probably least acceptable to the father when the child is a boy. This is especially true when the father has a strong concept of what masculinity is all about, equating it with vigorous activity, outdoor games, rough-and-tumble play, getting into fights and scrapes. The passive child may quickly become typed by such fathers as 'weak', 'sissy', 'unmanly', 'a mother's boy' and so on. This can lead to rejection by the father and the removal of his support and encouragement. Mothers, in my experience, tend to place a greater value on these characteristics, and will often take the child's side. This can lead to sharp conflicts within the home over the best child-rearing methods to adopt. The father may insist that they treat him in such a way as 'to make a man of him'. Where passivity is associated with anxiety, as it frequently is, this rough-and-ready approach can be little short of disastrous. Girls are usually allowed to be far more passive by both parents. Fathers who have a strong concept of what being 'manly' is all about frequently have an equally powerful, and no less mistaken, idea of what it takes to be truly 'feminine'. Here, the admired characteristics are obedience and docility.

Remember that the way the child responds is an inborn characteristic. The over-passive child is no more responsible for his approach to life than the over-active one. He or she can best be helped by being allowed that natural individuality, by not being forced to try and match a stereotyped image on the parents' part of what a little boy or little girl 'ought to be like'.

The Over-Anxious Under-Fives ('Response to Novelty' score of –6 or more)

Anxiety can show itself in many ways during this period, although it may not always be obvious that the root cause of a specific problem is this very damaging response. Anxiety also results from a low threshold of stimulation and an inability to adapt to change. Such infants tend to respond very vigorously to anything novel or unfamiliar, and to take a long time to accept any new situations. The child who is fearful of novelty is likely to reject attempts to persuade him or her to try new foods or drinks, to put on different clothes, or to sleep in a strange room. They may become extremely unsettled when moved to fresh surroundings, when introduced to strange adults or children, or when asked to tackle a chore they have never previously attempted. The slightest variation in routine can provoke an extreme response simply because these children are so highly sensitive to their surroundings. I have seen a four-year-old burst into uncontrollable tears because his mother tried a new hairstyle or wore a dress he had not seen before. Like Tom in our earlier example, these children have an acute awareness of their surroundings to a degree which others never possess. Not only do they see the world much more sharply and keenly, but images remain fresh for far longer. In a fairly short space of time, most people get so used to certain aspects of their environments that they cease to register. People who live by a railway line, for instance, may not even notice the passing trains within a few days of moving in, while their visitors will be very aware of every rattle and crash. The ultra-sensitive child is constantly in the position of those visitors. In the jargon of psychology, they take far longer to habituate to new stimulation than other people.

A highly perceptive temperament, combined with an intolerance for the kind of ambiguity represented by the novel and unfamiliar, can be a powerful intellectual force. When used to an individual's advantage, these qualities may allow a person to see things in a very original and creative way, and to be aware of possibilities which the less sensitive could easily overlook. Unfortunately, these children are particularly vulnerable to personality labelling during the first five years. Parents find them very difficult to cope with or relate to because they take such a long time to accept changes, because their reactions to quite minor upsets in routine can be so intense, and because the anxiety associated with this kind of temperament can make the child appear unfriendly and antagonistic. The relationship between the personality of the over-anxious child and the parents, especially the mother, is crucial. Research has shown that of the four possible combinations, two may be beneficial to both mother and child, while two present the maximum number of disadvantages to both.

1. *Calm Mother and Anxious Child:* a good match. One compensates for the other.
2. *Anxious Mother and Calm Child:* another good match because the less easily aroused child does little to increase the fears of an already uncertain mother.
3. *Anxious Mother and Anxious Child:* a bad match. Each heightens the fears of the other. Can prove a disaster for both of them.
4. *Very Passive Mother and Very Passive Child:* another bad match. The child never receives sufficient stimulation from the mother to develop successfully.

In Chapter eight, I will be dealing with ways in which the passive child can be stimulated, and in Chapter nine, I will be looking at the needs of the anxious adult and suggesting how fears can be reduced.

However patient and loving parents try to be, there usually comes a point when a battle of wills develops. The adults are determined that something will be done but the child is unable to oblige. The parents may insist that a chosen type of food is eaten, that a particular situation is confronted, or that the child conforms to their views of life. A failure to achieve these demands may result in punishments and the label of stubborn, obstinate, self-willed, or plain bloody-minded being firmly attached to the infant. Achieving a reasonable balance is never easy. It requires great perception and considerable powers of judgement. There are some situations which can be made much worse if the parent constantly gives way to the wishes of the child. (I will consider these in Chapter eight, when I look at the special needs of the anxious child.) At other times, it may be essential to allow the child to follow his own feelings, and not to force him to conform to your wishes. An understanding of the reasons why a child takes a particular attitude may make it easier for you to relate to him effectively. These inborn characteristics, so infuriating in the under-fives, can prove very valuable to the child later in life. When properly handled, these heightened perceptions can give creative insights which are denied the less responsive individual.

The Unsociable Under-Fives ('Social Attitudes' score of –6 or more).

Being a friendly child counts for a great deal in the eyes of most adults. Not unreasonably, we all respond more positively to people who show warmth and friendship towards us. Indeed, the fact that somebody obviously likes us is one of the major factors which determines whether or not we like them. Adults are usually keen that their children are well-liked by relatives, friends, and even visiting strangers, because it reflects favourably on their abilities as parents. On many occasions, calling at somebody's house to carry out tests on the children, I have been cautioned: 'You may not find him/her very co-operative today. He/she really is sociable by nature, but a bit moody. You've caught him/her on an off-day, I'm afraid.'

In adults and older children, being socially effective requires the mastering of certain basic skills. For example, having an interesting contribution to make, and being able to put forward your ideas effectively; being able to send out the right sort of body language signals and being sensitive to the moods and feelings of others. But sociability in children aged between about five months and three years is largely a matter of inborn characteristics. It is, primarily, a reflection of the child's responses to the unfamiliar and their general levels of arousal and activity. If the child is very anxious, he or she may avoid situations in which it is possible to learn and practise social skills. If very passive, they may never make sufficient effort to take advantage of such social encounters. Most infants pass through a phase, usually around nine months of age, when a previously happy acceptance of strangers gives way to a fearful wariness to anybody but their parents. Normally, this period is quickly passed through, and the earlier responses reassert themselves. But some infants never seem to overcome feelings of anxiety and uncertainty when confronting strangers.

As adults, we are so used to dealing with others that we usually fail to realise what a massive source of information and stimulation another human being is. There is no comparison between the complexity of responses needed to operate the most intricate and elaborate toy in the infant's nursery and those demanded during even the shortest and most detached encounter with a human. All such exchanges involve those taking part in a staggeringly complicated series of mental processes. There is a tumult of sights and sounds to be absorbed, analysed and acted upon. We have to be sensitive to the most subtle aspects, as well as the most obvious components of the interaction. We must be aware of nuances of body language, and interpret correctly the shades of meaning conveyed by tone and inflection; a movement of the eyes, a twitch of the lips, or a hesitation in delivery. Professor Ray Birdwhistell of the Annenberg School of Communication at the University of Pennsylvania, has calculated that, if one were to record on tape all the information involved in the course of one hour's interaction between two subjects, the manpower needed to analyse that flood of data would be the equivalent of the full lifetime efforts of roughly half the population of the United States!

As we grow older, we quickly learn to extract the information needed to make sense of each encounter, and to ignore the rest. Although we do so without realising it, this task does represent a highly skilled piece of behaviour which has taken a great deal of time and effort to perfect. By the time they are five, most children can do it fairly effectively for much of the time, although they are generally less good at interpreting exchanges absolutely correctly than are their slightly older brothers and sisters.

Children who have a very low threshold of arousal, who perceive the world so much more powerfully than others, are likely to find this task even harder to accomplish. Because they are especially sensitive to everything in their environment, filtering out the essential from the unnecessary is that much harder to accomplish. It takes longer, requires more effort, and demands a greater amount of practice. The unfortunate thing is that a child who appears to be unfriendly often prevents people from providing the practice so necessary if social learning is to take place. Without that experience, the novelty of relating to others will remain, the anxiety will never be reduced, and the skills needed to respond effectively to friendly approaches are unlikely to be attained.

The 'unfriendly' infant will grow up learning that it is easier to be a loner. He or she will stand on the sidelines when others are playing, be a spectator rather than a participant in group activities, and gradually find it harder and harder to relate successfully at anything but the most basic level. The only answer is to continue to provide such children with the opportunities for experiencing friendly exchanges during the first five years of life. This is, I am well aware, easier to say than to do. The practical difficulties are often tremendous. As a child gains a reputation for being unfriendly, party invitations tend to dry up. As a parent, you may be reluctant to expose others to your 'unfriendly' child, or to force the child to do something which, quite rightly, seems to you distressing for them. On the other hand, without sufficient practice, they will be unable to overcome their social difficulties. It may never be easy, because such exchanges make them so much more anxious than they do other children. But it will never be as easy — however hard it appears at the time — as during the first five years of life. Gentle support and understanding, combined with a reasonably firm insistence that they do make attempts at establishing friendly relationships, is the best approach. Avoid making out that you think they are doing something especially difficult, however. Never say to the child: 'I know you hate this, but it's for your own good.' I have heard mothers use this tactic, which is far more likely to do harm than to help. The child has received confirmation, almost been granted parental permission, to see the situation as hateful, difficult and distressing. Manipulate behind the scenes, but keep your motives, and your feelings, to yourself.

The Easily Distracted Under-Fives ('Span of Attention' score −6 or more).

The degree of persistence which the under-fives bring to any task depends on a number of factors, two of the most important being the temperament of the child and the nature of the activity. Children who are made anxious by novelty may pay very little attention to an unfamiliar pursuit, but persist with a familiar one long after a less easily aroused child has got bored and given up. A child who adapts very quickly to novelty may rapidly obtain all the information he or she feels can be gleaned from a task, while the child who adapts more slowly will continue to play happily. Very active children often attend to any one thing for only a brief period before something else attracts their attention and they rush off to play a new game.

The child who assimilates information rapidly may be regarded as less studious than the slower learner who spends more time studying a new toy or game. If forced to persist with an activity which he or she has already assimilated, boredom and disinterest are bound to follow.

Whether or not the child finds a particular game or toy interesting is a very subjective decision, and adult feeling on the matter usually bear little relationship to the way a child feels. Major toy manufacturers are well aware of the gulf which exists between grown-up views and the child's opinion about what constitutes a pleasurable pastime. As a result, they often employ panels of small children to tell their designers just what they think of a new range of toys.

Whether or not a child is persistent in some activity frequently plays an important part in the parents' assessment of his or her personality. But how persistence is judged varies considerably according to the personalities of the parents, their attitudes towards that particular task and the age of the child. For example, if the parents attach a great deal of importance to neatness, a child of, say, four or five, who approaches writing, drawing or modelling in what seems to them a slapdash and messy way is very likely to be censured. The parents are likely to criticise the presentation of work and to neglect the actual content. If the child continues to work in what they define as a careless manner, then this will be assessed as part of their personality: 'John is much too casual in his attitude,' the father may say. 'He's naturally disorganised.'

Parents who are less concerned with outward appearances, and more interested in what is being expressed, may never even notice such 'carelessness', and their assessments of the child's personality will be quite different as a result: 'John is very bold and creative,' they may tell you. 'He works quickly and confidently.' When it comes to making up your mind about your child, the degree of persistence and attentiveness shown may play an important part in your assessment of their personality. There is no disputing that they are extremely significant to intellectual success. Paying sufficient attention to absorb the main points of a problem, and having the persistence to keep searching for answers in the face of set-backs, are essential requirements in any mental task. It is in these two abilities that gifted children often show the greatest divergence from those whose inborn promise has not been realised.

But despite their importance, I would caution you against affording them much prominence when passing judgement on the under-fives. The variables which determine our interpretation of what constitutes persistence and attentiveness are far more complicated and numerous than is generally appreciated. Too many parents base their opinions on the following kind of reasoning:

(i)   The task is interesting, and the child should attend to it carefully and show persistence in solving the problems involved.

    (ii) The child does not pay attention, and is easily dis-
tracted.

    (iii) There is a lack of persistence, which is clearly shown in
the poor results.

    (iv) Therefore, the child lacks the motivation or the ability
to concentrate. So we should either give them different
tasks, or accept that they will never be able to cope with
intellectual challenges which, inevitably, require
attention and persistence.

This line of argument may seem reasonable, but is it right? Before deciding, one must question all the assumptions on which it is based. Is the task really interesting? The fact that it appears so to adult eyes is no proof that the child sees it that way. Is it too advanced for the child, who, not unreasonably, gives up as a result? Is an inability to come up with the right answer a result of inattentiveness or an ignorance of the necessary skills, or a lack of knowledge about the true nature of the givens, or the way in which the manipulations should be used, for example? Is the adult's assessment of the end product reasonable? Are faults being seen at the expense of the positive aspects of the answer given? Finally, is the adult's judgement of what constitutes persistence and attentiveness too subjective? These are the sorts of questions which should be asked before any assessment is made about a child's ability to attend. But, in my experience, they are seldom considered. Often on the most inconclusive fragments of information, the under-fives are labelled in a very definite way. They are held to be well suited to intellectual tasks requiring persistence, and provided with increasingly interesting and complex challenges. Or they are seen as being incapable of meeting one of the basic requirements of academic attainment. Once defined in a particular way, the attitude of all the adults the child encounters is likely to be profoundly influenced. That definition, and those encounters, will shape the future.

Chapter Seven

Getting On — By Getting On

Parents sometimes say to me: 'I don't want my child to be especially gifted, only happy and well adjusted.' This makes it sound as if they are being offered just two alternatives — giftedness or happiness. But there is no such painful choice to be made. Indeed, as I suggested in Chapter one, the fear of creating some kind of Frankenstein monster by encouraging the child's mental development is an important reason why some children are denied the chance to realise their natural brilliance.

Let me describe one, major piece of research which effectively demolishes the myth of restriction, once and for all. In 1921, the American psychologist Lewis Terman embarked on one of the longest and most remarkable studies ever undertaken. Terman, who had been responsible for early work on the IQ test, identified 1,500 Californian schoolchildren of both sexes who could be considered intellectually gifted. Their test scores placed them in the top 2 per cent of intelligence. During the years that followed, Terman and his collaborators watched every one of those 1,500 students carefully to discover whether early ability was matched by subsequent achievement in life. In the vast majority of cases the researchers found that this was indeed what happened. More than 80 per cent of the group finished in the professions and achieved considerable success in their chosen careers. By their early twenties this relatively small group of individuals had written ninety books and registered more than one hundred patents on new inventions. They had achieved higher status and better paid jobs than even the average college graduate. They were better adjusted, more socially successful and usually extremely popular. Far from their high intelligence preventing them from being happy and adjusting to everyday life, they were clearly happier, more fulfilled and better integrated into the community than less gifted individuals. What was more, probably as a result of their higher pay, greater job satisfaction and superior living conditions, their health and stamina were far better than average.

So intellectual giftedness is not bought at the price of social contentment or happiness. Indeed, an ability to get on with others can be of crucial importance in the successful development of intelligence and creativity. Social giftedness is just as important as giftedness in other areas of ability.

What are the qualities possessed by children who have well developed social skills? Roy Jarecky, an American psychologist, found out by following the progress of a group of 14-year-old boys during their first term in a big American school. Amongst the abilities which distinguished the socially successful, Jarecky found the following. They related to their companions and to adults on an equal basis, resisting insincere, artificial or patronising relationships. They were open and honest in their behaviour. They seemed free from emotional tension and were not afraid to express themselves openly, but their demonstrations of emotion were always relevant to the situation. They stimulated positive behaviour in others. They were enthusiastic youngsters who seemed to have the ability to cope with any social situation, managing to do so with a mixture of intelligence, humour and insight.

These are, I am sure you will agree, very desirable ways of behaving. They are likely to make the individuals easy to get along with and rewarding companions. Yet none of these skills arrived with the baby. All were learned during the earliest years of life. How they were taught by their socially gifted parents forms the subject of this chapter.

During the course of my research into giftedness I have

visited scores of homes in different parts of the world to interview children and their parents. As I am leaving one of the adults may remark: 'He was on his best behaviour today. . . .', or apologise: 'I am afraid he was in a bad mood. . . .'

The majority of parents want their children to be well-liked and highly regarded by other adults. In part, this may be because they believe the child's behaviour reflects the parents' skill in child-rearing. An ill-mannered, undisciplined infant shows the family in a bad light and is an embarrassment. But this is not the only consideration in the minds of most parents. They want their children to be liked because they know that this is important to future success. The child who makes a good impression at first meeting (remember the importance of the primacy effect described in the last chapter) is likely to get on better and faster than the socially inept. Knowing this from their own experience, they plead: 'Be good', or warn: 'Behave properly'.

But what exactly does 'being good' involve? How is the child expected to 'behave properly'? The exact types of behaviour vary quite widely from social class to social class, between countries and cultures. But the kinds of conduct most frequently mentioned when I ask parents to tell me what *they* mean by 'good behaviour' are as follows: not being a nuisance; not fidgeting during meals; not getting down from the table without permission; not speaking to an adult unless spoken to first; smiling or shaking hands when meeting an adult; remembering to say please and thank you; not passing personal comments; expressing gratitude when given something; looking interested when being talked to; not asking too many questions; not interrupting adults; not arguing when told to do something; not disobeying, not being too noisy; standing up when an adult comes into the room; not quarrelling with other children; not making a mess; not being impudent.

While probably far from complete, this list does cover most of the main components of 'best behaviour' which have been described to me. If you examine them carefully, you will see that they divide into two types of command. There are 'don't rules', which prohibit certain kinds of activities, and 'do' rules, which demand particular forms of conduct. The 'don't' rules include such things as not interrupting, not making too much noise or not making a mess. The 'do' rules involve shaking hands, saying please and thank you, looking interested, smiling and so on. A further analysis of these, and any other 'don't' or 'do' rules which you may use in your family, will reveal that the majority of 'don't' rules are designed for the convenience of adults, while most of the 'do' rules arise from social customs or cultural traditions. The sort of 'do' rules which a child learns vary greatly from one country and ethnic group to another, but 'don't' rules tend to be quite similar around the world.

The same sort of rules apply when children are playing together under the watchful eye of adults. Only now some of the 'don't' rules are used not simply for the convenience of the grown-ups, or for the safety of the individual child, but to protect children from one another. 'Being well behaved' in this context usually means abiding by such 'don't' rules as not yelling; not throwing toys; not hitting smaller children; not making too much mess; not spitting; not biting other children; not spoiling somebody else's game; not taking another child's toy. These and other prohibitions are aimed at providing a measure of peace for the adults and reasonable security for the children. 'Do' rules may include offering to share toys or sweets; helping smaller children; tidying away toys after use; co-operating with others, and so on. Although these usually make the adult's life easier, there is a strong element of social tradition in most of them. Amongst different cultures, for example, sharing and co-operation can either be strongly emphasised or greatly disapproved of.

Parents collecting children new to a playgroup may be told by the supervisor: 'He was no trouble at all, played quietly from the moment you left.' Or reproached with: 'She was a bit of a handful. Didn't settle at all.' Remarks like this are really a reflection of the extent to which a particular child's behaviour either matched or diverged from the 'do' and 'don't' rules which that adult regards as important. Every adult has an expectation of the way 'well mannered' children should behave. The more closely these are met, the higher their opinion of the child is likely to be. The greater the gap between adult expectations and a child's conduct, the more negative their impressions.

To a great extent, expectations about what constitutes good manners are subjective opinions which result from the adult's own upbringing, background and social attributes. Somebody who takes an 'old fashioned' view about polite behaviour is likely to have a longer list of 'don't' rules and 'do' rules than one who has a less conventional, more laissez-faire approach. A Victorian grandmother, her social time-clock set in the days when children were 'seen but not heard', is likely to value quiet, deferential behaviour on the part of the very young. A modern mother may expect her under-fives to be expressive and independent, rather than meekly respectful, in their dealings with adults.

But while there are extremes of viewpoint, with some adults demanding strict adherence to a lengthy catalogue of rules, and others employing none at all, most parents adopt a compromise position. In their view, children should be allowed to express themselves providing they do so fairly quietly. They have every right to their own views so long as these do not clash with what the grown-ups want to do. They need not be servile when meeting adults, but they should show respect. They do not have to agree with everything their elders tell them, but must not disagree too vocally.

If you have a traditional view of what is meant by good behaviour in young children, you will probably be thinking that this is perfectly right and proper. If you favour a more liberal and liberated approach, you may well be wondering whether it really matters that much how a child behaves?

Surely people of all ages should be valued as individuals, and judged on the merits of their ideas and interests, not on the basis of how well, or how badly, they conform to a set of social rules.

While I have some sympathy for this approach, experience suggests that 'good behaviour' does matter a great deal. Social skills, with all that this term implies about following certain 'don't' rules and knowing the necessary 'do' rules, *are* very important. Perhaps it should not be like this. Maybe the fault lies with adults. But the fact remains that children have to grow and succeed in the world as it is. Whatever views we have about the value of uninhibited self-expression and independence of action, an inability to meet the social expectations of parents and other influential adults can be extremely damaging to the child. The image which others have of them will affect their self-image. It will influence the opportunities open to them, either increasing or limiting their chances for stimulation and discovery. It will determine the way their failures are judged and their achievements received.

A child who is socially skilled in his, or her, dealings with adults quickly establishes a very positive image. The socially inadequate child, however able he may be in other directions, will make a bad impression.

Here is a story, drawn from the files of the National Association for Gifted Children in London, which well illustrates this point. Although it concerns an older child, we must remember that the way in which this boy behaved is a reflection of lessons learned during the first five years. One day an architect was visiting the home of a friend when he saw a clever drawing of an ornate doorway pinned up on the family display board. The perspective and detail were excellent, which made the man all the more astonished to learn that it had been drawn by the nine-year-old son of the family. Impressed, he invited the child to spend a few days of his holiday working with his design team. On the first day the boy was allowed to go out with a qualified surveyor who reported with astonishment:

'He took ten minutes to adjust to the technique of measured surveys and, from then on, was as good as any mature assistant.'

The boy loved the work and spent all his holidays in the office from then on. A year after he first started he was being allowed to sit in on discussions with clients and made a real contribution to the practice. The most significant comment in this report comes at the end where the architect notes: 'One might think there would be resentment within that office to so much precocity. But the truth is that, coupled with his remarkable ability to grasp the subject, he also retains the ability to integrate socially with very much older colleagues.' In other words, the boy was socially gifted as well as creatively talented. He was not overbearing or pompous about his abilities, he did not push himself forward or hang anxiously back when asked to do something novel. He was friendly, co-operative and agreeable, a pleasure to be with.

It was a wonderful opportunity for a talented child to gain real experience of life. But, however skilled his drawings, it is unlikely he would have been given the same chances had he made a negative impression on those adults who were in a position to help him. For young children, getting on with others successfully is the surest pathway to success in all areas of mental development.

Babies are socially precocious. They need relationships with other human beings and are eager for them. In order to enjoy the good opinion of adults and older children, infants must master the more important 'do' and 'don't' rules.

But simply carrying out these responses in a mechanical way is not enough. In the words of the old song: 'It ain't what you do, it's the way that you do it. . . .' that gets results. For example, the impression conveyed to an adult by a child who says 'Thank you' for something, but does so with downcast eyes and a sulky expression is likely to be fairly negative. The words combined with eye-contact and a bright smile will produce a far more positive impression and result in a greater liking for the child.

The way in which the behaviours involved in 'do' rules are successfully carried out is a subtle and complex process, involving skilled non-verbal as well as verbal responses. While the basic rules can be taught directly, by instruction or example, the presentation of these responses — the exact ways in which they are used — is seldom amenable to direct teaching. Usually it is learned by the child from copying the ways in which adults in the family, and outside it, behave. To a large extent, it reflects interactions between all the members of the family unit.

Teaching The 'Do' Rules

I will begin by looking at ways in which the 'do' rules can be taught most effectively. Then I will consider the teaching of the 'don't' rules, and finally look at some of the more important aspects of body language.

The 'do' rules are the easiest to teach during the first five years because they can be explained, demonstrated and then rewarded immediately they are carried out — such as noticing and encouraging the use of polite comments like 'Please' and 'Thank you'. A second important consideration is that the frequency and skill with which the child obeys a 'do' rule can normally be seen quite easily. If it is overlooked by the child, the mistake can be pointed out immediately. All this adds up to a nearly perfect learning situation, and, as a result, sensible 'do' rules should be mastered very quickly. The same advantages are seldom found when it comes to teaching 'don't' rules.

Let me illustrate these points by looking at the way a small child learns that very simple, but important 'do' rule in Western cultures — the handshake. A youngster who has been taught how to shake hands correctly at a first meeting with adults makes a very good impression. 'How polite', the adult thinks, returning the greeting. 'How nice to meet a child so young and so well mannered.'

Shaking hands is not just a matter of extending the arm, of course. It must be accompanied by other appropriate pieces of body language; a smile, eye-contact, and a firm grip. All these can be taught to the child by a demonstration combined with the simple explanation that this is the 'right' way to say hello to a grown-up. If you ensure that you greet other adults in this way when the child is present, the important 'do' rule will be mastered in no time at all. But, at first, you should provide immediate reinforcement for the action by smiling at the child, and, perhaps, commenting favourably on his conduct a little later: 'I am so pleased you shook hands with Mr Brown. He told me what a polite boy you were.'

Here, the three stages of successful learning — direct instruction, an adult model to follow, immediate reinforcement of the correct response — are easy to apply. Teaching 'don't' rules is harder because, for reasons which I will explain in a moment, it is much more difficult to follow this important sequence.

'Do' rules often seem illogical to modern eyes, because their origins lie deep in the social traditions of a particular culture. The handshake, for example, originated in a peaceful gesture indicating that no weapon was being carried. Then there is the 'do' rule, still followed by some sections of society, which insists that a man walk to the left side of the woman he is accompanying. This may seem illogical until one discovers that its original purpose was to enable a swordsman to have easy access to the sword, which hung on the left side.

'Do' rules change with the times, and there are many fewer today than there were even half a century ago, when bulky volumes of etiquette, really compilations of the necessary 'do' rules, exerted a powerful control over those in 'polite society'. But the 'do' rules which still remain are important pieces of social behaviour, and the child must master them. Some parents seem to believe that they will appear spontaneously, and that no specific lessons in how to behave are needed. It is true that those who have never been taught directly do pick up many of the most important 'do' rules simply by seeing the ways in which others act. But the quickest and most effective method is to teach them during the first five years. This can best be accomplished as follows:-

1.   Start out with a clear understanding of the 'do' rules you want the child to learn. If necessary, make a list of them.

2.   Do not try to teach them out of context. Whenever an appropriate occasion arises, tell the child exactly how they are expected to behave. If possible, demonstrate. Do not leave it too late. The earlier the lesson is taught, the easier it will be for the child to master.

3.   At first, reward every occasion on which the required 'do' rule is used. These reinforcements need not be lavish or elaborate; a warm smile, a nod, a word of praise, are all that is needed. But remember how important it is to reward a desired piece of behaviour *immediately*. Do not wait for an hour or so before making a favourable comment.

4.   Never reward the omission of a 'do' rule by carrying on as it if had been followed. In some circumstances, a gentle reminder will be enough, although this need not be a spoken one. Simply by carrying out the response yourself, you may jog the child's memory. On other occasions, you may feel that the child is deliberately testing you, perhaps to see if the 'do' rule is still in force. For example, the child has learned to say 'Please' when asking for something. She does not do so, and demands: 'Give me a sweet.' If you ignore the mistake, and give her a sweet, you will have rewarded the wrong sort of behaviour and made it more likely that the same thing will happen again. Point out the error and insist, gently but firmly, that the 'do' rule is obeyed before you go any further.

Children generally like learning 'do' rules. For one thing, they are behaviours which polite adults use, and the majority of youngsters enjoy being able to act in a grown-up manner.

They also enable the child to make a good impression with strangers, who are more likely to respond favourably towards them as a result. Finally, they provide clear guidance on how to act when meeting adults, something which causes a high level of anxiety in many young children. If they know how to behave, they have a basic structure on which to build their response to a situation.

Teaching The 'Don't' Rules

These are rather harder to teach, for several reasons. For a start, it is often difficult to assess how well they are being obeyed, as this is frequently a subjective decision which may change with the mood of the adult. For example, a 'do' rule such as shaking hands is easy to observe and judge. But what about a 'don't' rule like: 'Don't make too much noise.' On one occasion, you are laughing and joking with friends, and making a fair amount of noise yourself. The noise from the children, although loud, is acceptable. A few days later you are trying to concentrate on a difficult job, which has to be completed against a deadline. Anxiety over the task lowers your threshold of tolerance. An identical amount of noise from the children brings down your wrath on their heads. As I have said earlier, inconsistency of response is distressing for the child and hampers effective learning.

Another difficulty is that it is almost impossible to immediately reward compliance with the majority of 'don't' rules, the essential condition for rapid learning. Suppose you tell a child not to play with some ornaments, and at no time during that afternoon does he go anywhere near them. If you remember your instruction and the child's compliance later in the day, you might comment favourably. But this will be a delayed reinforcement, and, as we have seen, ineffective in helping to establish that particular way of responding. It is more than likely, however, that you will take their obedience for granted. You expect them to do as they are told, and see no reason for praising them for doing so. 'Don't' rules are usually punished when ignored rather than being rewarded when obeyed. This makes their learning difficult and sometimes unsatisfactory.

It is hard to give general guidance over the most appropriate 'don't' rules to employ, because the ones you consider necessary will vary according to your own attitude towards life, the temperament of the child, the warmth of relationships within the family, even on the kind of house or apartment in which you live, and the area in which it is located.

Parents who believe in regulating their children very closely, who live in a small apartment high above a busy street and have extremely active children, are likely to use a large number of 'don't' rules and apply them very firmly. Parents who want their children to enjoy the maximum amount of freedom, who live in a large house surrounded by open country, will probably have very few 'don't' rules.

In practice, the number and type of 'don't' rules used must be a matter of personal opinion. By my comparative studies of families which have children with exceptionally well developed mental abilities, with those where intellectual growth appears to have been considerably restricted, has led me to three firm conclusions.

If you want the inborn brilliance of your baby to be realised:

1.   *'Don't' rules should be used very sparingly.*
Employ only the absolute minimum necessary for the safety of the child and the successful adjustment of the child to the demands of society.

2.   *'Don't' rules must always be fair and logical.*
They must be capable of rational explanation, and you should make every effort to explain them.

3.   *'Don't' rules must be enforced consistently.*
Every child needs an ordered, logically structured world in

which to grow and learn. This can only be achieved if the rules remain constant and are consistently applied. Frequent changing of the rules, forbidding things one moment and tolerating them the next, can introduce a degree of uncertainty into the child's life which easily leads to learned helplessness.

If you have a very large number of 'don't' rules, several difficulties can arise. For a start, the child may have a hard job remembering them all, and you are likely to find it hard to enforce them consistently. If they are still strictly imposed, the child's freedom to explore and experiment will be severely curtailed and damage to mental development is bound to occur. I have already mentioned three justifications for 'don't' rules — to protect the child from harm; to help the child fit into society and meet adult expectations; and to give parents an easier time. All are equally valid, but you should appreciate the true purpose of each, and be honest about it, when introducing a 'don't' rule. One rule which is enforced under the guise of being in the best interests of the child when it is actually designed for the convenience of adults, is when something is sold under false colours. Do not underestimate the insights of children. They are quite capable of separating truth from falsehood, and if they decide that you have been dishonest about a prohibition, they may doubt both your integrity, the value of the rule itself and other such future prohibitions.

So far as introducing such rules in order to make your life more agreeable is concerned, the essential thing is to do so without feeling guilty. I know many parents feel very bad about curtailing the activities of their children simply because it is in their own best interests. While it is easy, and harmful, to be too selfish in this matter, you must indeed consider your own needs and feelings. You have every right to assert yourself and to make demands on your children, even small children. You are entitled to periods of peace and quiet, to opportunities for shared activities with your partner from which the children are excluded, to privacy when you want to be alone, and to time in which you can follow your own interests.

Provided these 'don't' rules are reasonable and fairly applied, children will not mind complying with them. But you should be willing to confer the same rights on the child. The rules about respecting privacy, appreciating the need to do things alone, and allowing periods of peace and quiet, should apply to the entire family, not only adults. If they are, then you will find them readily accepted. The important thing is to be honest about their purpose and consistent in their application. Where possible, teach 'don't' rules by transforming them into 'do' rules. This makes them easier for the child to learn and for you to monitor. For instance, instead of telling children: 'Don't be rude', show them specific ways of behaving politely. Emphasising the positive aspects of their conduct, and de-emphasise the negative aspects. Do not say: 'You are a rude little boy, and that is why you act like that.' Instead, tell the child: 'You are a polite little boy really, and polite boys do not act like that.'

Always look for good pieces of behaviour, and encourage them as strongly as possible while avoiding any rewards for bad conduct, especially when this is designed as an attention-seeking device. Remember that even a punishment can be rewarding for a small child who feels neglected. 'Don't' rules can never be expected to leave a vacuum, however severely they are enforced. The child must do something! That something should be a constructive, socially acceptable way of behaving. Work out what is required, and then eliminate the responses which you dislike by encouraging the desirable alternatives.

You may feel that none of this properly applies to the under-fives. It may be a good idea to explain things to older children, but at this early age, the child is too immature to either want or understand such explanations.

While it is certainly easier for parents simply to make rules and then enforce them, everything which I have learned about the under-fives convinces me that this is the wrong approach.

Use simple concepts, and explain in terms of the child's experiences, but never avoid an explanation. For example, suppose you tell them: 'Don't interrupt when grown-ups are talking', and refuse to explain why. The child cannot understand why this is necessary, especially since they will see that adults constantly interrupt one another! If you explain by adding 'because it's impolite', the child is unlikely to be any the wiser. What is 'impolite'? Far better to explain in these terms: 'The best and proper way to hold a conversation is for everybody to take their turns to speak. That way, we all get a chance to say what we want and to hear what others have to say. Sometimes, grown-ups forget this rule, and then it can be very muddling.' This enables the child to appreciate the logic of your rule and, believe me, the under-five are extremely receptive to logic when given the chance. But you must practise what you preach. If the child is talking, make sure you do not interrupt his or her conversation.

By allowing the child the chance to try and understand, you are widening his experience of life and helping him to respect essential 'don't' rules.

Speaking Without Talking — And Saying The Wrong Things

Robert was a seven-year-old with the unfortunate habit of smiling at the wrong moment. It may not sound like a very serious mistake, yet it was one of the problems which caused him to finish up in a school for maladjusted children. For some reason, he had come to associate high levels of anxiety with what seemed to be a grin of amusement. Whenever he was being scolded or punished, he would smile broadly and, in the opinion of the outraged adults, impudently. As a result, Robert was punished even more severely, and ended up with a whole range of behavioural difficulties.

This is a rather extreme example of the way in which saying the wrong things without saying a word can affect a child's successful development. Body language is important to everybody. .We all use a remarkable number of silent speech signals in everyday exchanges. Some we are well aware of and employ deliberately to convey a particular response; amusement, distaste, anger, and so on. But many more are used without our being aware of the fact, although they still play a crucial role in the kind of messages we silently transmit, and the way what we say with our voices is received. They involve such subtle factors as proximity to others, the use of eye-contact, and the direction in which gaze is broken; barely perceptible nods and shakes of the head, slight gestures of the hands and arms, leaning towards or away from the other person, and so on.

Children under the age of five make even wider use of body language, because, lacking verbal fluency, it is a far more important part of their system of communication. A child who is able to 'talk' confidently by means of gesture and gaze will be able to relate to other children far more effectively than the poor body talker. And it is just as important for the child to get body signals right when talking to adults. The errors need not be as obvious as Robert's ill-timed smiles in order to have a very adverse effect. They may involve nothing more than an incorrect use of eye-contact, a poor judgement about head movements, or a lack of synchronisation between words and gestures. The child, like the inept adult body-language talker, may not even notice that the wrong signals are being sent out. Recipients of such signals may not be directly aware of what is going wrong, but they will be very conscious of the fact that something is not quite right. They are left with a feeling of unease, a lack of empathy, an absence of closeness to the child. 'I don't know what it is about Francis,' one mother told me when we were discussing a neighbour's five-year-old, 'but I can't bring myself to like him. He's a polite enough little boy, but there's something strange about him.'

Frequently in these cases, analysis of video-recordings made of such children during exchanges with adults reveals a lack of body language ability. By comparison, analysis of recordings made of children who are able to convey a positive impression at first meetings always shows that they have a good grasp of body talk.

Learning body language is mainly a matter of experience. You can teach children to use the more obvious signals — smiles, for example — at appropriate times. But there is no way you could train the child to become fluent in all the complex subtleties of proficient non-verbal communication. For the most part, efficient silent speech is acquired by constant exposure to other children and adults who are, themselves, effective body talkers. In a survey which covered the silent speech skills of one hundred children in Britain and America, I did not find one child who was very competent in silent speech whose mothers, at least, were not equally gifted. By the same token, those children who showed the least ability had parents who were similarly ineffective.

Because children are so closely associated with their mothers for so much of the time during the early years, it is inevitable that mother should provide the primary model. But she is not the sole source of instruction; the father — especially where the relationship is a close one — brothers and sisters, adult relatives, other children and every adult with whom the child comes into frequent contact, can teach them something about non-verbal communication. This is just one of the reasons why children should gain experience of as many different people as possible, especially children of around their own age. It is also important for them to remain reasonably unhibited about making use of body language. To a great extent, the ways in which silent speech signals are used are socially and culturally determined. The French, for instance, tend to be more demonstrative in their use of gestures than the English. Successful body signals must always be appropriate to the culture concerned.

These, then, are some of the most effective ways of teaching the basic rules of social conduct. It may appear relatively straightforward, but problems can arise. An over-stringent application of the rules can restrict a child's mental progress. The price paid for 'good' behaviour can easily become intellectual failure.

Growing Promise — Growing Pains

Most parents, as I have said, have clear expectations about how their children should behave. Unfortunately, the 'don't' rules necessary for such 'good' behaviour frequently conflict with the ways in which a child must be allowed to behave if inborn brilliance is to be realised.

This clash can lead to emotional problems for the child, and cause acute distress and anxiety to the parents. An atmosphere of distrust may grow within the family, which damages all relationships and restricts the child's potential. There may be arguments between the parents as to the right approach, and between parents and child about the things they should be allowed to do. Faced with a choice between limiting mental growth and conforming to parental 'don't' rules, a child may well obey with an inevitable loss of individuality and independence. Equally, children may rebel, reject parental rules, and go their own way in an effort to retain that freedom which they regard as more important than the good opinions of others. When this happens, they will, inevitably, lose the sympathy, help and encouragement of their parents, responses which are every bit as important to successful mental growth as freedom of action. Either way, the result will be to diminish the potential for intellectual and creative development.

It is a painful dilemma. In order to allow a child to acquire those essential characteristics of thought and action that lead to intellectual achievement, parents may be forced to sacrifice the 'don't' rules which mark out their boundaries of good behaviour. By doing this, they may encourage the child to do things which many influential adults, teachers for example, find highly objectionable. As a result, adults will respond negatively to the child. However clever they are, the opportunities needed to take advantage of a well-developed mental ability may then be denied them. They will receive adverse reports and critical comment. Other children may not want to play with them. Their chances of rewarding social exchange will be greatly limited, and they will never learn the skills necessary to interact effectively during adolescence and adulthood. Their poor image in the eyes of others may lead to rebellious, aggressive, or indifferent behaviour as the child takes the line that — I am disliked anyhow, so let me give them something to think about; or simply shrugs off all opinions held as being unworthy of attention.

It is almost a double-bind situation, when nothing one can do is for the best. Almost but, fortunately, not quite. It is possible to impose 'don't' rules without simultaneously destroying the freedom necessary for mental growth. The expectations of adults do not have to be bought at the price of a child's intellectual potential. The vicious, negative spiral of mutually damaging responses can just as easily be a series of positive, mutually beneficial exchanges which are rewarding to both parents and children. I am not saying that it is an easy situation to achieve, but neither should it be regarded as an impossible dream.

The starting point is an understanding of those characteristics of thought and expression likely to be present in children being allowed to grow towards their full intellectual potential; and an appreciation of the ways in which these may conflict with adult expectations and 'don't' rules. In my work with gifted children, I have identified ten major areas of possible difficulty which are described below. First, I will list the characteristics of the child who is striving to realise his mental promise, and then consider some of the problems which may arise, together with the 'don't' rules liable to be violated.

1. *The child needs to develop keen powers of observation, a willingness to explore the unknown and the unusual; to be*

receptive to different ideas and to possess a strong sense of what is significant to his or her own lifestyle.

POSSIBLE PROBLEMS

Because the child is so eager for all kinds of new experiences, and wants to find out as much as possible in the shortest possible time, he may sometimes seem gullible or lacking in discrimination. Initially, he may be prepared to pay a lot of attention to ideas and activities which strike the adult as trivial and unworthy. If this really is the case, the successfully developing child will quickly reach the same conclusion and lose interest. But it is a decision which he must be allowed to reach for himself. What may seem unimportant to an adult can provide a great deal of pleasurable learning for the child. Let him follow that line of exploration as far as it will go. Do not impose your own value judgements.

Because they have strong ideas about things which are meaningful in their own terms, such children may reject or resist 'don't' rules which seem unreasonable or illogical. Try to ensure that any rules you impose to stop them doing something have a rationale which the child can see as relevant from their individual point of view.

Finally, the keen powers of observation and curiosity may cause acute embarrassment to adults, especially when perceptions are uninhibitedly expressed.

'Why does uncle's hair move about like that?' inquires a curious four-year-old. Uncle, who had hoped that his new toupée would pass unnoticed, is indignant. 'Can't you teach that child some manners?' he snaps. 'Don't' rules which prohibit this kind of sharp observation and information-seeking will limit the child's mental development to an unreasonable extent, although you might impose on them that asking personal questions may hurt the feelings of some grown-ups, and that they should ask you privately later on. But, apart from that, my view is that it is worth upsetting a few touchy grown-ups in order that the child learns as much as possible about the world.

2. *The child needs to develop a good memory so that vast amounts of information can be retained and used effectively.*

POSSIBLE PROBLEMS
A retentive memory means that the child learns far more quickly than most adults realise. Quite complex lessons can be mastered with only one or two trials. Take, for example, the case already mentioned of the nine-year-old boy who understood the rudiments of surveying after only ten minutes practice. Adults tend to believe that the very young are slow learners who have to be given the simplest possible explanations on as many occasions as possible. But this can lead successfully developing children to become quickly bored and frustrated. They dislike routine and drill because they have no need for such rote-learning methods. Having grasped the essentials, they want to get on as fast as possible, to discover ways of using their new knowledge. Parents who believe that education consists of memorising a great many facts may be especially upset by this kind of mental approach. They should try to understand that true learning involves using information, not simply storing it up like jars of preserve in a larder. Children who have a rapid grasp of methods and procedures become understandably restless when the same thing is repeated over and over again. They are quite likely to reject any 'don't' rules which place a value on slow learning traits, such as: 'Don't rush at things', 'Don't lose interest so quickly', 'Don't fidget when being shown something', 'Don't get bored with new toys'. 'Don't always want to be doing something different'.

3. *The child needs to have a great interest in how things work and why events happen, to search for and value truth, to reject anything that fails to match up to their high standards of logic.*

POSSIBLE PROBLEMS

Children who are good at asking questions require adults who are equally good at answering them. This does not necessarily mean knowing the right answer, but it does involve a willingness to look for that answer and not resort to some fobbing off response such as: 'Because I say so', 'Because it *does* happen', 'Because you're too little to understand something like that'.

Ask yourself how you would feel if given that kind of reply from another adult. You would probably be highly indignant and resentful at being taken for a fool. Children of all ages feel the same way. Restraints such as 'Don't say that', 'Don't ask that', 'Don't do that', will be considered stupid and illogical, and, in time, the adult may well come to be regarded in the same way. Children may be compelled to obey an instruction which they see as unreasonable through fear of punishment or out of love for the adult who makes the rule. But it will inevitably damage their mental growth and lower the respect they have for grown-ups as a source of information. Always come up with a sensible answer that respects the child's search for knowledge. If you do not know, say so. Suggest ways in which the answer might be found, perhaps by reference to books or, better still, by some kind of simple experiment which the child can carry out for himself. Here is how the father of one lively three-year-old answered the question: 'Why do ships float?' He might have said '. . .because they are full of air', but that would have meant little to even an intelligent three-year-old. So the inquiry became the subject of a bathtime experiment. All kinds of objects, from a lump of solid metal to cans, plastic cups and wooden blocks, were gathered together. A logical procedure was adopted, and each placed in the bath in turn. When those things which could float had been separated from those which sank, various other tests were carried out to see how the buoyant objects could be made to sink, and why. In this way, the child, who carried out all the experiments himself, learned a lot of valuable lessons, perhaps the most important one being that you can discover the answers to questions by carrying out interesting tests on the objects concerned.

Because children who have a hunger for knowledge usually combine it with a desire for practical insight, household objects may suffer at their hands. The father whose record player is pulled apart, or the mother whose favourite clock has its insides painstakingly dismantled may feel justifiably angry. High priority 'don't' rules about touching and breaking adult property will have been violated. Have such rules, by all means, but recognise the child's need for practical exploration. Give them grown-up things like clocks, pieces of machinery, and broken gadgets of all kinds to play with. Check first, of course, that there is nothing which could hurt them, such as jagged pieces of metal, glass valves or dials, and so on. Then let them dismantle to their heart's content.

4.   *The child needs to think critically about the way things happen, to have a healthy distrust for statements which are not supported by logic or evidence. They have a powerful need to prove things for themselves.*

POSSIBLE PROBLEMS
Children who have been encouraged to think critically about objects and ideas are unlikely to stop short at people. This can produce very negative and often extremely punishing responses from adults who seldom appreciate criticisms from small children. One bright four-year-old in my survey upset the nursery teacher on her very first afternoon at school. The woman pulled out a radio plug by yanking at the flex. There was a bang, a flash, and the lights went out: 'That's because you made all the wires come loose inside,' the child told her. 'You should never pull out a plug like that.'

Even an adult making that kind of comment under those conditions might have expected an icy response. The child was immediately scolded for being impertinent and the teacher formed a negative impression of her personality. This lasted throughout the girl's time in that teacher's class and adversely affected her mental development.

Critical attitudes towards adult behaviour by the under-fives can be very disturbing to some grown-ups. They violate basic 'don't' rules such as not being rude or impudent, not talking out of turn or being disrespectful. If this has happened to you, try and remember that a child of this age is not usually being deliberately impertinent or trying to be smart. He or she is probably passing a comment, or raising a question, which seems entirely reasonable and fair. By responding positively and encouraging critical evaluations of the actions of others, you help to increase self-confidence and build on the child's desire to find out about life.

5. *The child needs to be creative and inventive, to constantly seek new ways of doing things, and to be interested in creating and discovering.*

POSSIBLE PROBLEMS

In Chapter one I described how some adults demonstrate their love by giving expensive presents to their children. Often these are the kinds of toys they would really like to play with themselves. They are usually exciting and attractive. Not unreasonably it seems to them, adults who have paid large sums of money for an intricate toy get angry when that toy is damaged or destroyed. When toy cars are driven over the edge of the stairs to see what will happen, or a talking doll is minus a head and arms an hour or so after being handed over to the child. Such acts of 'vandalism' are likely to bring forth angry comments about the 'destructiveness' of small children and the opinion that it is a waste of time to give them 'decent toys'. One indignant father told me how he had given his four-year-old son a magnificent galleon, complete with sails. When he went up to the child's room to see how he was enjoying his expensive toy, the man found the boy playing with the packing which the boat had come in. The galleon itself, masts broken and sails hanging limp, lay abandoned. The child had quickly grown tired of a toy which allowed him very little scope for creative play. He preferred to exercise his creative skills and imagination on the polystyrene blocks which had held the vessel secure in its box. By neglecting the toy the child was violating 'don't' rules involving breaking things up, and 'do' rules about showing gratitude and consideration. Where such rules clash with a desire to experiment, the imaginative child is likely to come into severe conflict with adults. Bear in mind that the way you see a toy and the way a child responds to it are likely to be entirely different. The younger the child the greater this difference in perception is liable to be. Let him play with the toy in the way which stimulates him more effectively. If this involves damage to the toy then that must be accepted as part of the price to be paid for finding out.

6. *The child needs to concentrate on activities, to focus all his or her attention on the task in hand to an extent that everything else may be forgotten.*

POSSIBLE PROBLEMS
Most adults dislike being interrupted when they are trying to finish some piece of work, yet few have any qualms about interrupting an under-five who is busy and concentrating hard on a task.

'Let's see what you are doing,' they will demand, often plucking the half-finished work from the child's hands. If the response is an irritable one, or if their approach is simply ignored, they may well feel slighted and hurt. Because of the intense concentration which children can develop, other things may be driven from their minds. They may forget instructions to do some household chore, or ignore calls that a meal is ready, overlook commands to go to bed or tidy up. This can infringe 'don't' rules such as: 'Don't disobey an order'; 'Don't be rude to grown-ups'; 'Don't ignore other people'; 'Don't forget what I've told you'.

7. *The child needs to be alert, eager and enthusiastic about tackling new challenges.*

POSSIBLE PROBLEMS
It might seem strange that problems could arise because a child is alert and enthusiastic about things. Many parents complain bitterly because their sons and daughters seem so lacking in energy or alertness! But an eager, active, inquiring youngster is quite a handful to cope with, and often parents create 'don't' rules to try and bring the situation under control. They attempt to limit those inquisitive enthusiasms which lead the child to explore boldly and, perhaps, to get into trouble. They try to supress eagerness over activities of which they disapprove, while strongly encouraging enthusiasm for those things which interest them. I remember arriving at one house as the oldest boy, aged six, was about to be taken on a fishing expedition by his father, a keen angler. The child was sitting in his bedroom absorbed in the study of some beetles which he had just started keeping in an old fish tank. He was so occupied with the task, that he had ignored several calls to get ready. Finally, his mother came into the room and virtually dragged him away from the tank. As he was being bundled into a coat and scarf, his father grumbled: 'I can't understand what you see in those horrible bugs, David. Anybody would think you didn't want to come fishing with your Dad.'

Inquiring, active minds can easily break numerous 'don't' rules which are highly valued by parents: 'Don't get so excited'; 'Don't waste so much time on that sort of thing'; 'Don't be selfish'; 'Don't be so inquisitive'.

8. *The child has a need to set his or her own goals and work persistently towards them, overcoming obstacles and set-backs.*

POSSIBLE PROBLEMS
The old comment: 'I am determined, you are obstinate, he is

bloody minded', sometimes seems to be in the minds of parents whose children are persistent in working towards their goals. If that goal is one the parents value, there is usually no conflict, and, indeed, they will usually applaud and encourage such persistence. But many of the goals which seem important to the under-fives are meaningless to adults, because of the very different ways in which they see the world. The child who perseveres in some activity which is deemed insignificant or unworthy is likely to arouse the scorn and irritation of grown-ups. If they insist that the child find other things to do, a battle of wits may develop, with the child determined to go on with what is important to him while the parents use increasingly punishing responses in order to overcome this 'stubborness'. Once a child has gained the reputation, whether inside or outside the family, for being self-willed, such punishments may be swiftly employed. While waiting in a hardware store not long ago, I watched a child of about three playing with a collection of discarded pipes and old taps which lay in one corner. The little boy was finding out how they worked, turning them on and off and doing no harm to anybody, while learning valuable lessons for himself. Seeing what he was doing, the mother yelled for him to: 'Come here, away from those dirty things.' A moment later, before the child had any chance to obey, she ran across the shop and slapped him hard. 'I told you to come away from there', she shouted. Then, seeing the looks the other shoppers were giving her, said in an exasperated tone: 'He always wants to get his own way.'

The rules broken by this approach include: 'Don't be so obstinate'; 'Don't do anything we don't want you to do'; 'Don't work towards goals we don't value'.

9. *The child needs to find pleasure in mental activities, in the forming of original concepts and in seeking out fresh problems. Intellectual effort must be regarded as worthwhile for its own sake.*

POSSIBLE PROBLEMS

Children who like to think things out for themselves, and have taken the trouble to do so, often resist answers handed to them on a plate by adults. They constantly question and doubt. This is excellent for the growth of the intellect, but it can come into sharp conflict with parents who adhere to the prohibition: 'Don't do it your way, mine is better.' Children may not discover methods for doing things which are as rapid or effective as those which the parents suggest. If they try and fail, adults who believe in this 'don't' rule often use such failure to score points: 'I told you it wouldn't work. Perhaps you'll be sensible enough to listen to me in the future.' This makes the child anxious about taking an original view of things, and reduces the chance of doing so again. Far better for the child to follow his own line of reasoning and not succeed, than to stick blindly to a cook-book formula provided by an adult. If this approach works, the child will tend to accept other people's ideas in favour of his own in the future, even though he or she may have no real idea about how or why the procedure worked. When failure results from a child being mentally independent, never use it to confirm your superiority. Instead, help him to draw what lessons he can from the mistakes made. There is almost always something valuable to be derived from the worst blunder, even if this is only a warning not to adopt that particular method in the future. Look for the positive aspects, and make certain that the child sees and appreciates them as well. Use the negative elements only insofar as they can provide constructive insights.

10.   *The child needs to discover an individuality of thought and action, to acquire habits of self-reliance, and to accept the isolation which comes with taking an independent approach.*

POSSIBLE PROBLEMS

Having a truly original and independent way of looking at the world — essential elements in intellectual creativity —

sometimes means coming into conflict with the entrenched views of the majority. This can prove anxiety-producing for people of all ages, but especially for the very young, who have a strong need to conform.

In one report, prepared for me by the mother of two boys with well-developed mental abilities, there is a comment which nicely illustrates this need for acceptance by the majority. She was worried that her intelligent eight-year-old chose his friends from amongst the roughest, least academically successful boys in the class, even though he was sometimes fearful of them. She wrote: 'There were always two or three pupils in each class who did not get involved in brawls, disruption and coarseness, and I asked him why he didn't stick with them, rather than the others, of whom he was often afraid. He very logically pointed out that the "smart set" was not liked, and he was unpopular enough as it was, and would be more so if he spoke and behaved pleasantly.'

The extent to which a desire to confirm can influence one's judgement was clearly demonstrated by S.E. Asch, an American psychologist, in the early 'fifties. He asked small groups of volunteers to match up comparison lines with a standard line. For a while, there would be agreement, then, curiously, all the subjects but one insisted that a line which was obviously shorter or longer than the standard made the perfect match. What had happened was that the one dissenter was telling the truth, and all the others, at the instruction of the experimenter, were lying. Under these conditions, the lone objector was under strong pressure to change his mind and agree with the majority. In one third of the experiments which Asch conducted, this is exactly what did happen. The isolated subjects preferred to doubt the evidence of their own eyes and the judgement of their own brains rather than remain the odd man out.

The child who has grown confident about his intellectual abilities and uses his mind eagerly often comes into conflict with adults and other children. Like the naive individuals in

Asch's experiments, they are put under considerable social pressure not to step out of line. If they refuse to conform, the result may be increasing isolation. They are in frequent conflict with such 'don't' rules as not questioning what adults tell them, showing insufficient respect for the views of grown-ups, and not being the odd man out. Attempts to restrict mental development will always lead to tragic results. Either a loss of ability on the part of the child who conforms, or a loss of understanding between the nonconformist child and intimate adults.

Commenting on his research findings amongst 14-year-olds, psychologist Roy Jarecky described socially gifted behaviour as a vital and hitherto neglected human resource: 'The socially gifted person has an important function to perform in our society,' he says. 'His particular skills are as badly needed as those of the skilled technician and scientist.'

This is perfectly true. A high level of social ability is an important form of giftedness. But it is all the more valuable and helpful to society when combined with other gifts, such as creativity or intellectual precocity. These three skills form the ideal basis on which to build a successful, fulfilling and stimulating life. They are the gifts which the truly gifted parents allow their children to develop in full measure.

Chapter Eight

Growing Up Gifted

So far in this book we have looked at some of the important ways in which a child either grows to giftedness or develops tactics which result in under-achievement. Let me restate my views about how and why such failure occurs. On the basis of my researches, I believe that an inborn promise of brilliance, which the majority of babies possess, fails to be realised because the child is prevented from growing up gifted. The natural talents which should have been developed in response to positive lessons from the environment are restricted by negative lessons. It is not so much a matter of making children bright but of preventing them from learning to become stupid.

The gifted parent is one who enables this innate potential to be achieved. As I stressed in the first chapter, adult giftedness does not depend on high levels of intelligence, special educational attainment or material prosperity. The gifted parent may well have any or all of these attributes but such advantages will not guarantee the successful mental development of the child; nor will the absence of them — provided it is not too extreme — make failure inevitable.

I am often asked for specific advice about what constitutes a 'good' environment. As I indicated earlier, it is impossible to lay down such rules because each child is a unique individual. One can only judge whether a particular environment has been 'good' or 'bad' for a particular child by looking at the intellectual, creative and social abilities achieved. It is not impossible for a child to develop magnificently in a home which would be expected to retard mental growth. When this happens, it is often the case that the deprivation has acted as the spur which goaded the child on to greatness. However, such instances are far rarer than those where children are damaged, perhaps permanently, by a neglectful and understimulating environment. So while it is impossible to be specific, one can suggest various general child-rearing procedures which are most likely to have beneficial consequences for most children. The gifted parents who responded to my research questionnaires investigating various approaches to bringing up the under-fives, bore out the fact that these procedures are widely used.

In this chapter I want to look at these important procedures, to describe the research evidence which supports them, and to offer practical advice about how you can best use them to help your child. Towards the end of this chapter I will also be examining two major barriers to success; excessive anxiety and high levels of aggression. These produce problems for children of all ages, but they can most easily and effectively be controlled as they start to emerge during the early years.

I shall begin by considering three related concepts, all of which exert a major influence on the growth — or restriction — of inborn brilliance. We will start, as every baby does, by looking at the manner in which infants learn to understand themselves in relation to the world. The outcome of these lessons determines, to a very great extent, the ways in which the world is perceived. On this unique perception rests the self-image which the infant gradually begins to develop. From self-image, behaviours arise which either help or hinder growth. For example, the infant who comes to see the world as a logical place will develop logical tactics for solving the problems which that world presents. The child who perceives the world as illogical will not only be far more anxious but much less likely to approach the solving of problems in a logical manner. As a result, the child may come to believe that it is impossible to make sense of life and pointless to behave in a sensible manner. He or she will learn to be helpless all over again.

Helplessness And How It Happens

At birth the human baby is one of the most helpless creatures on earth. Without protection and almost constant attention, death is certain. As the baby grows, this physical helplessness slowly declines. The infant is able to move around more efficiently and begins to perform many of the complex activities needed for survival — such as feeding — without direct adult intervention. With greater physical maturity should come increasing self-confidence and self-reliance, without which inborn brilliance cannot develop successfully. What frequently happens, however, is that while children grow away from physical helplessness they also grow towards a different but more lasting destructive form of helplessness: a disbelief in their own capacity for influencing events. This results from the way in which adults have been responding to the infant's needs. Let us begin by examining the manner in which a baby begins to make sense of what psychologist William James termed 'the booming, buzzing world'.

Some of the most important early problems which the baby has to solve have to do with himself or herself in relation to the external word. A basic lesson to be mastered is just where the boundary lies between body and surroundings; what belongs to him and what belongs to somebody or something else? Are his fingers and toes his? Is his mother a part of his body? The answers to all these questions seems so obvious that one can hardly believe they ever presented us with problems. Yet these are the basic facts of life that a baby must learn; such information is not programmed into us at birth. For example, it takes quite a long while for the infant to arrive at an accurate understanding of the length of his arms. It is for this reason, rather than a lack of co-ordination, that babies tend to miss when they swipe at a swinging ball. In terms of survival it is efficient. After all, the child's arms are constantly growing so that no single programmed idea of length of reach would be any help.

How does the baby find out what belongs to him and what lies outside his bodily domain? One of the most important clues is the immediacy of feedback between thought and action. The baby thinks about wiggling his toes; the toes obediently move. In time, he comes to realise the significance of this relationship. He appreciates that the link between mental command and physical response is almost perfect. It is not an entirely perfect relationship because, of course, there are times when mental commands may not be followed by the required movements — because of cramp or fatigue, for example. But normally, we can say that they are under our control. Intention to do something and performance are synchronised.

This is the first lesson the baby learns; that it can move an arm in such a way that the thumb is thrust into the open mouth or the fingers come into view. The second lesson, and a less pleasant one, is that other things it once believed to be part of itself are not under such exact control. They are not synchronised. Perhaps the worst shock is to discover that the mother is a separate being. There is often a strong relationship between what the baby does and what the mother does, but it is not as perfect as the link between thought and body movement. The baby may learn, for instance, that if he cries, the mother will usually — but not always — pick him up. If he smiles, she frequently, but by no means invariably, smiles back. If he wriggles, she often pats or comforts him. The mother, in caring for her baby, provides a synchronisation between what he does and what she does. By this means, the child learns that although not everything is a part of him, he can exert control over important portions of his environment.

When the mother is very unresponsive, these essential lessons are far less easily learned, and may, indeed, hardly be learned at all.

The discouraged, apathetic mother just sits, passively holding the baby, without face-to-face communication,

much less active, playful mutual responses to the baby,'
comments psychologist, L.B. Murphy. 'The deprived baby
does not have the experience which . . . leads him to the
realistic expectation that reaching out, exploring the
outside, trying out new impact upon it, would bring pleasant
results.' (L.B. Murphy, *Play and Development* Ed. M.W.
Piers. New York, 1972.)

One of the most extreme cases which I have encountered of a
mother refusing to provide any feedback to her child's actions
came before the British Courts in 1977. The mother of a two-
year-old girl and a one-year-old boy believed that children
should be allowed to develop 'naturally', unaided by anybody.
Although they were physically well cared for, the children
never received encouragement or response for anything they
did. As a result, their mental development was severely
retarded, the boy was unable to sit upright, and the girl could
only make a series of grunting sounds.

While such instances of total unresponsiveness are probably
rare, very few babies receive the kind of synchronised feedback from adults which they both want and need in order to
develop fully. This is not due to a lack of interest or caring on
the part of their parents, but because they have insufficient
understanding of what is required.

Most mothers talk to their small babies, some talk a great
deal. But think about how they do this. The child is usually
lying flat on his back in a cot or else being held very close to the
adult's body; cradled in the grown-up's arms, snuggled against
the chest, or looking over the shoulder while being burped. In
these positions, the infant is quite unable to see in any detail
how the adult is responding to his face and arm movements.
The feedback is of the most general kind. It is pleasurable
because there is warmth and comfort, soothing sounds and
gentle movements against his skin. But the experience can
never be any more rewarding than that.

In order to establish effective two-way communication —

and infants of only a few months old can be highly competent social animals when given the chance — there must be a face-to-face exchange. After all, could *you* have a proper conversation any other way? If you think you could, then try it. Hold a discussion with your partner while standing back-to-back, or side-by-side, so that it becomes impossible to obtain any visual clues. You'll find it a strange and unsatisfactory way of talking together. Your baby feels the same.

In *The Secret Language of Your Child*, I described how animated conversations can take place between mother and baby provided the conditions are right. The baby should be sitting upright, comfortably supported in a secure seat, with the hands and arms, and preferably the legs as well, completely free to move around. The adult should be five or six feet away, the face level with that of the child. Under these circumstances, the two can enjoy a long and mutually satisfying exchange. The adult will have to do the verbal talking, of course, but the baby will talk excitedly using body language, smiling, giving or breaking eye-contact, moving hands and arms delightedly.

Such exchanges provide the baby with a vital learning experience. He can come to understand, through the powerful and direct feedback from the adult's features, how certain actions on his part produce responses from the other person. In this way, the baby discovers that the world can be controlled. That what he does matters. It has an effect on what goes on 'out there' in his environment. Infants who fail to master this basic lesson sufficiently well, or early enough, tend to believe that what they do is of little importance. Like the passive kittens in the experiment of Richard Held, they begin to regard themselves as more or less helpless when it comes to determining their own destiny.

What is the point of attempting to influence the course of events if you have no power of control? Realising this, the infant may become apathetic, depressed and undemanding. He asks for nothing from the world because he has reached the conclusion that any such pleas are pointless. He or she has learned to be helpless.

The idea that people, adults as much as children, could *learn* to become helpless arose from a series of experiments carried out by Martin Seligman during the 'sixties. His research involved two groups of dogs. One group was strapped into a hammock and given electric shocks from which they were quite unable to escape. Nothing the animals did, whether they barked, or whined, moved their heads or wagged their tails, made the slightest difference. They received the full series of shocks. The other group of dogs was given no shocks at all.

The animals were then tested in a special box which had two compartments divided by a barrier. In one compartment, the dogs received a shock, after a warning signal, but could escape the punishment quite easily by jumping over the dividing barrier into the 'safe' compartment. The dogs who had never before been shocked soon discovered this escape route. After a few trials, they became almost nonchalant about the experience. They would wait by the barrier, leap quickly over when the warning signal sounded, and so escape entirely. The behaviour of the previously shocked animals was different, so different that it struck the experimenters as bizarre. Instead of making any attempt to escape from their painful situation, most of the animals remained crouching helplessly in the shock compartment. Even when they were physically lifted over the barrier and shown how it was possible to avoid the punishment, they remained hunched and miserable on the wrong side of the barrier. They had learned from their experiences in the harness, when nothing they did made any difference to the number of shocks they received, that they were unable to control events. So powerful were these lessons, that even when they were given proof that it was possible to escape the shocks, by being manhandled over the barrier to safety, they refused to accept the fact.

Seligman believes that humans, like his experimental dogs, can learn to be helpless and, having learned that lesson, will respond in negative, ineffective ways to many situations; not

Grahame, a highly intelligent four-year-old, is seen solving block design problems in this sequence from a research film. The task was to match drawings with the coloured blocks. Notice the attention which the boy brings to each problem as his mother demonstrates the right way of doing

it, and the excitement with which he greets each success. This sequence does not show the persistence which was also brought to the task. These characteristics of attention, persistence and pleasure in achievement are typical of the child whose problem-solving potential is being realised.

simply to situations similar to those in which the lessons were learned, but to a wide range of challenges: 'Men and animals are born generalisers,' he says. 'The learning of helplessness is no exception.'

The under-fives are expert learners. They master good lessons and bad ones with equal ease. If the child learns that he can succeed, he will behave in such a way that the chances of success are very high. If he has learned to behave in a helpless way, then the likelihood of failure is equally strong. In the first case, success will confirm the child's prediction that he would be successful, and so make future attainments a good deal more probable. In the second, the failure will merely confirm the helpless child's belief that it is impossible to exert effective control over events. This kind of negative response, therefore, becomes more firmly established.

Let me give you two examples of these very different attitudes in action. During the course of my researches, I have made many hundreds of short video-tapes showing children solving simple block problems. All they have to do is fit together a series of small blocks so as to match a drawing in a book, or an example made up from another set of identical blocks.

Grahame is a four-year-old who has shown exceptional reading ability. By the age of two, he was able to read aloud from simple books. A couple of years later, he could tackle newspapers and even encyclopaedias. He is a lovely, self-confident child with a strong belief in his ability to control events. He sat down eagerly to play with the blocks, and the conversation between myself and the boy, in a slightly shortened and edited version, went like this:

'Do you know what we want you to do?'
'Yes.' Very confident, he sits on the edge of the chair, his expression eager. 'Can I start now? Good. Oh, this is easy. Have I done that right?'
'Look at the other blocks, do they look the same, Grahame?'

'Yes. I have done it right! Shall I do another?'
'Do this one, please.'
'Oh, that's easy!' He moves the blocks quickly and confidently.
'That's right!'

The designs get progressively more difficult, but, even when puzzled, Grahame does not lose faith in his ability. He moves his blocks more slowly, but still in a methodical way. Each success is greeted with delight. He is really excited by being able to copy the patterns. After a particularly difficult design which he eventually got right, he said: 'That was clever . . . I was clever to get that.' He was not boasting, nor was he asking for confirmation of his cleverness. He was stating it as a fact; and he was right.

Michael is a small, thin-faced boy of four with a diffident manner. He is rather shy about attempting the block puzzle at all, but finally and reluctantly, at the urging of his mother, he agrees. He sits well back in the chair, as far away from the table and the blocks as it is possible to get. He appears indifferent to the description of how the blocks go together, and does not seem to follow the example which is demonstrated.
'Do you know what we want you to do, Michael?' He looks uncertainly at his mother, and then slowly nods. For a few moments, nothing else happens.
'Do you think you'll be able to do it, Michael?'
'Don't know.'
'Are you going to try?'
'Yes.' He moves the blocks around slowly and hardly glances at the sample blocks which provide the design he is supposed to copy.
'Do you understand what we want you to do, Michael?'
'No. I can't do it.'
'Will you try?'
'All right.' He moves the blocks again and, almost by accident, it seems, matches the design. He stares at it.
'Do you think that's right?'

'I don't know.'

'Does it look the same as the others?'

'I suppose so.'

'Then you've done it right, haven't you?' He nods without any evident pleasure. I ask if he'll attempt another design, and again show him how the blocks go together. After a while, he manages to complete this design. But the next proves too difficult, even though it should have been well within his capabilities.

'Can't do it.'

'Are you sure?'

'Yes, can't do it. I can't, can I, Mum? I can't do it.'

The obvious conclusion from those two examples is that Grahame is very bright and Michael is unintelligent. This is the way many adults would be inclined to interpret the results. But it is wrong. Michael was no less capable, intellectually, of finishing the whole series of block problems than Grahame. It was just that they had learned different lessons from life about their inability to cope with challenges. 'What is often passed off as retardation or an IQ deficit may be the result of learned helplessness,' comments Martin Seligman. 'The child has learned that . . . nothing he does will be right. As he falls further behind, the helplessness deepens. Intelligence, no matter how high, cannot manifest itself if the child believes his own actions will have no effect.'

We have already looked at one of the ways in which children learn that it is possible to control events. First, the baby discovers that arm and leg movements can be commanded at will. This is achieved as a result of the exact relationship between mental instructions and physical movements; they are precisely synchronised. Then the infant learns that a less perfect, but still useful, relationship exists between what he does and what objects do. If a ball is pushed, it rolls away. If the rattle is dropped over the side of the pram, it vanishes. If the blanket is pulled, it moves towards him. He learns that control extends to many inanimate things in the surroundings.

The baby also discovers, very early on, that although his mother — and other familiar adults — are not a part of him, they frequently respond to his activities. He may not always like the reactions he gets, but he can clearly see that they are a result of something which he did; smiling, belching, bawling, emptying his bladder, kicking his legs, and so on.

No baby lives in such an unresponsive environment that these fundamental lessons fail to be mastered. They may be acquired far more slowly and ineffectively than ought to be the case, but they will be eventually absorbed. As the infant starts to crawl and handle a wider range of objects, his desire to control things comes up against two powerful restraints. The first is a lack of skill and strength due to physical immaturity, the second the restrictions imposed by adults. The first produces certain frustrations, and sometimes acute, but short lived, distress. It is quite common to find an infant bawling in misery because his arms are too short to reach a doorknob, or his hands too clumsy to play with a toy which an older child manipulates with ease. Such limitations are inevitable, but cause little lasting damage provided they do not occur too frequently. This can only be ensured by adjusting the infant's environment appropriately; by reducing the number of challenges which the toddler will be quite unable to cope with because of size and lack of strength or co-ordination.

The second set of restrictions depends entirely on the attitudes of the parents. How much freedom they allow their baby will vary according to their personal views about child-rearing. These opinions may be based on how their own parents treated them; on social custom and tradition; on any deeply held religious or philosophical opinions; on the books or magazine articles they have read, and so on. Some children will be raised in an atmosphere of great tolerance, where almost anything goes. Others will experience a very strictly controlled environment with many restrictions and prohibitions, perhaps enforced by physical punishment. So far as the actual concept of helplessness is concerned, it does not matter very much whether the response a child receives to a particular action is agreeable or unpleasant, whether it results in a reward or a punishment. What does matter is that the response is consistent and predictable, that a similar outcome invariably follows a particular activity on the part of the child. It is when this connection between what is done and what happens breaks down that helplessness can easily result.

Why Things Make Sense At All

People sometimes say that they live 'in a world where nothing makes sense'. If that really were the case, then life would be impossible. We are only able to survive because the physical world is, fundamentally, sensible, where there are physical laws which govern the way things happen: if you drop this book, it will fall to the ground; if you were to drop it in a space vehicle, it would simply float away. These are two very different results, but both are consistent, and therefore capable of making sense. For the purpose of understanding our surroundings, it makes no difference at all whether the book always floats up or always drops down — providing it does so consistently. If it occasionally floated away, sometimes fell, and now and then remained exactly where you had left it in mid-air, then you would start to doubt your sanity, with reason. One of the techniques of brain-washing is to create an artificial environment for your victim, where things no longer seem to obey fixed laws. Drugs are used to confuse the mind and disturb the senses, the floor of the room in which the brain-washed victim is housed tilts and shifts, the angles of the walls alter, furniture changes position and shape; projectors flash images on to screens around the room until the person can no longer distinguish between drug-induced dreams and filmed events. It is a place gone, literally, crazy, where previously-inviolate physical laws no longer seem to hold good.

The world of the under-fives can appear like that to them. Events frequently seem far from logical or sensible. They are at the mercy of powerful gods whose whims decide their every action, whose moods may be just as frightening and inexplicable to the small child as the vengeful deities of the pagan world. We are those gods, our attitudes and opinions, feelings, beliefs, anxieties, angers and prejudices are the often-erratic laws which control the lives of the very young.

A few years ago, I was carrying out some studies into the nature of stress with Dr Robert Sharpe (*Thrive on Stress*, Souvenir Press, London 1977). We were especially interested in reactions to stressful environments, and in finding out what brought about high levels of anxiety at work. One of the variables we examined was what difference the attitudes of bosses made to those who worked for them. Was a generous, easy-going employer less stressful to his or her employees than a dictatorial one? Would a boss who 'ran a tight ship' provoke more breakdowns, ulcers and resignations than the person who could not care less what the employees said, thought or did, provided the work was completed on time?

In the event, we found that the worst kind of employer, the one that most people said they found it difficult and disturbing to work for, was neither easy going nor a strict disciplinarian. It was the individual who could not make up his mind whether to be saintly or stern; who blew hot one day and cold the next; who could give a man praise and a raise for no apparent reason on Monday, and tear him into shreds for some trivial offence on Thursday. People who worked for a boss like that never knew where they were from one day to another. They could not judge the likely outcome of their efforts, and they felt helpless.

Children are put in this position far more often than adults. At least the disgruntled employee may shout back, walk out or demand more reasonable treatment. The under-fives, like their older brothers and sisters, can do none of these things. They can easily become helpless.

Martin is playing with his paint box on the polished dining room table, and making a bit of a mess. His father sees what is happening, smiles indulgently, and says nothing. Billy is doing the same thing. His father explodes with rage, and smacks him for spoiling the surface. Each has learned something different from his father's response. Martin will probably paint on the table again and anticipate that his father will be equally tolerant. Billy may well think twice before painting there again, but if he does, he will expect his father to be angry, and the outcome to be painful.

But suppose that next time Martin is quietly painting his father is furious and punishes him, while Billy gets no more than a few words of encouragement from his father. The result will be confusion. The world no longer will make as much sense as it did before; the law of cause and effect has failed. It may well be that, on the second occasion, Martin's father was already angry because of a row with his wife and took his rage out on the child, while Billy's father might have been in a better mood and prepared to tolerate a little spilled paint. Their motives for this change in response are most unlikely to be explained to their children, and would probably be incomprehensible if they were. All Martin and Billy know is that life is unfair and uncertain. This do not make sense. If they go on not making sense long enough, then the boys will have no way of knowing what is expected of them. They will become increasingly helpless.

Some children may respond to this helplessness with anxiety and withdrawal. They will shun almost every activity which is likely to produce an unpredictable outcome, and their fears may quickly generalise to a wide range of behaviour. They will even stop doing things where the response is reasonably favourable and consistent, because they have begun to believe that nothing can be safely predicted; no adults can be trusted; no outcome taken for granted.

If they are to be indiscriminately punished anyhow, they seem to argue, then it may as well be for something as for nothing. So they strike out aggressively in all directions. Anticipating that punishment will follow the most innocent of activities, they willingly provide adults with sounder reasons for their anger and assaults.

The inconsistent response of adults is a fast way to produce helplessness in children. But consistent praise or consistent blame, whether or not the circumstances warrant it, can be equally damaging, and for the same reasons. These irrational responses deny the individual, whether adult or child, control over events. If you are always praised, no matter how indifferent or downright bad you know your actions or your work to have been, or if you are always blamed and punished, no matter how good or successful you know your work has been, then you are helpless. Why try your hardest if second, third or even fourth-best receive the same acclaim? Why worry about getting things right if you are going to be punished whatever happens?

Children who are constantly told that their every action is perfect, wonderful, the sign of true genius, can learn helplessness just as rapidly as the child who is constantly being punished and scolded. For the child to make sense of the world, the world has got to make sense to them.

What The Child Tells Himself About Himself

Here is a short conversation I had recently:

'Why do you think you couldn't do that block problem?'
'Because I'm dumb. I'm really stupid.'
'Do you really believe that?'
'Oh, sure. I don't have any sense at all. Just stupid . . . you know. That's it.'

A fairly bleak self-image, I am sure you will agree, and bad enough if coming from an adult. But Anne, who lives in an expensive New York apartment with her lawyer father, and sees herself in that dismal light, is just four. Nor is she the only under-five to think so badly of her abilities; I have met many who believed themselves incapable of almost any intellectual, social or creative task. When five-year-old Sean from London is asked to try a simple numerical test, he says at once:

'Can't do that. That's numbers, isn't it? Well, I can't do numbers.'
'Why not try, perhaps you could?'
'Not numbers. I can't.'
'Just look at it.'
'No, I can't,' he pushes the test away. 'Not numbers.'

Catherine, aged four, is asked to paint a picture. She looks unhappy.

'I don't like pictures.'
'Why not?'
'I don't know how to do them.'
'Why not try?'
'No, I can't.'

Everybody has a self-image. Sometimes, it more or less matches the view others have, but often there are considerable differences. What we see as a piece of smart behaviour on our part, somebody else may regard as devious. Our firmly stated opinions may strike others as prejudice. Natural modesty, which we consider a desirable trait, may appear as a lack of confidence. How we see ourselves plays a major part in deciding how we will respond to challenges and demands. This applies to children just as much as to adults.

We have already seen how a very negative self-image, a belief that nothing one does will have any effect, can greatly diminish a child's ability, while a positive self-image will enable it to grow. By changing the child's self-image from negative to positive, therefore, it should be possible dramatically to alter his or her abilities. But this is quite hard to do. It requires patient and careful behaviour modification over a period of several months if permanent changes in self-image are to be brought about. Short term change in self-image, however, can sometimes be produced much more rapidly by more drastic means. This was demonstrated a few years ago by Dr Vladimir Raikov, a leading Soviet psycho-neurologist. A group of Russian schoolchildren and university students were selected on the basis of having very average academic abilities. These were children who had neither especially strong self-images nor particularly negative ones. What would happen, Dr Raikov wondered, if they considered themselves geniuses instead? To find out, he put the group into a state of deep hypnosis, and then told them that they were all highly gifted.

A series of tests followed, and the results confirmed that the children were, indeed, capable of brilliance. For example, in one test they were told to strike out a particular letter of the alphabet every time it occurred in a sentence of 300 letters. They did so in half the time normally required. They were then told to memorise a list of foreign words and write down as many as they could remember. Their performance after hypnosis was four times better than it had been before. Later in the experiment, they were persuaded that they were highly creative artists, and told to produce a drawing. The standard was far higher than had been achieved prior to hypnosis.

What had changed? Not the talents and skills of the children. It was simply that they had dramatically altered their self-images. They achieved a high level of academic success because they now believed themselves capable of doing so. Unfortunately, the effects were short lived. After a time the original, restricting self-images resurfaced and their newly-distributed abilities sank back to the earlier levels. Hypnosis is not the answer to long term change, but that experiment did provide a compelling illustration of what might be achieved by a change for the better in the self-image of the older child. And it underlines the need to ensure that the lessons learned during the first five years of life do not include those of helplessness.

Enrichment Procedures

1. *Helplessness Is Learned – Avoid Teaching It.*
Your baby learns to control events through the active experience of seeing that a relationship exists between what he does and what happens. Some of the earliest and most basic lessons come from observing his own body, but a need rapidly arises for experience of outside interactions.

You, the parent, are the most sensitive, responsive, complex and exciting source of stimulation and synchronised feedback in your baby's environment. Teach your baby that what he does has an effect on what happens by letting him take the lead. Do not see your baby as a creature who can only respond to you. Provide plenty of experience of responding to him. Let him initiate 'conversations' using a whole range of body language. Do not feel embarrassed about doing this — I know that some parents find it. awkward at first, but this initial uncertainty and discomfort will vanish with a little practice. Trust your baby. Do not worry about passing control into his domain. It is only by constantly allowing him such experiences that he can quickly and efficiently learn how to master and control events. Respond as warmly and as sensitively as you can once the first eye-contact has been established between you. Now and then you can initiate an exchange but be willing, most of the time, to follow his lead by responding to his face and body movements. During these conversations, talk to the baby with words as well as with expressions and gestures. In this way, the child gets an experience not only of synchronised movements but of words linked to non-verbal communication. This is valuable when it comes to developing speech. Place the baby in a comfortable, secure seat — as described before in this chapter — so that you can enjoy face-to-face dialogue. You will quickly discover that your baby can easily regulate the 'conversations' by looking away, by smiling, frowning, and making pre-vocal movements of his mouth.

Allow the baby as wide an experience of objects as possible.

Not just infant toys, but all kinds of safe household objects. By safe, I mean the usual common sense precautions about things not small enough to swallow, sharp enough to eat, soft enough to suffocate, and so on. Remember that every baby is a natural scientist who needs to make practical experiments on the world to understand how things work.

2.   *Helplessness arises when there is a lack of synchronisation between what a person does and what happens to them.*
If you fail to respond in any way to your child, he or she cannot know how a particular activity has been received. Always react in some way, but not always with praise or criticism because that is, effectively, a non-synchronised response. It tells children nothing about their behaviour. Every child needs a structured, logical world in which to grow up. Make rules for the safety of the child and the protection of your property, but keep them to an essential minimum, and keep to them. Do not blow hot one day and cold the next; be consistent. The world must make sense, and that means that it must be predictable.

3.   *A negative self-image is one of the most powerful brakes on brilliance that exists.*
If your child comes to see himself or herself as helpless, a poor self-image is bound to develop. This will cripple mental growth and prevent social progress.

One of the key differences I have observed in the attitude of children with special abilities is their strong, positive self-image. It may not generalise to everything they do, but in what they do well they are usually extremely confident — and with good reason. Each success assures them they really are competent. It is a constant confirmation of their talents and skills. Success breeds successful self-imagery, while a positive self-image helps to ensure success.

4.   *If a job's worth doing, it's worth doing badly. . . .*
Many adults see the result of a child's efforts in very polarised

terms. They are perfectionists who will only use terms like good or bad, right or wrong, success or failure. Banish these extremes from your mind when looking at the efforts of the very young. A far better term than failure, where children are concerned, is non-success. The five-year-old who has managed to write a short descriptive passage, but formed the words badly, may not have achieved the level of success you expected, but he or she has not failed either. Important lessons have been learned. Set-backs are not merely useful, they are essential. Every child has to discover how to handle mistakes and deal with criticism.

In an experiment designed to explore the importance of learning to cope with errors, a researcher took a group of ten to thirteen-year-olds who were the worst at mathematics in a school of 750 pupils; all of these children tended to give up within moments of being presented with a mathematical problem. They were divided into two groups. Both received 25 days special training, but one group was set only simple problems and never allowed to fail. When they did, their mistakes were glossed over or ignored. The other group was set easy problems and tough ones. The experiment was designed to ensure that they experienced set-backs as well as successes. At the end of the training period, both groups received the same test, which consisted of a mixture of simple and difficult problems. The group which had enjoyed an easy, success-filled twenty-five days went to pieces as soon as they came across a difficult problem, while the others tackled all the problems successfully.

We all fear the unknown. Until something has been experienced and dealt with, it produces anxiety, a response which directly inhibits logical reasoning. Failure is no exception. Do not try to protect your child against not being able to do things, but regard all set-backs in a constructive light. Do not look for mistakes or notice only what has not been achieved. See, instead, what has been accomplished and build from there.

5. *Discourage unnecessary dependency.*

Examine some of your current child-rearing attitudes in the light of the comments I made earlier. Be as objective as possible, and see if you can apply any of them to your own rules and regulations. Anxiety on your part, arising for a number of reasons, may well be contributing to your child's lack of independence. Such anxiety will not disappear merely as a result of acknowledging it, however. In Chapter nine, I will be describing positive and practical steps which you can take to help yourself to help your child.

Give Baby The Freedom To Grow

The barriers of a playpen restrict mental as well as physical exploration. An infant imprisoned within the bars of a pen quickly exhausts the small amount of stimulation possible from the toys and other playthings left to 'amuse' him. Once this has happened he is most likely to grow bored and miserable. Certainly, he will be unable to give his brain that essential mental exercise necessary for successful growth. Valuable growing time is being wasted. You may feel that a playpen is essential to safeguard the child physically. You may also take the view that penning the baby helps to protect your valuable property at the same time. These are not unreasonable considerations but they do not need to be achieved at the expense of the infant's mental development. It is possible to provide the crawling infant with surroundings which are safe for everybody, and which offer the greatest possible opportunity for essential intellectual stimulation.

Enrichment procedures involve making the widest possible area as safe as possible for exploration and discovery. It is more time consuming than the use of a playpen, but the long term rewards make the effort well worthwhile. Here are some of the more important steps you will have to take:

1. Vacuum the carpet very carefully to pick up any pins or

other sharp items which might cause harm.

2.   Remove ornaments which the child might reach and pull over. Do not under-estimate the strength of the toddler nor the height of grasp.

3.   Cap all power points so that small fingers cannot explore them.

4.   Make certain that windows are closed and firmly clasped.

5.   Stairs have a great fascination for children who have just started to crawl; be certain they are well barricaded.

6.   Remove all harmful substances from reach, including household polishes, cleaning fluids, aerosol sprays, every kind of medication, and such items as baby aspirin, bottles of spirit or beer, ink, paint remover and so on. All of these will exert a great attraction for the exploring infant.

7.   Watch out for electric cables trailing to desk or table lamps, radio sets and televisions. Remove them for the time the child is being allowed free access to the rooms.

Subject to these precautions, the child should be given as much freedom as possible to explore room after room. Hard surfaces, such as linoleum-covered floors, will make it easier for the baby to crawl, but the knees should be protected by a well-padded romper suit. Never under-estimate the speed of movement which a crawling child can achieve. If you turn your back for only a moment, the infant may have vanished from view. It is especially important to bear this in mind during explorations out of doors, which should form a regular part of the baby's programme from the earliest weeks. As soon as the infant is old enough, allow him to sit up and survey the world instead of being confined to the bottom of a deep, hooded pram.

An interesting link has been found between levels of intelligence and the time of year when the baby was born. A possible explanation is that children born in summer seem generally brighter than winter babies because they are able to experience a wider range of environments in the first few weeks of life. Winter babies, confined to their homes until the weather improves, are denied this additional stimulation. Give your baby every opportunity to see as much as possible and investigate everything he possibly can. Such experiences are the tools that build the mind.

How To Talk To Children

Research has shown that many adults talk far too slowly to the under-fives. They bring down their rate of word-delivery to around 100 words per minute on the assumption that young children will only be able to grasp their meaning at this speed. While it is essential to speak clearly, slowness of delivery is disliked by the majority of youngsters. The most appropriate speed is around 175 words per minute, although you can talk at rates of up to 200 words per minute, if necessary. As a guide, a delivery rate of 175 words per minute would mean reading aloud to this point in this paragraph in about 34 seconds — or approximately 30 seconds for 200 words per minute.

What you say to the child is, of course, even more important than the rate at which it is said. I believe it is important to avoid nursery terms, to call things by their correct adult names, and not to be afraid to use long words when necessary. You should also be as fluent as possible when giving the child directions or instructions. Children who fail to acquire a sufficiently wide vocabulary during the first five years of life are seriously disadvantaged when they start school. Variations in language ability are considered by some researchers to be one of the most striking differences between children from poor backgrounds and those from homes which provide plenty of intellectual enrichment. The less fluent child not only uses far fewer words but is less able to understand complex sentences, and speaks in short, simple phrases. The parents of such children usually give them orders in much sharper and less informative ways than the more articulate parents of verbally proficient children. For instance, a mother of limited verbal ability may simply tell her child to: 'Stop that at once!' or 'Don't do that again.' A more reasoned, explanatory approach not only reduces the anxiety associated with forbidden activities, but it provides the child with sufficient information to understand why the prohibition has been introduced in the first place.

The disadvantages produced by an environment devoid of sufficient language experience do not usually reveal themselves until about 20 months of age. But, after this, the gulf in abilities between the different types of upbringing become increasingly obvious and serious.

To master language successfully, the child needs periods of face-to-face contact with an adult. It is not enough to chat to the baby while you are busy with something else. The conversations need to be distinct activities in themselves. Arrange the baby, as described earlier, so that you are at the same level and can exchange body signals. Talk quite normally, as you would to another adult. Do not be afraid to use a wide range of words to describe things as vividly as possible. If you are talking about objects in the room, point to them. If you are discussing parts of the body, indicate them first on your body, and then on the baby's. Pause now and then to give the baby a chance to 'talk' back. He or she will not do so in words, of course, but in body language. There is a detailed description of how such exchanges evolve and how to interpret the silent speech signals in my book *The Secret Language of Your Child* (Souvenir Press, London, 1978).

How To Correct Correctly

Some parents have a horror of striking their children, while others appear to use physical punishment as a first rather than a last resort. Although I regard with unqualified disgust the ritualistic corporal punishment handed out by some parents and teachers, I have found no evidence to suggest that the occasional slap did any harm to a developing intellect.

Whether it did any good or was actually necessary is another matter. This depends on the temperament of the child, the context within which the blow is administered, and the relationship between child and parent. There is some evidence that physical punishment, when frequently used, is associated with aggression in the child, a point which I shall consider later in this chapter. But there is no reason to suppose that occasional, light smacks will damage the child. There are, however, some verbal methods of control which are extremely damaging, and far longer lasting in effect than an irritated slap. There are more apt ways to correct behaviour in the under-fives which I will discuss here, and also later in this chapter under the heading of aggression. But for the moment, let us look at some of the wrong methods of correction.

1. *Never use comparisons between children as a basis for punishment.*
Avoid making comments such as: 'You are a naughty child, not half as nice as your sister. Why not behave like her?'

2. *Never use terms of abuse as a form of punishment.*
Do not tell the child he is 'stupid', 'ignorant', 'wicked', 'filthy', and so on. These terms provide the child with material for a negative self-image while denying him any constructive feedback.

3. *Never withdraw love as a punishment.*
Do not tell the child you can no longer love him or her because of what has been done. The child will either come to believe it and be made extremely anxious, or else realise that you do not really mean what you say, in which case your credibility will be diminished.

4. *Never punish a long time after the event.*
We have already seen that delayed rewards are ineffective in changing behaviour. Long delayed punishments have the same

inappropriate effect, especially where the under-fives are concerned. Their span of memory is often too poor for them to connect the correction with the activity for which they have been punished.

5.   *Never threaten using your partner as a weapon.*
Mothers at their wits' end sometimes warn: 'Wait until your father gets home, and see what happens.' Since the fuss may well have blown over by the time father returns, this is quickly seen to be an empty threat. Even if the predicted punishment does occur, it will be so delayed as to have no effect on the misconduct. Furthermore, by building up the father or the mother as a bogie in this way, the child is likely to develop a completely distorted image of the absent parent.

If a child persists in being disobedient, I suggest two possible courses of action. The first is to make quite certain that your instructions are clearly understood. It may be that the child does not really know what you mean, or doubts that you really mean it. Kneel down close to the child, so that you are face to face. Hold the child's head firmly, with your palms pressing against each cheek so that they have to look at you. Then explain carefully and clearly why they must not go on with what they are doing. If they continue after this precise command, then the most effective method of control is to use a procedure called 'time out'. This is especially useful with aggressive behaviour or where children persist in some activity despite every warning.

To understand 'time out', it is necessary to look at the behaviour you would like changed, and to see it in terms of the reinforcements received by the child for carrying it out. You may say that there are no rewards, that the child is scolded and punished. But such attention, in itself, may be very reinforcing for some children. It is better to be shouted at, the attention-seeking child may feel, than to be ignored; preferable to feel the pain of the slap than to feel that you are not the centre of adult attention.

If the punishments themselves are serving to reward the behaviour, more punishment is merely going to increase the rate of undesirable activities. To curtail them, these rewards must be removed. 'Time out' works by doing just this. It is punishment mainly in the sense that it denies the child the reinforcers which were resulting from that way of behaving. To instigate 'time out', you will need a spare room, not a cupboard or an attic or surroundings which are frightening to the child; simply an ordinary room without any amusements, toys, books, puzzles or games. When the child disobeys, after the kind of clear warning I have suggested, take him without further comment of any kind and place him in the 'time out' room. Say nothing by way of explanation or condemnation, and be as neutral in your expression as you can be. The child may well be watching for the slightest indication that the misconduct has got through to you. 'Time out' should not be continued for more than five or six minutes. Usually, three or four minutes will be sufficient. The behaviour which you want to change may not alter immediately after 'time out' has been introduced, but it should soon decline in frequency, and provided every incident is followed by a period in the 'time out' room, should eventually cease completely.

Rewarding Behaviour

We have looked at ways of correcting behaviour disapproved of by parents. But it is no less important to reward and encourage activities which are in the child's best interests. You should never withhold praise or recognition on the grounds that: 'They ought to do that anyhow.' It is very important during the first five years to establish desirable ways of behaving as securely as possible, since once the child starts formal education, there may be pressures to act in a less constructive manner. These will be most firmly and effectively resisted if the child has a well established repertoire of appropriate responses to social or intellectual demands.

Avoid the error of over-rewarding. If the child is doing something intrinsically interesting, providing additional, unnecessary rewards may actually make the task seem less attractive. For example, if the child is happily painting and you tell him that if he carries on painting quietly for the next hour, you will give him some sweets, his motives for wanting to paint may well change. Now, instead of finding pleasure in the task itself, he may merely be filling in time so as to gain a reward.

When asked for comments on a piece of work, always be specific in your praise and your criticism. Never offer general congratulations, such as: 'How very pretty. What a nice thing to have done', as such vague remarks provide children with nothing of value. They need practical feedback on all possible occasions. You might say, for example: 'The drawing is very good. You've got the detail just right, but I think that the colour is put on too carelessly.'

If you are impressed with some result, say so clearly, do not take the opportunity for scoring points off the child: 'Very nice, but why couldn't you do that yesterday? Why can't you try your best all the time?'

Try not to be too eager to help. I have already mentioned the frustration some adults feel when they watch a young child struggling with some task. Be patient, do not show your anxiety. The child can quickly discover that it pays to play dumb if the answer is always handed to him on a plate. Let him learn to deal with failure as well as success.

The Importance Of Play

'Play is paradoxical behaviour', comments Dr Sussana Millar in her book *The Psychology of Play*.

> 'Exploring what is familiar, practising what has already been mastered, friendly aggression, sex without coition, excitement about nothing, social behaviour not defined by a specific common activity or by social structure, pretence not intended to deceive. . . .'

Every parent knows that children devote a lot of time to what is termed 'playing' and gain considerable enjoyment from it. In the past, psychologists believed that they also learned a great deal, especially about social relationships. This last assumption still holds true. Playing *is* an important way for children to discover how they can relate to one another, and many play activities serve a serious social purpose for the under-fives. The exchange of toys, sharing games, co-operation in group activities, the taking of toys, and struggles for possession of a coveted plaything, are all ways in which the pecking order of the group is determined and maintained.

Doubts, however, have arisen about the value of play as a means of learning. It was long believed that this was an essential function of the seemingly aimless periods of play indulged in by the young of many species; that they were rehearsing the skills which would be needed in adult life. Young lions and kittens played at stalking and slaying one another. Small children, copying adult activities, discovered ways of doing things in a relaxed, informal way. This once-widely-held view has now been challenged by some psychologists. They agree that a certain amount of learning does occur during haphazard play but that more effective methods exist for teaching important, basic skills to the under-fives. Their research has suggested that the best procedure is a combination of direct instruction followed by the opportunity to practise in a play situation. It is important to give a careful demonstration of what must be done, and not to move too quickly. Adults who are very practised at some routine activity usually carry out the manipulations so rapidly that the child is unable to follow them. Try to break the procedure being taught, whether this is tying a shoe lace or building a model house, into a series of logical stages. Make certain that each step is fully understood before going on to the next.

Children who are developing their minds correctly will welcome this kind of precise instruction. They are eager to learn exact methods of manipulation in order to have a foundation of effective skills on which to create for themselves. Teaching children practical ways of doing things will not limit their imagination, but will provide them with the means for successful expansion. For this reason, the slightly more formal teaching approach found in nursery schools is likely to be of greater advantage to the bright child than the slightly more haphazard, free-and-easy atmosphere of play groups. The schools established by the great Italian pioneer, Dr Maria Montessori, are especially effective. They provide a sensible, structured system which allows each child to develop at his or her own pace under the guidance of a directress — they are not called teachers or supervisors — trained in the Montessori method. The schools can be found in most major cities in Britain and Europe.

When teaching the child yourself, keep the following key points in mind:

1.   Allow the child to participate actively in organising the lessons.
2.   Allow the child to make mistakes and cope with the consequences, so long as these do not involve physical danger.
3.   Reward initiative, curiosity and the asking of questions.
4.   Encourage exploration and invention. Demonstrate the basic procedures for each activity, but then allow the child to experiment with different methods.
5.   Build your teaching around the child's inborn need to find out about the world. Each lesson should relate to problems which are relevant to the child's own interests.
6.   Do not try to impose knowledge on the child too early, or he will simply become confused and bored.

Passive children may appear reluctant to take part in learning games at first, especially if these involve vigorous activity. This can be especially frustrating for more active brothers and sisters, or for parents who regard the physical pursuits as especially important. (Bear in mind the points made in Chapter six about the inborn nature of many responses.) Your child is not adopting a passive manner from laziness or to spite you in some way. Respect the child's feelings, and try not to impose your views about how children should behave too strongly. At the same time, provide as much stimulation as possible in areas which appeal to them, playing games of skill such as chess, painting, model making and building with construction kits. The passive baby can best be stimulated by ensuring plenty of face-to-face dialogue opportunities with adults.

The Barrier Behaviours

There are two different types of behaviour which can act as powerful barriers to successful mental development. These are the most obvious and potent causes of failure in the older child, and they are deeply rooted in the first five years of life. The behaviours, which are only damaging when consistently present at a high level, are aggression and anxiety.

The very aggressive or highly anxious child is disadvantaged in many crucial ways. Not only is the child directly limited beause his brain never gets the chance to function effectively, but he is also indirectly limited through the adverse responses he produces in adults. As a result, both groups of children can soon become restricted intellectually as well as socially. It is important that such children be helped before they start formal schooling, where the problems are more likely to get worse and cause great damage.

Helping The Aggressive Infant

Aggressive children are exhausting even for trained adults. Their behaviour is often so offensive and intolerable that it becomes increasingly hard — even for the most loving and sympathetic of parents — to forgive and forget. Typical activities of the very aggressive child include bullying, destruction of property, the teasing of animals and behaviour which appears deliberately calculated to hurt and upset others.

There is no instant solution to such problems. The aggressive child cannot be transformed into a friendly, sociable youngster in a matter of a few days or even a few weeks. But it would be wrong to conclude that change is impossible, and that the behaviour will simply have to be tolerated. Happily, permanent change for the better can be brought about. There are practical steps which the parents of very aggressive children can take to reduce the number of violent outbursts while, at the same time, building up the frequency of socially desirable responses.

Start by ridding yourself of folklore wisdom about the nature of aggression in children. It is not something which little boys do 'naturally'; it does not signify 'wickedness'; nor does it occur because the child 'once had the fevers'. The only reason any of us do anything is because that behaviour has come to be seen as the most rewarding answer we can find to a particular set of problems. If the response did not seem to provide an answer, it would not be rewarding. If it was not rewarding, it would not be carried out. Understanding very aggressive, or excessively anxious, behaviour in children depends on the appreciation of this basic truth, and then applying it to every occasion in which that particular kind of response occurs.

The answers people find to problems confronting them do not have to be right in order to be helpful and rewarding, at least in the short term. Some of them will strike others as being foolish and ineffective in the extreme. For instance, the answer which an alcoholic has found to a whole range of his problems, is alcohol. It is a mind-numbing 'medication' which provides a temporary answer to such problems as loneliness, anxiety, and feelings of inadequacy. Its long-term effects are such that more problems are created than are ever solved, but it does seem to the sufferer to provide immediate relief; so long as the misery of the present is taken care of, the future can look after itself.

Aggression can be regarded as another short term answer,

one way a child, or an adult, has found of solving problems which they can see no other way of dealing with. For example, a boy has never learned the social skills necessary for making friends, taking the lead and winning by persuasion. He wants to be looked up to and followed — if not willingly from admiration, then reluctantly through fear. His aggressive behaviour provides an answer, but it will probably not be his only answer to every situation. Although adults who have labelled a child as a bully may believe he is aggressive on all possible occasions, the truth is usually quite different. There are times when even a persistent bully will behave reasonably and co-operate well. The child who gets into frequent fights at school may be kind and considerate towards his younger brothers. The girl who destroys her sister's belongings may treat those of a friend with care and respect.

Before you can take any steps to change such anti-social behaviour, it is essential to find out precisely under which circumstances the answer of aggression is being used. This requires written notes. It is not enough to rely on memory. You need to keep the kind of careful records which a scientist would make during the course of an experiment. Every incident of aggressive behaviour during the course of, say, a week or ten days should be written down at the time it happens. Note the place, who was present, the precise nature of the aggressive behaviour, and the consequence for the child. Was an adult hit, another child struck, something deliberately broken or a game demolished? Was the child responsible scolded, smacked, sent from the room, or begged to be better? Record also all the desirable behaviour on the part of the aggressive youngster: times of quiet play with other children, the sharing of games or the offering of toys, co-operation with an adult. This will provide you with objective information about the child's behaviour. You may find, for a start, that some pattern emerges. That the child is most aggressive when particular children or adults are present, when bored with some activity, after being defeated in a game, while being teased, or when being ignored.

It may be that there is so much aggression, one cannot pick out certain situations or circumstances more likely to lead to aggression than any others. In either event, do not waste too much time trying to work out *why* the aggressive behaviour takes place. The first essential, for both you and the child, is to reduce it. Start by deciding which kinds of aggression are most distressing. Do you find fighting with brothers and sisters more frequent or more troublesome than fights with neighbouring children, for instance?

Now, from your records, try to discover what kind of rewards the aggressive conduct offers the child. Look at the sort of problems for which this response has come to provide an answer. Does aggression follow teasing by an older child? Could it be an answer which brings teasing to an abrupt halt and so obtains the reward of stopping an unpleasant verbal attack? Does it produce attention from the adults and so offer an answer to the problem of not getting enough of the limelight? Does it enable the child to spoil the games of others, and so attempt to answer the problem of being neglected by them (implying that if I cannot play, nobody will)? Is it an answer to frustration resulting from defeat in a game? Is it a way of resolving the conflict between a strong self-image and the inability to beat another child fairly? Or a physical expression of a statement of contempt for the game itself, saying in effect: 'Who wants to play a stupid game like that anyhow? That's what I think of it. . . .'

You will now have identified certain kinds of aggressive response and, hopefully, been able to decide how the rewards which sustain that type of conduct are being produced. Your aim from this point must be twofold: to reduce the incidents of aggressive behaviour in that particular situation, and to provide the child with more desirable and more rewarding answers. Remember, it is not possible just to take away a response, as one might extract a rotten tooth, and leave nothing in its place. The child cannot simply stop behaving. It will always be doing something, and that something should, ideally, be the socially acceptable activity which you desire.

Start by eliminating the rewards which aggression produces. If teasing is the problem, make it clear to both children that their behaviour is unacceptable. If it occurs again, put them both into 'time out' (in separate rooms, of course). Aggression which is designed to produce attention from adults can also be dealt with by 'time out'.

At the same time, help the child positively. Teasing is likely to occur outside the family and beyond your control just as frequently as it does between brothers and sisters. Many children find this extremely distressing, usually because they have no weapon with which to fight it — except the answers of aggression or tears. Teach them more effective means, assertive behaviour which allows them to express their feelings of contempt for the child who is doing the teasing. Or simply to shrug it off. This can be practised, perhaps in the form of a 'play drama' between you and the child. Very quickly, the teased child will find that it can be more fun and more satisfying to respond in this way.

If the child's aggression is an attention-seeking device, then first establish that they are really being given their fair share of attention — or is their complaint perhaps justified? Certainly, as the child starts to show aggressive behaviour, your favourable interactions are likely to decline simply because they are so unrewarding to be with. Combine 'time out' with periods during which you reward sociable behaviour by taking a clear interest in the child, not just paying them attention which they have to share with other children or household chores.

Aggression which occurs because the child is excluded from others' games, or lacks the ability to win when playing, can best be dealt with by a combination of 'time out' and training, training in the social skills needed to co-operate with others and in the tactics necessary to win at different kinds of games. In the first case, direct, verbal instruction should be sufficient with older children. Tell them that they will be liked better if they share their toys, if they invent their own games instead of disrupting the activities of others, and so on. Provide them with some games which they can offer to the rest of their group. Failure at games may be due to a lack of practice. Play with them. Watch out for their difficulties, and patiently show them how to do things better.

At the same time, start to reward positive behaviour immediately it occurs. You can do this by praise and encouraging comment, but be positive. Do not hark back to old habits and make wounding comparisons: 'I am so pleased you've decided to behave properly at last.'

Another method of reward is called a 'Token Economy'. You draw up a contract with the child (with four or five-year-olds this can be an actual written document). In return for certain behaviour, you will award a token. This can be a plastic button, foreign coin and so on. By collecting tokens, they can 'buy' themselves treats, such as extra time to watch TV, another bedtime story, some sweets, and so on. Using tokens means it is possible to reward desirable behaviour immediately, thus providing the most powerful possible learning situation.

The immediate effects of this approach may be to increase the incidents of aggression, but do not be discouraged. This is quite normal. It only shows that the child is fighting back with the same old methods which proved so effective in the past. Persist, and the aggression will decline and finally disappear.

At the same time that you are making these beneficial changes, take a long, cool look at your own lifestyle. How much of a model for aggression is provided by relationships within the family? How do you and your partner resolve difficulties? By furious rows or reasoned discussions? How do you punish disobedience in the children? By scolding or using physical aggression against them? There is little point in trying to persuade even a young child that aggression is not the answer if you continually behave as though it was.

The aggressive child is hardly ever a happy child. Often, he or she is desperately keen to find better answers to their problems, but old responses shackle them. These children will react very favourably to a practical, caring approach, which recognises their difficulties and offers them a new way of coping with life.

How To Help The Anxious Child

One of the most successful problem-solvers I have ever watched in action amongst the under-fives was one of the most anxious and, initially, least co-operative. She was a very shy four-year-old who had great difficulty in relating to strangers. When she was finally persuaded to try her hand at the tests, however, she completed them in less than half the usual time. Quickly and confidently, she produced the right answers without any hesitation or apparent effort. Although the problems which I used in my research were not designed to assess IQ, there was no doubt in my mind that had she tackled a standard intelligence test with the same assured expertise, her rating would have been extremely high; if, and it is a big if, she could have been persuaded to attempt it in the first place. My guess was that she would either have refused or, out of anxiety, raced through the sets of problems without giving herself a proper chance.

There are many children who disadvantage themselves in this way. They are so anxious in social situations that they remain passive observers, never able to bring themselves to take part, and, as a result, never learning essential interpersonal skills. Other children are less fearful in social situations than when challenged by some more formal learning problem. Their high levels of anxiety make them see every task as being far more complex than it really is. Their subjective assessment of eventual failure is high. They never give their brains a chance, and they fail. After a while, they may use the strategy of failure as a way of getting along in life; appealing for help to adults or other children, crying and looking distressed when compelled to make any real effort. They are children who, when they start school, will become very adept at reading the body language of their teachers. If pressed to answer, they will mumble something non-committal, watching for encouragement or disapproval in the teacher's expression. Most adults are much more obvious in their feelings than they realise, and it is not difficult for anxious children to know when they are getting something right, or if they are heading in the wrong direction. They sometimes develop a technique of speaking so indistinctly that the teacher is not really certain what has been said. But, since most teachers have a vested interest in their children appearing bright and knowledgeable, the missing information is, quite unwittingly, provided by the teachers themselves. They believe, because they want to believe, that the child has said the right thing and given a sensible answer. If this strategy is rewarded, the child will seize upon it eagerly as the best way of avoiding the anxiety associated with mental effort. Avoidance which leads to a reduction in tension and fear is a rewarded response, a response which will, therefore, be very likely to occur again.

By the time anxious children start formal education, it may be too late to help them control social or intellectual fears. Certainly, it is going to be far more difficult than during the first five years.

I have often found that anxious children have equally anxious parents, and the first step could be for the adults to examine their own reactions to situations which they find unpleasant. If these are avoidance tactics, then a more realistic approach should be adopted. How this may be achieved will be described in the next chapter.

So far as the child's behaviour is concerned, you should proceed as for the aggressive child and start by keeping a record, over a week or ten days, of every occasion when the child seems to be restricted by excessive anxiety — when invited out to play with friends, perhaps, or for an outing with the parents of other children; when attending play group or nursery school, or when being asked to attempt some challenging task. The exact response should be noted as well as the way in which *you* reacted. Did the child: cry or have a tantrum; refuse point blank to attempt the task; beg you not to force the issue; become clinging and fearful? What did you do? Insist that the child go through with the challenge? Allow him to avoid it? Get angry and scold?

What you are looking for are the 'rewards' which have established the anxiety response. In most cases, these will be avoidance. Such reinforcers must then be withdrawn, which probably means compelling children to go through with the feared behaviour, insisting that they greet and talk to visitors, that they go to parties, accept invitations to outings, and so on. There may be difficulties at first, refusals and tears. The longer the avoidance has been carried out, the more difficult it will be. But unless the tactic of refusing to confront challenges is got rid of in the early years, it may prove very resistant to change later on in life.

One procedure which has been used with great success by my colleague Dr William Mitchell, at the Institute of Behaviour Therapy, involves vivid imagery. The under-fives usually have very powerful imaginations, and these can be used to help them overcome particular anxieties. The child is encouraged to picture himself in some situation where he feels especially confident and happy. For example, one youngster had developed a phobia about dogs and would scream with terror even in the presence of a puppy. His pride and joy was a sketchboard on which he propelled himself expertly around the neighbourhood. So he was encouraged to picture himself on a super skateboard, a high speed, brilliantly painted creation, with chrome wheel hubs and silky smooth bearings. He was helped to develop a vivid image of himself on this skateboard, zooming powerfully around the streets. Then a small dog was introduced into the scene, all in his imagination, of course. He was told to picture himself skating quickly past the dog and not feeling anxious. Over several sessions, the dog image was made larger, fiercer and closer. It was done very carefully and patiently, so that the child never became anxious. After a time, his phobia disappeared, not just in his imagination but in real life as well.

The type of vivid imagery you choose will depend on the personality of the child. Some may want to imagine themselves accompanied by a powerful magician who helps to keep them safe, while others will be more enthusiastic about picturing themselves as a bionic man! By working through their fears progressively, in the imagination, you can reduce any anxiety they actually feel. Start with situations which cause them very little anxiety and work slowly through a lost of their fears until they are coping easily and confidently with the things they dread most. This is a very effective method of helping children to overcome many types of anxiety. But it demands careful planning and persistence on the part of the adult. If you feel you lack either the time or the patience to carry this procedure through, then it is best not to attempt the approach at all. Vivid imagery which is tried and fails may end up by making the child more anxious than before.

Make certain that the child understands exactly what is involved in attempting a task or accepting an invitation. Sometimes they are confused and very fearful as a result. I remember the case of one child who became terrified of going to visit a school friend. In time, this unexplicable anxiety spread to visiting other friends as well. Her mother was bewildered because, up to that time, her daughter had been a very sociable child. Some patient questioning revealed the fact that the four-year-old had overheard an adult conversation about her friend's mother during which one grown-up had commented: 'I pity her husband. She's a real dragon when angry.' The child was convinced that the woman could turn herself into a real, fire-breathing monster, and, quite reasonably, felt terrified of seeing her again.

Try to manipulate events so that initial attempts to tackle

challenges head on are rewarded. Ensure that early party attending involves a few, familiar friends. Do not throw the child into the deep end of a big, noisy party with many strange faces. When setting a problem, make certain at first that the child can succeed. If there is anxiety about meeting strangers, give as much practice as possible. Invite friends and neighbours around to your home — since the child will feel less anxious on familiar territory — and ask them to be particularly responsive to the child. The more regular and rewarding the previously anxiety-producing activity becomes, the less fearful will be the response.

So far in this book I have concentrated on the needs and feelings of the child. But your needs and feelings as a parent are just as important. The way the under-fives feel about the world and about you will be tremendously influenced by the way in which you feel about them. It is quite unrealistic, and totally unreasonable, to consider family interactions only from the viewpoint of the children. In the next chapter, I will be looking at ways in which you can effectively help your child by helping yourself.

Chapter Nine

Helping Yourself To Help Your Child

In the drama of modern family life, parents seem to be increasingly cast as villains. It is their lack of expertise which creates social misfits; their failures of understanding which lead to adolescent hostility and rebellion; their inability to meet the needs of sons and daughters which produces maladjusted children. Faced with such charges, many parents feel justly accused. Arraigned for incompetence before the tribunal of public opinion, they plead guilty without any evidence being offered.

No period of history has been more child-orientated than ours, nor produced parents who regard themselves as so inadequate. After generations when they could do no wrong, many parents now feel themselves incapable of doing anything right. Anxiety seems almost endemic in middle-class Western households. Bombarded by the views of experts and the cautions of specialists, their failures condemned and their successes taken for granted, it is hardly surprising that parents should respond in this way. Professor A.H. Halsey must have expressed the confusion of many when he commented in a Reith Lecture in 1972:

'Fathers, and more especially mothers, inhabit a world which takes away their control and simultaneously insists on their responsibility for the fate of their children. . . . They are increasingly made to feel amateurs in a difficult professional world.'

If you regard this book as one more voice of accusation, then these comments may seem somewhat curious. Rather like the prosecutor rising to make a plea on behalf of the defendant! But, in suggesting that children are taught to be stupid, and that these lessons must, inevitably, stem largely from their parents, I am not attributing blame, but attempting to explain probable causes. I have not been trying to produce an indictment but an inquiry into causes. The object of my work and the purpose of this book have been to discover and describe some of these causes; it has never been to condemn or to censure. The statements that parents are responsible for determining the mental growth of their children is intended as a starting point for constructive change in attitudes, not as a source of further anxiety.

I said a moment ago that parental self-confidence has been dangerously eroded. The danger exists because the level of confidence with which a task is approached influences its apparent difficulty and determines the motivation to continue. The greater the difficulties, the higher the associated anxiety. The more anxiety is felt, the less confidence one can muster to achieve a successful outcome. And so the increasingly vicious and damaging circle continues.

At least part of the problem, I believe, is that many young parents have a quite distorted impression of what bringing up children involves. Very often, they have a highly romanticised view, based on glossy colour photographs in baby magazines and soft-focus television commercials for child-care products. Faced with the reality of crying, constant demands for attention, sickness and soiled nappies, they are ill prepared to cope. Many books on bringing up children seem to adopt a similarly unrealistic approach. The basic advice may be excellent, but it often depends on parents being endlessly patient, having almost inexhaustible energy, no other demands on their time, and nothing other than the welfare of the child to occupy their minds. Furthermore, the emphasis is always on the effects of the adults on the child. The parents are constantly pictured as taking an active role and determining, quite independently of the infant, what attitudes they will adopt. Neither assumption is correct.

As a parent, you will hardly need convincing on the first point. You know only too well that you get tired, feel unwell, lose your patience, are short of time to get everything done, and have many concerns and worries other than those directly involved in bringing up children. The fact that your child exerts a powerful influence on you and, even when only a few days old, can direct and control your behaviour, may come as more of a surprise. Until recently, the extent of the child's effects on parents was a neglected area of study, and many psychologists regarded it as of little significance. Today, as a result of several detailed studies, its real importance in determining the course of family relationships is widely recognised. Some of this new knowledge has been obtained from research into baby battering, an increasingly widespread phenomenon in Europe and the United States. The low incidence of reporting such assaults makes it impossible to put an accurate figure on the number of babies and infants who are violently beaten by their parents each year; but the number probably runs into millions. When baby-battering parents are taken before the courts, they themselves are often severely punished and described in such terms as 'wicked', 'evil', 'viciously sadistic'. While I am not condoning attacks on children, there are, surely, few parents who have not read of such cases and reflected that they too have known moments when they would willingly have assaulted their own children. Reporting the findings of some studies in their book *Child Effects on Adults*, Richard Bell and Lawrence Harper comment that:

'Many of the parents felt that they had been abused by the child, not that they had abused the child. . . . It is quite typical to find that only one child in a family is abused. . . . The child who has been battered is often transferred to a foster home. In some instances, it has been reported that battered children have been abused in a foster home, transferred, and abused in another foster home.'

Clearly, these children are exerting a powerful and, for themselves, dangerous and even disastrous influence on adults. Amongst the behaviour which is most likely to produce such assaults are constant fussing, strange and very irritating cries and other exasperating conduct. These unpopular activities are certainly not any fault of the child. There is evidence to suggest that they may be connected with difficulties due to such things as premature delivery and low birth weight. (amongst battered children, this runs as high as 40 per cent). But neither can the assaults which result be considered entirely the fault of the adults. The unintentional provocation provided by the babies must be seen as a prime factor in the battering.

The starting point for helping yourself to help your child is to recognise the two-way influence of cause and effect, and to accept that parents are just as human as children. You cannot hope for any real chance of success in relating to children if you begin from an unrealistic belief in your own capabilities. If you are convinced that, as a mother or father, you are never supposed to lose your temper; enjoy yourself without the children; get tired; bored; depressed, and occasionally fed-up with the whole idea of being a parent, then doing any of these things will make you feel guilty. In a recent book, (*The Anxiety Antidote*, Souvenir Press, London, 1979), Dr Robert Sharpe and I discussed some of the reasons why people feel anxious. One of the causes we considered was the discrepancy between self-image and actual performance. People with an unreasonably high opinion of their own abilities and talents become extremely anxious when they are unable to live up to those expectations.

We are not saying that you should under-estimate yourself and avoid trying to do things at which you may fail. One should always aim as high as possible, *but within a realistic framework.* Instead of saying: 'I can do that easily. . . .' and then growing anxious if failure results, it is far more sensible to tell yourself: 'It may be difficult. But I have succeeded in similar tasks before and should be able to do it again.' This is the approach which one must always teach phobics when helping them to overcome their fears. They must never tell themselves: 'I shall succeed without any trouble,' because the consequences of a set-back are so much worse.

Sometimes, it helps to externalise your feelings. Instead of keeping them bottled up, write them down. Draw up a list of your expectations and the chances you have, in your view, of achieving them. Cold print on a sheet of paper tends to produce a degree of objectivity which is impossible while the same hopes and fears are locked away in your brain. The ancient exhortation above the temple of the oracle at Delphi — 'Know thyself' — has lost none of its truth down the centuries.

The starting point for change must be where you are now, not where you would like to believe yourself to be. If you see yourself as having endless patience, then outbursts of irritation may cause shock and guilt: 'How could I behave like that? I am so long suffering.' Accept that you are easily irritated, and the behaviour, while you may not like it overmuch, will not cause you such surprise. Having accepted a low level of patience as one of your ways of responding to pressure, you can then set about making changes in your attitude. If you believe that parents should always be available for their children to consult, at any time of day or night, then your resentment at constant badgering may upset you and create feelings of anxiety: 'How can I be so selfish and unresponsive?' Accept that we all need time to ourselves, that you have a perfect right to want a period during every day when you do not have to think about the children and what they want. Occasional selfishness is nothing to be ashamed of. It is essential. How can one properly allow freedom of self-expression in others if you deny it to yourself?

Mothers have often said to me: 'I can't seem to cope any longer. I get tired easily.' They see it as a failing on their part, evidence of their unsuitability as a parent. But there is nothing unusual or shameful in getting tired. We each have different amounts of energy to expend, although everybody gets tired eventually. A husband coming home from a day at the office feels entitled to his weariness, but if a woman experiences the same tiredness, she often feels guilty.

As well as recognising your human needs, you should also form a realistic opinion about the abilities of your children. I do not mean that you should under-estimate them. Certainly during the first five years of life you should have the highest possible expectations for their potential abilities. But this does not mean trying to force them at a pace, or in a direction, which is unaccceptable to them. Talented adults are often eager that their children should show the same abilities, and will strongly encourage them to do so. By forcing the child in this way, they may well destroy interest in the very activities they are trying to promote. Respect the child's independence. Make life an hors d'oeuvre with the greatest possible variety, not a compulsory set meal.

Setting yourself impossible goals for behaviour, creating an unrealistic self-image and then attempting to live up to it, is a short sighted policy. If you try to give everything, you may end up effectively giving nothing. The child who has come to rely on his parents for everything often ends up receiving nothing.

'Children of two years of age can have evolved into delightful companions who have free and easy social relationships, and who, at the same time, have maintained a profound curiosity about the world at large', comments Dr Burton L. White, director of the Pre-School Project at Harvard, in his book *The First Three Years of Life*. 'Or they can have developed into beings whose world revolves almost exclusively around an older adult (usually the mother), in a manner such that the mother is badgered from morning to night by a kind of consuming desire on the part of a two-year-old to monopolize her time and attention.'

Such an outcome disadvantages everybody concerned. The child may grow anxious about developing social relationships with other adults and children, and become so involved in that one, exclusive source of stimulation, that all others are neglected. For the parent, the endless demands are exhausting, and can result in a rejection of the child or a loss of independence. Even when the adult manages to avoid these pitfalls, there will be an unpleasant and potentially harmful increase in levels of stress.

Learning To Handle Stress

In a recently published study I examined stress levels in men and women following a wide range of occupations, and closely monitored them over a period of weeks. The occupations included business executives, stunt drivers, parachutists and mothers with young children. It was this last group, rather than those in obviously dangerous or demanding jobs, who were found to suffer from the most consistently high levels of stress. (see *Thrive on Stress* by Dr Robert Sharpe and David Lewis, Souvenir Press, London 1977).

While a controlled amount of stress can be highly beneficial, prolonged exposure to excessive pressures can quickly become mentally and physically damaging. Because few mothers realise that they are working in a high stress environment, the effects can be even more distressing. The businessman who begins to suffer the effects of the rat-race can always tell himself: 'It's not me, it's my wretched job.' Few women appreciate that they are under even greater levels of stress than their husbands. When they start to feel ill or fail to cope, they tell themselves: 'It can't be my work. It must be me.' Many men regard their homes as tranquil, relaxed places, and their wives as leading tranquil and relaxed lives, working at their own pace, untroubled by constant demands on their time and attention. Many, I know, envy the apparent ease of the house-wife's work; no commuting on crowded trains and buses, no employers breathing down your neck, no headaches about deadlines, no need to rush out for a hasty snack at mid-morning. Husbands who have this false image of what is involved in running a home and looking after small children are likely to feel baffled and irritated if their wives complain of exhaustion and frayed nerves at the end of the day.

The truth is very different. In terms of every bodily measure for stress we made, from heart rate to changes in the electrical conductivity of the skin, the mothers of under-fives in our study were more anxious for longer periods of the day than their desk-bound husbands. When something went wrong, if one of the children had an accident, or they began to run seriously behind schedule for instance, their stress peaks were often higher than those of businessmen faced with a disaster in the office. At times, their level of physical arousal reached that seen in stunt drivers in the seconds before they rolled a car on to its roof, or parachutists just prior to their jumping from the aircraft.

In order to be able to handle stress successfully, the first essential is to realise it is present in your life. Stunt men, parachutists, and high-powered executives are well aware of the fact. Often the peaks of stress, those moments when adrenalin starts to surge through the body, are part of the attraction. They get a kick out of being strongly physically aroused. Housewives seldom appreciate just how great an amount of stress they themselves have to endure. As a result, they regard the very natural physical and mental responses to pressure which they experience as a kind of weakness. What right have they to feel tired when they are at home all day? Lack of obvious reasons for their distress makes them feel anxious, miserable and guilty.

Start by accepting that homes, however peaceful they seem to outsiders, are places of stress. The stresses present may be rather different to those normally found in business, but they are no less distressing, so keep a watch for the special areas of stress in your own life. Keep notes, as suggested when observing aggressive or anxious children, so that you have a permanent record of the times of day, the situations and the circumstances in which you feel especially tense or least able to cope.

My own study indicated five areas of stress which were likely to influence the lives of young mothers. To help you analyse your own lifestyle in terms of these pressure points, they have been incorporated into a 30 statement check list. To carry out the analysis, simply tick those statements which describe some aspect of your own behaviour.

1. I feel lonely and isolated at home.
2. If my child cut himself badly, I would not know what to do.
3. I find it very difficult to express my inner feelings to my child.
4. I feel I am responsible for failings in my child.
5. I feel constantly tired and unable to cope.
6. I am frightened that my child will have an accident.
7. I find it hard to sleep at night.
8. I am distressed by constant crying and waking at night by my baby.
9. I have frequent shouting matches with my child.
10. I seldom visit, or am visited by, friends.
11. I have no interests outside the home.
12. I never get a chance to eat more than a snack in the mornings.
13. I hit my child and then regret having done so.
14. I often worry that my child no longer loves me.
15. If my child received a bad electric shock, I would not know what to do.
16. I lack confidence in myself as a mother.
17. I find I have frequent headaches.

18. I find myself sitting and doing nothing for long periods.
19. I worry about not having everything finished by the time my partner comes home.
20. I am constantly badgered for attention by my child.
21. I feel that my home has become a prison.
22. If my child swallowed something hazardous, I would not know how to help him/her.
23. I feel that my baby cries a lot because I am handling him/her wrongly.
24. I feel there is no one to whom I can turn for advice.
25. There are frequent occasions when my child and I do not speak to one another.
26. I believe that if my child turns out badly, it will be my fault.
27. I spend most of my day cooped up in my home and take little exercise in the fresh air.
28. I feel guilty because I do not love my child as much as I should.
29. I never seem to have enough energy for all the demands made on me.
30. I am afraid I have spoiled my child.

Hot To Make Use Of Your Answers

The five special areas of stress which our study indicated are listed below. The numbers following each one refer to the above statements. Six were included in the checklist for each type of stressor. If you ticked three or more in any one area of stress, then I suggest you read the appropriate section below. If you found yourself in disagreement with the majority of statements, it may still be helpful to read through the sections where you did have any score at all, although the result does suggest that your level of daily stress is not unreasonable. You may also find it useful to look at the description of relaxation procedures.

Stressors

1. *Guilt over presumed errors in child rearing.*
This type of fear was quite frequently encountered. It is indicated by positive responses to statements: 4; 8; 23; 26; 28; 30.

2. *Boredom with household routine.*
A lack of stimulation in the surroundings is not usually recognised as a source of stress, but boredom is an important stressor. This type of difficulty was admitted by nearly 90% of women in our study. It is indicated by positive responses to statements: 1; 10; 11; 18; 19; 21.

3. *Breakdown in relationship with child.*
Although less common, this stressor was a source of great anxiety to a significant number of women. It is indicated by a positive response to statements: 3; 9; 13; 14; 20; 25.

4. *Fear of the unknown.*
A lack of knowledge about what to do in the case of an emergency is a worry for many young mothers, especially when they are cut off from their own family or friendly older women. Small incidents can become magnified out of all proportion. Mothers in isolated houses or high rise apartments lacking a telephone felt especially vulnerable to accidents. It is indicated by positive responses to statements: 2; 6; 15; 16; 22; 24.

5. *Lack of physical stamina.*
Feeling constantly tired, worried, and unable to cope with household demands is an underlying stressor which may reveal itself in any, or all, of the above areas of special concern. Not surprisingly, perhaps, this basic problem was found mainly in young mothers with several children living in cramped accommodation, amongst mothers who had to go out to work, and amongst those trying to exist on a lower than average income. The presence of this stressor is indicated by positive responses to statements: 5; 7; 12; 17; 27; 29.

Successful Stressor Control

GUILT

The feeling that a child has been spoiled, harmed, or in some way fatally mishandled is a common source of guilt-induced stress. Several psychologists and psychiatrists have noted the damaging consequences of the 'illusion of omnipotence' which results from taking too much notice of the wrong sort of information. Dr McIntosh, president of Barnard College, New York, has remarked that some young parents:

> 'Have acquired fixed opinions . . . which set their future responsibilities in a most terrifying light . . . all the experts seem to be saying to them: "Even the most innocent-appearing act or carelessly spoken word may harm a child or damage his future happiness."'

Doctors Thomas, Chess and Birch, whose long term study of temperament was described in Chapter six, have commented:

> 'What has impressed us over the years has been the destructive impact on parents of the prevalent concept that they are the exclusive determinants of disturbances in the child's development. Many of the mothers of problem children develop enormous guilt feelings due to the assumption that they must necessarily be solely responsible for their children's emotional difficulties. With this guilt comes anxiety, defensiveness, increased pressures on the children, and even hostility towards them for "exposing" the mother's inadequacy by their disturbed behaviour.'

Their work has shown that basic characteristics of temperament are inborn. They cannot be greatly influenced by child-rearing methods, nor can they be changed. All that the parent can do is to apply the most appropriate child-rearing methods for that particular kind of temperament. This means being flexible and adapting your approach to match the needs of the individual. The mistake is to believe that because a child-care practice is recommended by a particular expert, and seems to work with most children, it will be desirable for yours.

A good example of mistaken guilt feelings can be found in night-waking and crying by babies. In the past, regular waking and crying have been attributed to handling methods used by the parents. Experts have advised either that babies be left to cry or be immediately soothed. The implication has been that parents are to blame if their babies do not sleep through the night. Waking at night is one of the most common complaints mothers make about their children. It adds to their exhaustion the following morning, and may make it much harder for them to respond affectionately. This is especially likely if they already feel guilty for causing the infant to adopt such an unsociable routine.

However, a recent study carried out by the Institute of Child Health in London, has shown that night-waking is related to birth difficulties and is not connected with parental handling. The research showed that problems at birth, such as late delivery, a long delay between birth and the first cry, forceps delivery, and so on, can result in a high proportion of night-wakers. The mother's reaction to her baby's crying has no part to play in creating the condition.

Try to accept that certain responses are part of the baby's inherited make-up, no more your 'fault' or responsibility than eye or hair colouring. You can best help by recognising and valuing differences, by accepting them as part of the individuality of the child, and by not using them as a source of guilt and stress.

BOREDOM

Young mothers in particular often feel guilty about being bored. They wonder how other women manage to keep so busy and interested, and imagine that it is some failure of character.

Perhaps they do not love their family or value their homes sufficiently. In fact, any sort of routine work becomes boring in a fairly short space of time. That is, it no longer provides sufficient reinforcers to maintain a high level of interest and motivation. Large proportions of most working days contain routine activities which provide little stimulation. But when you are working with others, different sources of interest can often be established, such as gossip and looking forward to a tea break and a longer chat, exchanging views and information. The isolated housewife lacks any such escape from boredom, and is often extremely lonely. A recent survey varried out by Dr David Drazin of the Schlackman Research Organisation found that one in four British women was lonely and that marriage was often no cure. The greatest amount of loneliness was found in the 16 to 24 age group. Those who lived in large industrial towns were the worst affected, followed by women living in small villages.

Boredom and loneliness can lead to apathy and indifference to household chores, or an obsessional desire to keep the home in a state of almost clinical cleanliness. The final outcome of both can be deep depression. I need hardly say that all these states of mind disadvantage not only the woman but every member of her family. The damage is especially great for the under-fives, who look to their mothers as a primary source of stimulation.

It is impossible to suggest any ready-made answers to this widespread and disabling social problem. Each individual must find a solution that best fits her own needs; but there are a number of practical steps which can be taken. I offer them here not as a cook-book formula for the happy life, but as guides to methods which others have found helpful in the past.

1.   Recognise that boredom is quite a natural response to any environment which provides too few rewards (reinforcers) for the activities you have to undertake. Remember also that any behaviour which fails to be followed by some kind of a reward

is likely to decline. The housewife who spends hours each morning doing nothing except miserably contemplating her tedious day is actually carrying out a response which has come to be more rewarding, in some way, than the household routines themselves. If you feel bored, then do not also feel bad about feeling bored. It is a normal and natural reaction to a certain set of circumstances. To break out of these unrewarding responses, practical steps will have to be taken.

2.   Do not try to overcome a lack of stimulation by inventing work for yourself, by cleaning rooms which are already virtually spotless. There is very little reward in that, and you may become obsessional about it if this approach is followed for too long. At best, it will only increase the tedium of routine work.

3.   Working to a time-table is a way some people use in order to put themselves under pressure. Usually key points in the time-table are determined by outside factors such as getting the family off to work, picking children up from school, preparing a midday or evening meal, and so on. But between these benchmarks of the day, you may find it helpful to organise the remaining work in a precise manner. Try to vary the time-table routine from day to day so that tasks are tackled in a different rotation. It will not be much variation, of course, but every little change helps reduce the tedium by a certain amount. If there are some jobs which you especially detest: ironing, washing, or making the beds, for example, then try not to group all these tasks together. Separate them by doing other, more enjoyable chores in between, and follow each with some rewarding activity. A morning break, lunch, watching afternoon television, or whatever else you enjoy. By doing this, you will be reinforcing the carrying out of the least attractive jobs of the day.

4.   Planning work like this usually provides more free time which you can devote to yourself and to your child. Make the most of these opportunities for providing stimulation for both of you. With the infant of only a few months old, spend

some time in conversation training, as described in Chapter three. Older children can be helped to master a whole range of skills more easily. Why not teach your baby to read? Lessons can begin as early as twelve months, and will the child a valuable headstart on learning. There are a number of methods available, most of which depend on using very big print and associating words with familiar objects. First of all, for example, the child may be taught to read the word MUMMY written in large, bold letters, and held against you. Then the child begins to learn different parts of the body in the same way. The names of household items — chairs, beds, table, cupboard and so on — can be taught by using labels attached to the furniture.

With older under-fives, plan trips which you can make together to places of interest. Do not just go there, but prepare for each expedition carefully. Get the child to draw up a programme. Use brochures, magazine pictures, newspaper cuttings and so on to create a source book. During the visit, collect whatever free, handout material is provided, and include this in the book. But let the child direct the work, in order to gain experience in planning activities.

5.   Use some of the free time for yourself as well, for activities you can enjoy away from the children. One idea might be to go on some training course which will help you become more confident in handling household emergencies; (see FEAR OF THE UNKNOWN, below).

6.   If organisation is required to make these trips possible, such as having somebody to look after younger children during an outing, then organise yourself. Do not wait around for somebody else to do the spadework for you. Put a small advertisement in one of the local stores or newspaper, inviting mothers in a similar situation to contact you. You may gain further publicity by writing to the letters page of your local newspaper or asking the editor if a news item can be published about your intention to form a local self-help group. The advantages of co-operation with other mothers are consider-

able, quite apart from being able to work out a rota for baby sitting. Children benefit from going on outings in small groups; not only is it more fun, but they also learn valuable lessons in social relationships. It is often possible to arrange for organisations to send speakers to talk to a group. For example, the police might provide an expert to talk about crime prevention, the fire service might send a speaker on safety in the home, the ambulance or first aid organisations give a lecture on coping with medical emergencies, and so on. It may be quite easy, as an organised group, to arrange tours of interesting local factories, the local newspaper offices, radio or TV stations. All this will provide you with an interesting activity outside the home, and the children with extremely important learning opportunities.

7. The difficulty with boredom is that it breeds more boredom. After a while, making any attempts at change seem such an effort, that it is easier and less stressful to simply wallow in tedium. The first step in breaking out of this situation is always the most difficult. there are no ways of making it any easier. You must simply tell yourself very firmly that this is the course of action to be taken, and then go ahead and do it. If you have friends living nearby who are in the same position, then try and get their support. Companionship at the start smoothes out many anxieties. These may be further reduced by carrying out some relaxation training in the way described below.

BREAKDOWN IN RELATIONSHIP

This often arises partly, at least, from the previous stressor. Bored parents find it hard to relate to children, especially if they are seen as a major factor in the tedious existence which the adults are forced to follow. Women who had interesting, involving jobs before becoming pregnant are often particularly — and perhaps reasonably — frustrated by inactivity and household routine. Over-dependency is frequently a cause of parental alienation. The child whose demands are unending and of great intensity may create a situation which adults find intolerable. They complain bitterly, and justifiably, of never being allowed a moment's peace or privacy.

But dependency is a learned response on the part of the child. It develops because demanding behaviour is rewarded, not every time perhaps, but sufficiently often to make it an important source of reinforcement. If the irritating dependency is to be reduced, both for your sake and the child's, then a new set of responses to demands must be adopted.

Perhaps you feel that such advice is more easily given than followed? That was certainly the view of one weary father: 'It may be OK in theory,' he told me. 'But it's quite impractical. My two little daughters know I like to spend an hour or so every Saturday watching sport on TV. They've been told over and over again not to interrupt me, but they take no notice.'

I asked him what he did when they invaded his leisure time. He answered that sometimes he shouted and sent them from the room, sometimes he tried to ignore them, now and then he simply abandoned his programme and played with them. It was hardly any wonder, given that reaction, that the girls had learned not to take any notice of his 'keep away' rule. Some of the time, it is true, they received very little reward for their unwelcome invasions. But now and again, they did. Such occasional reinforcers are powerful in establishing a pattern of behaviour. Just consider, for a moment, how easily one can become hooked on playing a fruit machine. You start off full of good intentions. Only a certain amount of money will be wasted. You will definitely quit after it has all been spent. Then once or twice you win, so you carry on playing. You lose more than you intended, but you keep on pulling the handle and feeding in the coins. The machine is providing you with what that father gave his daughters, a 'variable ratio reinforcer'. You never know, when the handle is pulled, whether it will be a win or a loss. They never knew when they ran into the room whether they would be scolded, or rewarded with a game. The pain of watching your money vanish into the bandit is more than made up for by the thrill of hearing coins clattering into the winnings tray. The pleasure the girls got from having attention at a time when it was suppose to be denied them compensated for the punishments which they sometimes received.

If good relationships are to be developed and maintained beyond the 'five year factor', then mutual independence within the family must be taught as early as possible. You should not feel guilty about denying the child constant attention, and the child should not come to expect it. Make this one of the first lessons you teach, but be consistent. If you have set aside time to follow your own activities, then strictly enforce the regulations.

Beware of fake affection and expressing insincere feelings. Small children are quite capable of telling the difference, especially when the body language gives the lie to the words which are being uttered. A tense and obviously disenchanted mother tells her child flatly: 'Of course Mummy loves you, darling,' but the child is not fooled for a moment. In time, these devalued terms of endearment can become punishing rejections. A chilling experience which illustrates the way children may come to regard 'loving words' is described by the American teacher, John Holt. He asked his class to write up on the blackboard things which they hated to be called, the kind of insults which really got under their skin. Many were predictable — 'idiot', 'slob', 'dope', 'stupid' — but the remainder surprised him. They were all terms of affection: — 'dearie', 'honey', 'love', 'sweetness'. As these words were chalked up, the children vigorously expressed their hatred and contempt for them. It was the same kind of contempt which, these children believed, was being directed against them by parents who abused the language of love by applying endearments dishonestly and hypocritically.

Children are often very unlovable, and when they are, you should assert your right to tell them so. But there is no need to tell them you hate them, which is hopefully untrue, or that you will never love them again, or that your love depends exclusively on their doing what you want them to do. Expression of honest emotions never needs to be this cruel; it is quite enough to say that you dislike what they are doing or that you feel too tired to respond to it. The under-fives are generally very honest and open about their feelings. It is a frankness which many quickly learn to inhibit, but mostly they wear their hearts on their sleeves and have a spontaneity of expression which contrasts markedly and favourably with adult attitudes. Honesty should begin with self-honesty, then expand to honesty in relationships with other adults. Only then, perhaps, can you be certain of responding openly and freely with children. But a start can be made by refusing to use words of love at times when you feel exactly the opposite emotion.

If your relationships are bad at the present time, try to pin-point the reasons why in as objective a manner as possible. Do not put all the blame on either the child or yourself. Bear in mind that there is a constant interaction of behaviours, with both adult and child responses influencing one another. Many children go through a rebellious period around the age of two, which can make life very difficult. But try to be patient and remember that this is likely to be a passing phase.

Good relationships are especially important to parents who want to teach their children ways of expanding their minds. Effective help can only occur in an atmosphere of genuine trust, affection and co-operation.

'You cannot expect to be able to "turn on" good attitudes during the teaching hour if at every other time you feel frustrated, angry, or guilty in your child's presence,' comments Professor D.H. Stott in his excellent guide *The Parent as Teacher*. 'If you cannot understand why your efforts to discipline or stimulate him meet with no success, you may take it out on him rather than admit you are failing as a parent. Helplessness can breed rejection.'

I do not believe that there are any major disasters which cause the breakdown of relationships between human beings, any more than there is usually one reason for an accident. Both result from an accumulation of small incidents and events, unimportant in themselves, but whose cumulative effect may prove catastrophic. It is best to try to correct the situations at source. Never allow minor grievances to accumulate to a point where things begin to get out of control. If something is going wrong in the relationship with your child, do not ignore it in the hope of a spontaneous change. Work out what is wrong and then set about putting matters right.

FEAR OF THE UNKNOWN

Straightforward ignorance, rather than any more complex or profound problems, is a major source of anxiety. Ignorance comes in two guises: not knowing things and believing inaccurate information. As the American humourist, Henry Wheeler Shaw, once remarked: 'The trouble with people is not that they don't know, but that they know so much that ain't so.' A lack of knowledge in some areas of life is especially widespread, serious and often harmful. This is especially true about sex education, but it also applies to all kinds of essential domestic knowledge. For example, simple first aid which could mean the difference between life and death, basic home safety precautions such as checking electrical installations, and so on. Parents should master these essential subjects, not only in order to know what to do in an emergency, but so as to reduce anxiety about possible accidents. The average household is not only a highly stressful environment, as I mentioned earlier, it is also one of the most physically hazardous. The majority of serious accidents each year take place not in commerce and industry, but in the 'safety' of the home.

If you feel concerned about your lack of knowledge, then take practical steps to put matters right. Check with your local library for books on the subjects; and for information about any groups in your area which provide instruction, ask your

Citizens Advice Bureau. But find out, and start putting your mind at ease. Of all the stressors which can aflict parents, this one is the easiest to resolve.

LACK OF PHYSICAL STAMINA

Mental attitudes are important, but they are not the only methods of reducing anxiety, nor the only causes of excessive stress. It is impossible to divorce them from one's physical condition. If you are constantly tired, lacking in stamina, feeling unwell, it is very hard to develop a positive and optimistic approach towards life. Good health is the goal of almost everybody, but the possession of very few. The reasons are not difficult to understand. The majority of people recognise the importance of taking exercise, eating properly, not smoking or drinking to excess, and then do exactly the opposite. Much of what I am going to say now will be all too familiar to most people. I am sure you will agree with everything, accept it could make a difference to your fitness, and then forget all about it. However, if only for the sake of those few people determined enough to make lasting changes in their lifestyle for the sake of their health, here are five rules to follow:-

1.   Good health cannot be stored up like power in a charged battery. It must be worked at continually. Occasional spurts of effort on diet, exercise, cutting out cigarettes, and so on, will not make much long term difference. Furthermore, because their own short term effects tend to be punishing — doing without favourite foods, getting stiff muscles, feeling irritable — these *régimes* are unlikely to be kept up for long. Some people are able to make abrupt changes in lifestyle, stopping cigarettes from one day to the next, for instance, but for most of us, gradual changes are easier to accept. With cigarettes work out how many you smoke each day, and then cut down by perhaps one or two for the first week. In the second week, reduce your intake further, and so on. The success factor offers

a detailed programme for cutting down on smoking.

Housework involves considerable physical labour, and many women are far healthier than their desk-bound husbands as a result. But exercise in the fresh air is equally important to good health.

2.   Try to start the day with a meal which includes protein (eggs, bacon, cheese, fish) as well as carbohydrates (bread, sugar, cereals). This helps to maintain a high blood/glucose level throughout the morning. A breakfast high in carbohydrate and little else, is rapidly converted to blood glucose and burned as energy. This accounts for the mid-morning dip in energy which many people experience. By including protein in your first meal, you cause the level to stay at an energy-giving high throughout the morning.

3.   Your appetite at breakfast will be improved if you have eaten only a light meal last thing at night. This is because hunger depends on the levels of glucose in the blood supply. A heavy meal followed by sleep means that the 'appetite centre' of the brain is not stimulated first thing next day. As a result, you cannot face anything more than a cup of coffee. The exertions of the morning quickly use up your energy supply, and you feel hungry around midday.

4.   Good sleep is essential to health, yet many people find it very hard to get a proper night's rest. You will sleep more easily by leaving your problems outside the bedroom door. Try not to spend the hour or so before going to bed worrying about life or working tensely. Relax with music, an unstimulating television programme, or a restful book. If you are unable to sleep, do not lie in bed tossing and turning, otherwise bed will become associated with not being able to sleep. Get up, do a little work of a routine nature, listen to music or read, then return to bed. Repeat this process, and you will eventually fall asleep. More importantly, you will have broken the habit which many poor sleepers have of going to bed to lie awake.

5.   Relaxation is a valuable way of restoring peace of mind. It can be used to help you unwind at the end of a busy day, to help

you prepare for restful sleep, or to control excessive nerves in some especially difficult situation. Detailed advice about relaxation methods can be found in *The Anxiety Antidote* (by Dr Robert Sharpe and myself; Souvenir Press, London, 1979).

Here is a short description of one type of relaxation procedure which you may find helpful.

Find a suitable room, preferably quiet and darkened. Make it clear you do not want to be disturbed. If alone, take the telephone off the hook. Loosen all tight clothing, and remove your shoes. Now lie on a bed or couch, or sit in a comfortable chair with your legs stretched out. Have your arms by your side. For the first few moments, just flop out. Let your body sink deeper and deeper into the bed or chair. Now focus your mind on different areas of the body in turn. Start with your feet and ankles. Let these muscles unwind completely. Feel the tension draining away from them. Now move up to your thighs and buttocks. Again, bring all your attention to bear on just this area of the body. Feel the tension easing away. The next parts to consider are the stomach and chest. Keep your breathing light and regular. When you are concentrating on the chest, feel the air passing in and out of the lungs as you breathe. Now it is the turn of your hands and wrists, then your arms, and finally your shoulders, neck and face. These are often areas of especially high tension because most people hold their heads too rigidly and their face muscles far too tightly.

When each part of the body has been considered, turn your mind to some pleasant, relaxing scene. Perhaps a warm beach or a country meadow. Try to picture the scene as vividly as possible; feel the heat of the sun on your face and body, imagine the scent of the sea or warm grass. Hold this image as you let your body unwind and relax still further. Ten minutes spent relaxing like this each day will ease away the strains and anxieties of the day in the most natural and effective manner imaginable.

Chapter Ten

Beginning Before Birth

The gifted parent begins to help realise the child's potential from the moment of conception, not the day of birth. Indeed there is evidence to suggest that the actual moment of conception itself can influence the long term ability of the baby. I have already mentioned, in Chapter eight, the discovery that a link may exist between the month of birth and the growth of mental abilities. In this chapter I want to consider this, and other factors, which are likely to have an important part to play in the realisation of potential. Let us begin by looking at the intriguing relationship between higher levels of intelligence and the month of birth. One of the reasons for this relationship is thought to lie in the fact that a baby born at the start of summer is able to enjoy a much greater range of stimulating environments at a far earlier age. But there may be other factors involved as well. It could be that the higher external temperatures of summer adversely affect the development of the baby in the womb. This suggests that the month of conception is as important as the month of birth. A recent survey carried out by Thomas McNeill, an American research psychologist, has shown that the highest levels of intelligence, combined with the lowest rates of mentally disturbed adults, was found in babies conceived between December and February. The lowest levels of intelligence and the highest rates of later mental disturbance occurred in those conceived during what are normally the hottest months of the year, June to August. In McNeill's study, which covered 17 North American clinics, summer conceptions were found to be linked to a whole range of intellectual problems; poor reading, arithmetic difficulties, an inability to concentrate, and even speech impediments.

Professor Richard Lynn, of the New University of Ulster, feels that anxiety on the mother's part may be an equally significant contributor to these findings. Such anxiety, he believes, is influenced by the climate. He has examined the anxiety levels of several countries by studying such indicators as the number of suicides and car accidents, the proportion of the population who smoke heavily, become alcoholics, commit suicide or have heart attacks. The most relevant variation he has found when relating anxieties to the weather is in the number of thunderstorms. Those countries which have high anxiety levels, France, Italy and Japan, for instance, also have the most thunderstorms. Countries with fewer thunderstorms, Ireland, Holland, Canada and Britain, have lower anxiety levels. Significantly perhaps, the peak of the thunderstorm season in Britain comes in the summer months, and the overall annual pattern follows quite closely on the pattern for conceptions resulting in lower levels of intelligence and increased mental disturbances.

Stress in the mother during pregnancy is undoubtedly an important factor in the mental growth of the child. A survey carried out in the late 'fifties by Professor D.H. Stott looked at the relationship between mental retardation and such stresses as marriage difficulties, illness, housing problems, and death in the family. It was found that 49 per cent of the mothers of retarded children had one of these experiences during pregnancy. When all types of stresses were taken into account, the figure rose to 66 per cent.

There may also be a connection between a mother's anxiety during pregnancy and the health of her child. Many children suffer pains from very early in life. They experience stomach trouble when young, and, by adolescence, may have headaches, migraines, and so called 'growing pains'. A twenty-year study carried out by Dr John Apley, a consultant at

Bristol's Royal Hospital for Sick Children, has shown that a small minority of many such illnesses are due to organic causes. In every other case, the pain, although no less real, existed only in the child's mind. It was the result of an over-stimulated nervous system which, in turn, could be related to family stress problems. We have already seen some of the behavioural difficulties which this can produce.

There is also a link between the way a mother eats during pregnancy and the development of her baby's brain. From three months before birth to six months after, the infant is especially vulnerable to dietary deficiencies. Damage to the brain cells which occurs as a result of insufficient vitamins, a lack of protein or an absence of other crucial elements may prove irreversible. It cannot be made good even when the older child is properly fed.

This is not usually a threat to babies in the affluent west, although it is a major problem in Third World countries. During pregnancy, all mothers should ensure that they follow prescribed diets and eat well balanced meals of fresh, properly prepared food. After birth, the best food for the child is mother's milk, which favours the growth of brain cells. Cow's milk, by contrast, encourages rapid body growth and builds muscle. Other advantages of breast feeding, which have been found by a leading researcher in this field, Professor Stig Sjolin of Sweden, include protection against infection, a reduced risk of allergic illness like eczema, a lower chance of obesity, and an improved relationship between mother and child.

Finally, it should be mentioned that there is clear evidence of a link between birth order and the development of high intelligence. A study carried out by Anne Roe, in the early 'fifties, looked at the attributes of 64 of the most eminent scientists in America. Amongst the many points of interest which emerged was the fact that 53 per cent were first born children, a few others were effectively the first born, as an earlier child had died, while the majority of those remaining had an age gap averaging five years between them and older brothers or sisters. Dr Roe's findings have since been confirmed by several other studies which leave no doubt that first born are advantaged unless there is a span of at least four years between the children. There are likely to be a number of reasons for this, perhaps the most important being that the first child receives the undivided attention of parents. All their time, and other resources, can be devoted to the one child. The growing infant has adults, rather than young children, on whom to model his behaviour, and this, together with the constant stimulation, leads to greater independence, a more confident outlook on life, and a greater chance for early learning.

The findings of my own research amongst gifted children bears out all the points raised above. Not all of them were first born, indeed a large number had two elder siblings, and were born to slightly older parents. This may be significant, since there is some research evidence to show that fathers over thirty are rather more likely to have children whose inborn potential is realised. The result could, of course, be due to their bringing a more mature and patient attitude towards child-rearing than younger men. Where the child had older brothers or sisters, there was, in every case, an age gap of at least three years, and usually much longer between them. So far as dates of conception are concerned, only five per cent were conceived during the, seemingly, unfavourable June to August period. The majority (45 per cent) were conceived during the spring (March-May); 30 per cent in the autumn (September-November) while 20 per cent were conceived in the winter period (December-February).

My research also revealed that 70 per cent were breast fed for at least the first seven weeks of life. Breast feeding was usually associated with early contact between mother and baby, a circumstance which is known to produce a powerful bond formation. A high proportion of the mothers were non-smokers, but of those who did smoke, only ten per cent said they had continued to do so during pregnancy.

Stress was reported as being a particular problem by 25 per cent of the mothers, and it is interesting to note that amongst this group, there was a high proportion of children with some kind of behavioural difficulties. One cannot assume, of course, that these problems were a direct result of pre-natal stress. They might equally be due to a continuation of stress difficulties within the family after birth. But there seems no doubt that high anxiety amongst the parents, especially in the mother, is responsible for a wide range of problems in the under-fives.

If one were planning a family so as to give each child the best chance in life, the available research evidence would suggest the following guiding principles:

1.   Conceive during the latter part of the autumn, in October or November. The normal term of pregnancy will then allow the child to be born at the start of the summer. This provides the maximum scope for stimulation, combined with the coolest outside temperatures. (These dates are, of course, based on the climate in the Northern hemisphere).

2.   Eat sensibly during pregnancy, making sure to include plenty of protein sources in your diet.

3.   Try to remain as calm as possible. Relaxation training will help here.

4.   Do not smoke or drink alcohol (at all).

5.   Insist on being allowed to hold the baby immediately after birth, preferably with a naked infant held against your bare body. This ensures the best possible chance of a strong bond being formed.

6.   Breast feed the child.

7.   Plan your family so that there is a gap of at least four years between each child. The less the age gap, the more disadvantaged the subsequent children.

These are the key points which developmental studies have indicated. They do not mean, of course, that any other conditions will make it impossible for the child to grow to brilliance. But they do suggest that, with planning, a child can be greatly advantaged even before birth.

From the first squeal of life, your baby's successful growth depends not primarily on him, or on you, but on the interaction between you. The infant's inborn temperament will influence your responses and feelings just as crucially as your behaviour affects him. The importance of this mutual stimulation, of the constant and dynamic interplay between mother and baby, cannot be too strongly emphasised. But it does not take place in isolation. For the baby, the cocoon provided first by the womb and then by the exclusive intimacy of that one, vital relationship, soon changes and expands. The adult is always aware of external influences; of the feelings of partner, family and friends; of events which elate or depress. These too must affect the outcome of the dance of life which binds mother and infant so closely, and compels each to match the rhythm of the other so exactly.

By his or her fifth birthday, the child whose promise is being realised should be capable of understanding and exerting a degree of control over many of the main influences of his life. Only by doing so can the progress of the first five years be maintained. But even then, there will be difficulties, problems and unexpected hazards along the road to successful intellectual, creative and social growth. What these are, and how one can attempt to overcome them, will be discussed in the final chapter.

Chapter Eleven

Beyond the First Five Years

It would be agreeable to report that successful mental growth during early life guaranteed continued success beyond the first five years, but sadly, this is by no means the case. While it is certainly impossible for a child whose intellectual development has been stunted in these crucial years subsequently to realise that inborn promise, progress can always be halted. The intelligent, achieving five-year-old may well suffer a marked, and perhaps lasting, decline in abilities soon after starting school. The creative five-year-old may rapidly come to the conclusion that originality and imagination are not the best ways of ensuring success in the classroom, and that comfortable conventionality pays better dividends.

The father of a very intelligent girl, who attended her first school six months earlier than most, reports that: 'Intellectually, school has not been a success. Before she started, she was reading and writing well. She was also doing simple arithmetic with much enjoyment. In spite of two interviews with the headmaster, we haven't persuaded the school to provide her with material suitable for her abilities. She has progressed very slowly through an elementary reading scheme. Her writing has regressed, and so has her drawing. Only very clever educators could have achieved the level of regression that we have seen. Lucy's main new skill is the ability to *act* her age.'

This is an all too familiar story. Of the parents of gifted children in Britain and America whom I have interviewed, more than 70 per cent complained of the same problems.

Teachers unable to understand the nature of true intelligence and creativity in the very young; education officials who would not be able to recognise a gifted child if they tripped over one on their way to work; timetables as rigid and implacable as a caste system; curricula geared to the needs of the least capable; and schools which have become temples for limited learning, places where intellectual precocity and true creativity are daily sacrificed in the name of routine, rote and the examination syllabus, self-perpetuating monuments to mental mediocrity.

It is not just that they operate a laissez-faire arrangement where the especially bright and determined child might, somehow, fight through to success. There is frequently an active suppression of talent, a deliberate denial of the stimulation needed to satisfy a mind which, for five years, had been encouraged to inquire and initiate. The mother of a highly intelligent five-year-old who experienced great difficulties in settling to the, for him, undemanding routine of the classroom, says: 'I think his teacher did her best for him. She told me one evening that as he had read all of the class library books, and gone through the second year infants' syllabus, (this was in his first year at primary school) she had asked the head of the Junior School, same building, if he could have books from the Junior Library, and perhaps the first Junior book for English, but he had said it was entirely out of the question.'

The mother of a seven-year-old girl was told by her head mistress that the child was lacking in any academic ability. Her class teacher complained that she was 'always asking to do things, just like a little old woman,' and added that she was the least intelligent child in her class. An educational psychologist later estimated her IQ at 140 (which places her in the highly gifted category), and said that she was under-achieving at that school by 50 per cent. A change of schools worked wonders, and she now consistently scores in excess of 90 per cent in science, music and mathematics.

The fact that a different school was able to bring out her true intellectual talents clearly shows that the worst does not have to happen. I am certainly not saying that all schools are damaging places in which to try and learn, or that every teacher is an insensitive oaf with no interest in developing the intellects of his or her pupils. There are certainly many enlightened schools, and many more teachers who do all they can, within a repressive system, to help and encourage each of their students. But such places and such people are, in my experience, in the minority. The politics of Tsarist Russia were once described as 'absolutism moderated by assassination'. So perhaps the educational system of the West might be considered as 'absolutism moderated by incompetence'! Too many schools are conveyor belts for the mind, processing the brightest and the best into examination fodder, taking intelligent five-year-olds in at one end, and ensuring that, after ten or more years of exposure to education, they mostly come out all too average. It has been said that a camel is a horse designed by a committee. Education, it sometimes seems, is in the hands of a committee designed by a camel.

One educational psychologist, L.S. Hollingworth, writing in the 1940s, estimated that in an ordinary school, children with an IQ of 140 wasted half their time, and those with an IQ of 170 wasted almost all their time:

'In one case, one of the most tangible results of a child's brightness was an increase in the amount of laundering that his mother had to do because the youngster cleaned the blackboards and erasers while her classmates were working at their lessons. Frequently, a bright child becomes a strain upon the teacher, especially if the teacher resents pupils who know more than he, or if the child not only knows much, but also shown no hesitation in parading his knowledge and correcting others.'

Today, more than 30 years later, the situation has certainly not improved. Indeed, it seems likely that there is even more wastage, simply because the level of creativity and intelligence shown by pupils entering the school system is likely to be far higher than it was even ten years ago. This raising of the average levels is due to greater stimulation during the first five years, from parents with a better understanding of the needs of the very young, and from play groups and nursery schools.

Henry Collis, director of the London based National Association for Gifted Children, believes that in Britain at least 100,000 bright children go through their entire school careers unrecognised by either teachers or parents. In America, the number is thought to be well over one million. And these are children whose first five years have helped them to realise at least part of their inborn potential. The remainder of those who fail to achieve intellectual development have been brought down even before they reached the first hurdle.

The fate of the exceptional child whose ability goes unrecognised is seldom a happy one. Often, he or she is blamed by adults for not trying hard enough, for failures and set-backs caused by the attitudes of the adults themselves:

'These children are often lazy, because it is all too easy for them to keep up to the standards set by their friends,' says Henry Collis. 'Because they under-achieve, they withdraw into themselves, lose interest in what happens at school, and often turn to aggression, disruption and delinquency.'

An example of the worst that can happen came to light in Britain a few years ago when a boy with an intelligence rating which would place him in the genius class was sent to a home for maladjusted children. His mother explained: 'He was unpopular with his teachers, and most of them regarded him as a damned nuisance because he felt that his lessons were a waste of time.'

'It is often taken for granted . . . that the gifted child is equally valued by teachers and by parents, in the classroom and at home; that he is held an equally good prospect by teachers and by parents to succeed as an adult; and that the children themselves want to be gifted,' comment American psychologists, Jacob Getzels and Philip Jackson. 'It can be demonstrated that none of these assumptions regarding the value of the gifted child can be held without question. Empirical data related to these assumptions indicate that the gifted child is *not* equally valued by teachers and by parents, in the classroom and at home; he is *not* held to be an equally good prospect by teachers and parents to succeed as an adult; and children themselves do *not* necessarily want to be gifted, at least not in the traditional sense of the word (*In Phi Delta Kappa* Vol. 40. No. 2. November, 1958).

This statement is supported by the results of a survey which formed part of my study of exceptional children. Their parents were asked to rank the following ten characteristics in order of the importance they would attach to each when deciding whether their child was 'gifted'.

1. Favourable teachers' report when starting school.
2. Ability to do sums correctly at early age.
3. Ability to read earlier than expected.
4. Neatness in written work.
5. Rapid understanding of problems.
6. Constant asking of questions.
7. Interest in books or games demanding intellectual skill.
8. Ability to draw neatly or copy pictures from books acurately.
9. Number of fantasy games of imaginative stories invented.
10. Desire to explore possibilities of creative materials in novel ways.

The characteristics seen as most important by 90 per cent of the parents were those described in statements five and six — the rapid understanding of problems and a constant asking of questions. Those seen as least important by parents were a favourable school report, which was placed last by 45 per cent of parents, and in the last three by 95 per cent of parents; and neatness in written work and an ability to draw neatly which were also placed in the last three by 90 per cent of the parents.

However, when primary school teachers were asked to rank the same characteristics, they placed those which the parents considered least important — school report and neatness in written work and in drawing — as being amongst the most significant indications of ability. They also saw a rapid understanding of problems as useful, although it was placed in the first three by only 25 per cent of teachers and always below neatness in written work. Perhaps because of the disruption it causes in a crowded classroom, the constant asking of questions was placed in the last three by 85 per cent of teachers.

It was interesting that neither parents nor teachers considered the more creative talents described by statements nine and ten — fantasy games and creative exploration of materials — as being especially important. This suggests that adults are able to assess the kind of convergent thinking ability involved in formal problem-solving more easily than divergent creativity. One could conclude that the highly creative child is even less likely to have his or her special talents noticed at home or in the classroom than the more conventionally able individual.

The ability to read or do sums in advance of the 'normal' age was well regarded by parents, being placed in the first five by 70 per cent of parents, but seen as significant by only 20 per cent of teachers. Many, in fact, expressed open disapproval of early reading: 'I always think it a shame when children can read before they come to school,' one teacher told me. 'They miss so much.' This is not an uncommon response, and the advice many parents receive from teachers is not to do any teaching of these basic skills. One mother was told bluntly: 'Train him to keep quiet, do as he is told, and make sure he arrives on time.

Leave the teaching to the professionals.'

In view of the major differences between what teachers and parents consider bright behaviour, it is hardly surprising that many mothers and fathers feel anxiety rather than pride if their children appear especially intelligent or creative. Some, indeed, are ashamed of the fact, and warn their children 'not to act too brainy', in case they are looked on as 'odd' or 'different'.

'One of the most mistaken ideas is that every parent wants to have a gifted child,' says Henry Collis. 'Not a bit of it. They want clever, or even very clever children, who will pass exams and keep them in their dotage. But, except in the case of those who are themselves extremely able, they tend to have a mistrust of the gifted, and the problems which can arise.'

It is clear that in depressing ability and encouraging the kind of mental approach that will produce good results in examinations, teachers and schools are not acting in defiance of what many, perhaps the majority, of parents want for their children. Indeed, if they were to adopt any other approach in the present social climate, there would probably be an outcry, mass sackings, and the rapid closures of any schools deviating from the conventional educational line. Although individual parents may protest that their children are being held back, most encourage them to conform, to produce the kind of work which will ensure good class marks, favourable reports and successful examination passes. The acquisition of facts rather than the development of an ability to manipulate those facts in original and insightful ways is still the criterion for academic achievement. Examinations are no longer a means to an end (that is, the assessment of understanding and knowledge), but an end in themselves. If you doubt this, consider the fact that all places of education, from primary school to university, from the humblest establishment to Oxford and Cambridge,

Harvard and Princetown, prepare their students with the utmost care for every examination. There are trial runs on the kind of questions likely to be asked, special coaching in the topics which have been presented most frequently in previous papers, revision sessions in which the right sort of answers are rehearsed. What would happen if such massive predigestion of course work failed to take place? The most likely answer is that few, if any, would pass.

The answer will be given that, however unsatisfactory and ineffective examinations may be, they are the only possible way of assessing a person's level of learning and education. They may be fallible instruments of detection, wrong more often than they are right, but without them where would we be? What standards could we apply? How would the intellectual sheep be separated from the production-line fodder goats? While diplomas and examination passes remain the major considerations, the rule of thumb by which achievement is measured, this costly and time consuming paper-chase must continue. The biological law, which I mentioned in Chapter two, and which states that structure and function are always related, has equal truth in education. The function is to obtain examination passes, the structure is determined by that all-powerful need. That structure dictates the way in which the minds of the children are moulded. They are now frequently and ruthlessly streamed into various academic interests. Knowledge has been chopped like salami sausage at a super-market into convenient categories and packages. Its price tag is the transformation of learning into a series of precise and elaborate rituals in which the acquisition of facts is the primary objective; the surrender of individuality and creativity; and the decline in a belief in the importance of discovery.

How To Help The Older Child

Teachers often complain that parents take no interest in their children; that, once they have been sent off to school they are virtually abandoned to their fate. You can only help the older children by working closely, and preferably harmoniously, with their teachers. Watch out for indications of anxiety and stress on the part of the child; bed-wetting, sleepless nights, nightmares, an apathetic approach to work, even a reluctance to go to school at all. School phobia is a very much more common difficulty than most parents realise. The child who always seems to become ill just as the holiday ends, who makes a scene every morning before going to school, or who plays truant must not be punished but helped. Monitor progress by looking at school work on a week by week basis, do not wait for end of term reports to tell you how well or badly they are doing. Make a point of attending PTA meetings and of getting to know those teachers most concerned with your child. A perfect partnership between home and school, built on mutual trust and regard, is about as rare as a truly happy marriage! But such co-operation is essential to the best interests of the child.

Early training in social skills will enable children to present their abilities in the most acceptable way, by which I do not mean that they will be ashamed of their talents or try to suppress their skills; nor should they be reluctant to express knowledge openly and confidently. But there are ways of achieving all of this without alienating adults and making themselves unpopular with their classmates.

If the child lacks sufficient stimulation during school hours, try to compensate him or her at other times. Provide ample opportunities for enquiry and discovery. Here, for example, are twelve activities which are especially valuable:-

1.   Study the sciences: astronomy, geology, meteorology.
2.   Study philosophy, psychology, sociology.
3.   Carry out some independent research.
4.   Produce a home newspaper or magazine with neighbourhood news.
5.   Learn typing. Old machines suitable for beginners can be

picked up quite cheaply.
6. Go to classes in music, ballet, drama.
7. Assist slow learners in class.
8. Write poetry.
9. Write a book of original stories.
10. Dismantle and rebuild old electronic equipment. Parts of sophisticated but obsolete communications and computer systems can be bought very cheaply at electronics stores.
11. Gain experiences by working in free time in offices or factories. This may be difficult to arrange, but it can prove very valuable for the older child. If agreement is reached with some suitably qualified person, it is essential that the child be given proper tasks to do, as in the case of the architect described in Chapter seven. Just being allowed to hang around or be forced to do menial tasks will only produce boredom and perhaps a dislike of work in general.
12. Learn photograhy, take pictures and produce final prints. This requires some capital investment, although second hand photographic equipment can often be found at bargain prices. Look in the classified advertisements of local papers for amateurs who are giving up and selling complete darkrooms.

Help, encouragement and guidance in all these, and similar activities, will provide some of the mental nourishment which schools may be denying. Even if you feel that the particular school is exceptionally stimulating and receptive to intelligent children, you should see that, away from the classroom, interests are still as extensive as possible.

But do not be afraid of approaching the school to see if the child's mind cannot be more successfully stimulated in the classroom. Perhaps it would be possible to move to a higher class or take certain subjects with older children? If the school is unhelpful, then change schools, if this is at all possible. There are many instances of a previously under-achieving child suddenly beginning to flourish academically following a move of this kind.

Many parents with exceptional children feel isolated and uncertain how best to help them. Joining a society which brings together parents in a similar situation can provide support and practical advice. There are five such associations in America and one in Britain. You will find the address in the acknowledgements section at the start of this book.

Why The World Needs Intelligent Children

If you are the parents of an under-five, you may well be wondering if it is in anybody's best interests to try and awaken his or her mind. Would the child not be happier if left to amble quietly through life, moderately able, modestly successful? Would you not be made less anxious by a child who was compliant and conformist, undemanding in needs, unspectacular in ambitions? There can be no denying that this may well be the easiest course for all concerned. But that does not make it the right one to follow. A blind man never has to look on human suffering, need never see poverty or destruction. But nobody would seriously advocate blindness as a means to contentment. By denying the child a right to realise his inborn abilities, you are, effectively, encouraging a perhaps more dreadful form of blindness, the lack of vision that goes with a dull, unquestioning mind.

The world needs intelligent people. Indeed, our very survival may depend on raising the general level of mental abilities many times in the course of the next few decades. I do not mean that we must become technologically smarter, but possessed of a more visionary and creative intelligence that works towards long term goals rather than constantly seeking short term gains.

I said earlier in this book that our chosen survival strategy was to be more intelligent than any other species on earth. So far it has proved successful, but our achievements, in evolutionary terms, are still insignificant. The dinosaurs flourished for some 140 million years before disappearing in less than a century. We have endured, in a civilised state, for only a few thousand years. There is no certainty that we shall do as well, let alone better, than the dinosaurs. We should rid ourselves of the impudent belief that our species will inevitably prosper. Nature bestows no divine rights of survival. These have to be won. In the game of evolution, the prize is to exist; the single, terrible penalty is extinction, and extinction means for ever. If mankind goes the way of the dinosaurs, it will not be because we are too clever for our own good, as some suggest, but because we were not clever enough. In the battle for survival, the weapon which natural selection has handed to us is mental ability. The battle will only be one if those weapons are the best available. At present, they seem barely equal to the challenge.

A story is told about a millionaire who devoted his life and his fortune to a search for the world's greatest philosopher. He died with his quest unfinished, and at the gates of Heaven asked Saint Peter to give him the answer which he had been unable to find while alive. The saint pointed down to earth where an old man sat before a workbench. There is the man you were seeking,' he said gently. 'There is the world's greatest philosopher.' 'But I know him well,' protested the millionaire. 'He is only a poor shoemaker.' 'That is true,' agreed Saint Peter. 'But had his life been different he would have been the world's greatest philosopher.'

How many opportunities for achievement are lost in the earliest years of life? We can never know. But the number must run into billions. It is an enormous and tragic waste of ability when just one squandered talent would be too many.

'Children are unrealised geniuses,' wrote Anatole France at the start of this century. Only today are we starting to appreciate the full truth and significance of that comment. 'What is needed is a change in the entire intellectual climate in which we — the parents and the teachers — as well as the children, function,' comment the psychologists Jacob Getzels and Philip Jackson in their book *Creativity and Intelligence*. 'We need alteration in parental attitudes towards giftedness and towards success, change in the attitudes of teachers towards highly creative students, and in the attitudes the children themselves acquire even before they come to school.'

Your baby was born to be brilliant. Whether or not that potential is to be achieved will depend on you. Recognising your child's real potential is the first essential step towards realising it. Providing the child with the environment which will allow that promise to grow into the reality of superior intellectual, creative and social abilities is both the challenge and the reward of being a gifted parent.

Bibliography

The following books formed part of the references for this work. I have listed only those which are the most readily available and easily accessible for the general reader. Those marked with an asterisk are slightly more difficult, for the non-specialist, than the remainder. All offer valuable insights and fresh understandings of the fascinating and important process of growing up. They are listed in alphabetical order based on the surname of the senior author.

AMBROSE, A. (Ed) *Stimulation in Early Infancy*, Academic Press, 1969.*

BARBE, W. B. and Renzulli, J. S. *Psychology and Education of the Gifted.* Halsted Press (John Wiley and Sons. N. Y.) 1975.

BECK, J. *How to Raise a Brighter Child*, Souvenir Press, 1968.

BELL, R. Q. and Harper, L. V. *Child Effects on Adults* Lawrence Erlbaum Associates, 1977.

BLOCK, N. and Dworkin, G. *The IQ Controversy – Critical Readings*, Quartet Books. 1977.

BRUNER, J. S., Jolly, M. R. and Sylva, K. (Eds) *Play. Its Role in Development and Evolution*, 1976.

BRUNER, S. J. *Beyond the Information Given*, George Allen and Unwin, 1974.*

BUTCHER, H. J. *Human Intelligence*, Methune, 1968.

BUTCHER, H. J. and Lomax *Readings in Human Intelligence*, Methuen, 1972.

CIBA Foundation Symposium *Parent-Infant Interaction*, Elsevier. Excerpta Medica, 1975.*

CLARKE, A. M., and Clarke, A. D. B. *Early Experience-Myth and Evidence*, Open Books Ltd, 1976.

DAVIE, R., Butler, N., Goldstein, H. (Ed) *From Birth to Seven: Studies in Child Development*, Longman, 1972.

DENENBERG, V. H. *Education of the Infant and Young Child*, Academic Press, 1970.*

DOMAN, G. *Teach Your Baby To Read*, Jonathan Cape Ltd, 1965.

DOMAN, G. *What To Do About Your Brain-Injured Child*, Jonathan Cape Ltd, 1975.

DONALDSON, M. *Children's Minds*, Collins, 1978.

EYSENCK, H. J. *The Inequality of Man*, Temple Smith, 1973.

FOSS, B. (Ed) *New Perspectives in Child Development*, Penguin, 1974.

GESELL, A., Ilg, F. L., Ames, L. B. *The Child From Five To Ten*, Hamish Hamilton. 1973.

HEIM, M. *Intelligence and Personality – Their Assessment and Relationship*, Pengion, 1970.

HOLT, J. *Escape from Childhood*, Penguin, 1975.

HOLT, J. *How Children Fail*, Penguin, 1969.

HUDSON, L. *Frames of Mind – Ability, Perception and Self-Perception in the Arts and Sciences*, Methuen, 1968.

IBUKA, M. *Kindergartern is Too Late*, Souvenir Press, 1977.

JENSON, A. R. *Educatability and Group Differences*, University Press, 1973.

JERSLID, L. D., Telford, C. W., Sawrey, J. M. *Child Psychology*, Prentice Hall, 1975.*

LEVIN, J. R., Allen, V. L. *Cognitive Learning in Children – Theories and Strategies*, Academic Press, 1976*

LEWIS, D. *The Secret Language of Your Child*, Souvenir Press, 1978

LOVELL, M. *How Children Grow – From Conception to Two*, Routledge & Kegan Paul, 1975.

MATTERSON, E. M. *Play with a Purpose for Under-Sevens* , Penguin, 1975.

MILLAR, S. *The Psychology of Play*, Penguin, 1977.

MURPHY, L. B. (Ed) *Play and Development*, M. W. Piens (NV), 1972

MUSSEN, P. H. (Ed) *Carmichael's Manual of Child Psychology*, John Wiley and Sons, 1970.*

PAIGET, J. *The Origin of Intelligence in the Child*, Routledge & Kegan Paul, 1953.*

PILLING, D., Pringle, M. K. *Controversial Issues in Child Development*, Elek, 1978.*

ROGERS, S. (Ed) *Children and Language – Readings in Early Language and Socialisation*, Oxford University Press, 1975.*

SCHAFFER, H. R. *Studies in Mother-Infant Interaction*, Academic Press, 1977.*

SELIGMAN, M. E. P. *Helplessness – On Depression, Development and Death*, Freeman, 1975.

SHARPE, R., Lewis, D. *The Anxiety Antidote – How to Beat the Fear Response*, Souvenir Press, 1979.

SPOCK, B. *Baby and Child Care*, Bodley Head, 1958.

SPARKMAN, B., Carmichael, A. *Blueprint for a Brighter Child*, David and Charles, 1975.

STOTT, D. H. *The Parent and Teacher*, University of London Press, 1972.

STRAIN, P. S., Cooke, T. P., Apolloni, T. *Teaching Exceptional Children*, Academic Press, 1976.*

TIZARD, B., Harvey, D. (Eds) *Biology of Play*, Spastics International Medical Publications, 1977

TYLER, L. E. *The Psychology of Human Differences*, Prentice-Hall, 1965.

VURPILLOT, E. *The Visual World of the Child*, George Allen and Unwin, 1976.

WHITE, B. L. *The First Three Years of Life*, W. H. Allen, 1978.*

WOOD, M. E. Children: *The Development of Personality and Behaviour*, George Harrap, 1973.*